Ioana Pârvulescu

Jonah

and

His Daughter

Jonah and His Daughter
by Ioana Pârvulescu

Frist published as Prevestirea
by Humanitas, Romania (2020)

Text © Ioana Pârvulescu
Translation © Alistair Ian Blyth

The right of Ioana Pârvulescu, to be identified
as the author of this work has been asserted
in accordance with the Copyright, Designs and
Patents Act, 1988

First published in 2024 by Istros Books
London, United Kingdom
www.istrosbooks.com

Cover image: Mihail Coşuleţu
Design and layout: pikavejica.com

ISBN: 978-1-912545-377

The publishers would like to thank the Fundatia
Spandugino, Bucharest, for their support in
the translation and production of this book,
without which its publication would not have
been possible.

The translation and publication of this book was
supported by

Spandugino Foundation
Education and Culture for a Better Future

Ioana Pârvulescu

Jonah and His Daughter

*translated
from the Romanian by*

Alistair Ian Blyth

istrosbooks

Dedicated to the fathers

Contents

PROLOGUE
IN THE 21ST CENTURY

.

Dear Iona,
Great, thank you! Your interview will be held in French. I send you your schedule:

16.30: Librebook stand (no. 130) – Facebook Live interview
with Anna Rydholm (Social Media Team of European
Commission)
17.00: Librebook stand (no. 130) – Cocktail
18.00: Place de l'Europe (no. 205) – "What's the European Union
Prize for Literature?"
19.00: End

Best regards, Roberta

Ever since I started corresponding by e-mail in English, people have often referred to me as *Iona*. In English, the spellchecker automatically changes the *oa* in Ioana, a name it doesn't recognise, to an *o*, which it thinks more plausible. It's true, Iona does occur as a woman's first name, and here I only have to think of violinist and conductor Iona Brown. At first the alteration vexed me. With its full complement of vowels, my name encapsulated the name of my maternal grandmother, Ana, and my paternal great-grandmother, who was also an Ana, not to mention the many Ioans in my family, the name of the street where I grew up, Strada Sfîntu Ioan—Saint John Street—and the saint himself, whose feast falls on the eve of my birthday. Iona sounded too abrupt to me, too masculine. In Romanian, Iona is the name of a minor prophet who was quick to anger. But the more I studied it, both the name and the biblical character himself became very dear to me. I began to understand Iona, to understand Jonah. Like all true artists, he was exceptionally courageous, and he was the first, in his own way and long before Jesus, to have vanquished death after three days. I think he was the only person to have stood up to God in a natural way, through dialogue, perhaps because he imagined that a human being, created after the image and likeness of the Lord, could speak to Him as His peer and dare to say something other than what was strictly expected of him.

The reason his story is so beautiful and so human is because it is about deadly monsters that play a double part and which in the end are life savers, about the need for darkness, about fear and running away, about passion, about getting involved or standing aloof, about being human or separate from humanity, about dying, being born again and, yes, wishing to die many times, even if you believe yourself to have been chosen by God. About how you can become cruel, even while being good, and how you can become good, even while being bad. It is a total story. It sets the imagination working. It sets you in motion. It puts you to the test. It makes you feel things you've never felt before.

And another thing I noticed: everybody smiles when it comes to Jonah.

I realised that reality was tugging me by the sleeve: to write about the life of Jonah became almost an obligation. The task seemed as hard to me as that which God gave the rightful bearer of the name. I had countless reasons not to complete the task, to try to get out of it. In the end, nobody else knew about it apart from me and, presumably, God. The same as Jonah, I tried to run away, to flee in the opposite direction. How easy it would have been to write a minor novel about some (disastrous) love affair set in the present day! But no, the idea pursued me wherever I might be, like the eye of God, which sees all. And at intervals I would receive yet another e-mail: *Dear Iona*. In the end, I couldn't go on hiding.

The descendants of the patriarchs are here, they live among us, as someone once said, without knowing who her ancestors were, more likely than not. If we reckon that there are an average of three generations per century (in biblical times, there were actually more), then we are separated from Jonah, who probably lived in the eighth century BC, by around ninety generations. That wouldn't be all that many, if it weren't that the trail gets lost. On one side of my family tree, I have a record of twelve generations: surnames, first names, certificates of baptism and marriage. Farther back than that, history is silent. But if I were able to keep digging back in time, I would finally reach the parents of parents who were contemporaries of Jonah.

For a writer, a thousand or two thousand years are, as the Psalmist said, but as yesterday: they sweep by like a dream.

BOOK ONE

Much Sky,
Earth, Water

You could have been my son

'Peace be with you!'

The man thus greeted made a deep bow of the head, as was customary, but he spoke no reply. He sat on the ground, his heels tucked under him, and from beneath his long linen shirt could be divined firm, rounded thighs. He was hollowing a piece of wood in his lap, probably to make a wine cup like the two finished ones that rested beside him among wood chips. He looked up at the stranger garbed in white, and the sun, a little past its zenith, stabbed his eyes. He shaded his brows with his hand the better to see the face of the guest. He could see only that it was an old man with a grey, wavy beard covering his hollow cheeks and that he wore rings in his ears. The hands, which once must have been very delicate, held the reins of a mule, and on each forefinger, there glinted a ring set with precious stones, one of them gold, the other silver. Despite his small stature, something lofty, even commanding could be read in his bearing, betokening one who knew what he wanted and why he had come.

'A drop of water for me and my old beast, if you would be so kind. The servants will make do for themselves. We have come from the ends of the earth ...'

The man on the ground looked at him suspiciously, without saying anything, prompting the visitor to explain:

'From a place called Tarshish. "The ends of the earth." True, this day we have come only from Jaffa—' and here he pointed his head to the south—'but at my age it is still a long and weary way ... I set foot on dry land in Joppa. I have also come through Jerusalem. A place of huge crowds, people of all different stripes, too. Hustle and bustle and din everywhere. I can't abide all that: the clatter of horses' hooves day and night, the shrieks of women scolding their children, the gawpers every step of the way, the constant shouts of the market traders hawking their olive oil, their fish, their grain, their dried fruit, the howls of the thieves whose chastisement is meted out on their hides, and by night, the hoarse whispers from the craws of … Actually, for me, I think some wine would do better than water,' he said with a sigh and a meaningful look at one of the finished cups, 'since the animals don't have any use for such a beverage. I'd personally rather not let water pass my lips if at all possible.'

The man on the ground rose to his feet without delay, obeying the strict laws of hospitality. He took the dun beast by the reins, quickly led it to the nearby well, and set it to the trough. The mule plunged its muzzle in the water straight away, spraying droplets all around. Shortly thereafter the guest received sweet wine in a freshly whittled cup. The old man drank with the same insatiable thirst as the mule, likewise spraying drops of his drink. The host stood looking at his guest with impatience, however, as if he could hardly wait to be rid of him.

'You must be Jonah ben Amithai,' said the old man cheerfully. 'I knew your father well, may his memory be praised forever more. Or maybe he's still alive? I would be overjoyed to find out he is.'

'No,' said the man named Jonah curtly, without volunteering details.

He noted only that the question ought to have come first, but it was obvious that the guest was one of those fearful people who countenances the worst before hoping for the best.

'When, or, rather, how did he die?' asked the stranger with obvious curiosity, pointing an extended thumb at his cup, a sign easily understood, at which Jonah poured him another measure of the honey-coloured wine.

'Ten days. Today's the tenth. Didn't wake up. Morning of the Sabbath.'

'In his sleep, you mean to say? What a lucky man! And it was you who found him?'

Jonah nodded, increasingly morose. He didn't care for long talk, and this old man's tongue itched to wag, keeping Jonah from his business. It was business he wished to finish. And that meant in silence. The grief caused by his father's death was in any event still too raw to share with every unannounced traveller passing through Gat-Hefer on his way from Tarshish, or 'the ends of the earth', wherever they might be, too raw for him to fritter away the day with every stranger, even if the stranger in question had, so it would seem, known his departed father well.

'I'm your father's cousin,' said the old man, as if hearing what Jonah was thinking, 'and I met you once, if you can call the occasion that—it was when they cut your foreskin and gave you the name Jonah, or "Dove". All our names are loans from the Lord and they're reflections of the world, but I expect you know that from your father. You were such a lovely little baby when you were eight days old, my little Dove. After they unwrapped your swaddling clothes, you paddled your thin little legs, like a frog, not at all like a bird, screaming at the top of your lungs with your thin little voice all the while, till you were red in the face. You wouldn't stop. To tell the truth, I'd never have thought you'd grow up to have such thick legs and such a deep voice! Or cheeks bristling with such a curly black beard! I wasn't even sure you'd live, even though your shrill squeals showed you wanted something from this life ... I wonder, is that young, beautiful mother of yours still alive? Or has she departed to Adonai too?'

This time he put the question in the right order.

'Yes,' muttered Jonah.

'Yes, she departed, or yes, she's alive?'

'Yes, alive. Not young.'

'Praised be the Lord! Because she's alive, I mean! I really must see her straight away. Tell her that Jacob ben Benjamin is here, her relative from Tarshish, from across the Big Sea. Or rather, a relative of her husband, Amithai, unfortunately deceased, as you say. Which would make me your uncle.' The old man then added in a voice suddenly tremulous, shaking his head along with his gold earrings: 'Didn't they ever tell you about me?'

'Not at home,' answered Jonah, in a voice trying to be gentle, but which came out rather harshly.

'All the better! Better that way! I need to get used to the thought that instead of a rosy-cheeked, cheerful woman possessed of those contours most pleasing to the male eye, with breasts like two young roes that are twins, as the wise Solomon put it last century, utterly inaccurately, yet so enticingly—just between ourselves, your mother's dugs were swollen with milk at the time—her long neck wrapped around with strings of pearls, her black hair, glossy beneath her gauzy veil, her teeth like pearls, her lips aflame with the promise of delight, and that instead of a ripe young bride, dressed in gauzy linen, I shall see an old crone. I shouldn't be surprised if she were toothless too!'

'No,' said Jonah, who had never heard anybody talk like this before. 'No, no. She's beautiful. Has all her teeth. Black hair.'

For him, so sparing with words, it was a long reply. It showed he was troubled.

'Glory unto Thee, O Lord! I fled to the ends of the earth from her and the cousin she chose in wedlock, since in youth the blood runs hot and will not be denied. Youth is a terrible time, believe me, nephew: rife with errors and downright ridiculous.'

Jonah, still a young man, made no reply.

'You could have been my own son, my little Dove: Jonah ben Jacob ben Benjamin. You would have turned out nimbler of speech, for poor Amithai, blessed be his memory, trundled his words like boulders, he found it hard to dislodge them from his mouth, but even so, it was plain to see that not I but he was the "True", as his name betokens: A good heart and a good cousin, albeit irascible and superstitious. But I won't find fault with him now that he has so easily slipped away into sleep. That lad always had the luck ... You know, my child, folk ought to bid each other a "good death" rather than a "good night"! If you show me where, then I'll lay myself down to sleep till your mother comes, even though I hope the good fortune of dying in my sleep does not befall me on this of all days, before this white-haired old man has a chance to see once more her who has lost neither all her beauty nor her teeth.'

It seemed that they had nothing more to say to each other, even though the essential thing, which is to say, the purpose of the visit, had still not been revealed. Jacob didn't share it with him, for a reason known to him alone, and Jonah wasn't in the habit of speaking when not asked, nor was he curious by nature, and so, after he took the stranger up to the flat roof, shaded on two sides by an old vine, and where there was a straw mattress, he went back to his whittling, with a frown on his face. It was then that he heard a cry that froze the blood in his veins. It was difficult to tell whether it came from man, woman, or beast, but from the sound of it, it was mostly likely beast. Jacob, who had only just gone up to the roof, descended in a hurry.

Then the miracle took place

Gat-Hefer nestled among rolling hills, where the aridity was less intense than in the rest of the land. In spring you could see verdure speckled with red poppies, and in summer, among the thistles, a host of yellow wildflowers bloomed in the stunted grass. Between the boundless silk of the sky above and the stony earth divided into family plots passed down from father to son for all eternity, the Galileans of that small settlement toiled —like all those before them and all those that would come after them—and, full of hope or fear, they awaited the coming of the Messiah. The women milled the flour between two round grindstones in the yards of their houses, where they also baked the bread and raised the children. The men broke the soil and cleared it of stones, they cultivated the vines, which they toiled to water when the rain refused to fall, and they made the wine, which was rather sweet, but at least lent them joy and an appetite to life, while life itself ever followed the same allotted course. They would often make the journey south to Jerusalem or to Jaffa, a town they could even glimpse from home, white in the distance. They would go there on business, to barter goods and learn the latest news. Or else Jerusalem and Jaffa would come to them, in the form of merchants and travellers full of stories, like Jacob ben Benjamin, who was good at talking and nothing else, in Jonah's opinion. But very soon, this judgement on Jonah's part would turn out to have been hasty. For, Jacob had other skills than facility at spinning a yarn.

The cry had come from neither man nor beast, but from a mother. While the woman was bickering over nothing with a neighbour, her child had quickly clambered like a little beetle up the quite low stone rim of the nearby well, from which Jonah had drawn water for his uncle's mule and whose heavy lid had been left open. The mother had kept an eye on her child the whole time but let her out of her sight for an instant, a single instant. Such evil accidents the folk of Gat-Hefer named the will of God. The child had fallen down the well just as the woman turned to call her, and so she saw with her own eyes the horror she would never forget. The shaft was deep, and above it was a pulley from whose rope hung two large, wide-mouthed clay pots, an empty one above, the other down below, in the water. The two men ran to the well, the old man more slowly than his nephew and breathing through his mouth stertorously.

Jonah grasped the rope with both hands. His foot was too long to fit inside the vessel. So, he curtly ordered the women, who were wailing incomprehensibly, and his uncle, who was still panting, to lower it down the shaft while he clung to the rope. Luckily for them, right then the neighbour's eldest son came running up, a sturdy youth. They lowered Jonah making fierce exertion. Jonah swayed on the rope and the stone walls of the shaft flayed his skin as he banged against them. The mother gnashed her teeth and her fingers turned white from how tightly she held the rope. The neighbour, who was pretty and slim, and her son let out the rope hand over hand and braced themselves with their whole bodies. The uncle stood and watched. Abruptly, the weight yielded, a vessel full of water rose to the top and the neighbour propped it against the side of the well. The mother of the fallen child peeled her fingers from the rope and shook them to relieve their numbness. They had heard a splash and then silence. In the black water that had till now reflected a small, round, empty sky, they could now see nothing but the top of Jonah's head. Nobody could remember when the well had been sunk, but it was the first time it had swallowed anybody.

The head of the mother obnubilated the disk of blueness at the top of the well shaft in the instant when the hoarse command rose from below, hitting her full in the face: 'Pull!' They pulled up the vessel with great ease as the second bucket, having been emptied into the trough, descended. When it reached them, the vessel held in its hollow a frail, huddled child, her head hanging limply to one side, her eyes closed. She gave no sign of life, and the same animal cry as before made itself heard again. The woman clasped her inert child to her breast in horror and howled more than wept. A few older children had now come running, open-mouthed.

Jonah's God—for he had a god, a god all of his own—then made plain the purpose of Jacob ben Benjamin's arrival in Gat-Hefer that very afternoon. The old man gently moved the woman aside, he laid the dead infant on the ground—it was a little girl, probably not yet two years old, with a swarthy face and locks of hair plastered to her cheeks—and began to press her little chest, with his thin, ring-bedecked fingers, using a method known only to him, counting to twelve aloud. And he held his lips to the child's as if kissing them. The mother could not look, she was now mutely shaking, but her pretty neighbour fastened her eyes on the old man, sensing something magnificent.

The miracle then occurred and the drowned little girl was brought spluttering back to life as Jacob spat out the water from the well: in the end, water had indeed passed his lips.

'I learned this from the sailors. I came here by sea from Iberia, a voyage that lasted months— I even lost count of the months. I grew sick of so much sky and so much water and so much ship. Ten times I saw the full moon reflected in the waves and I passed through many ports, the last being Joppa,' he said in a voice suddenly weary. 'During a storm worse than you could ever imagine, with watery mountains and chasms that all but wrecked us, a man fell overboard, just as the winds and the rain died down. His comrades managed to fish out his body, they pumped the water from his chest, but him they were unable to bring back to life … Also, where I come from, I practise the art of healing,' the old man explained to the woman, who, insane with joy was kissing his dusty sandals. He felt a wet tickling of his feet and he softly pushed the happy mother aside. The goodness of such eventualities the folk of Gat-Hefer named the will of God.

Jonah they were unable to pull up from the well straight away. They had to call on some of the men folk to drag him back up. His skin hung in tatters, his shirt was heavy with water, his fingertips were corrugated. When he saw the little girl resting in the crook of her mother's tanned arm, with her little head poking above the woman's shoulder, her two dark eyes gazing at him in suspicion, Jonah's purple lips broke into a radiant smile.

'Your smile is just like your mother's!' said his uncle, pleasantly surprised.

Could it have been Jonah who forgot to push the lid of the well back in place after he fetched water for his guest? Nobody is now able to say. If so, then at least he didn't kill anybody by his action. Not everybody has such luck, my dear child … I remember that many times folk didn't bother to push the heavy lid back in place. True, so many children die that some mothers from hereabouts don't make the effort. And, yes, there are many families whose members don't care what happens to each other. But here, in our family, Jonah's family, things have always been different.

Father, Father!

After my grandfather Amithai died, whom I loved more than my mother and father put together, since my mother snuffed it giving birth and was nothing but a legend to me, and since my father didn't trouble himself at all about me, even though he was alive and had no other children back then, time passed very slowly. Fathers pay no attention to their daughters, as you yourself can see, because they know that they're not the ones who will perpetuate their name and deeds, that they're nothing but temporary guests in the family, staying for about fifteen years at the most, after which they leave forever to join the family of a husband who takes everything from them and gives them children in return.

In the ten days after the death of my grandfather, the sun neither rose nor set for me. When the father of my father Jonah was alive, he made the sun race across the sky, as if driving it from behind like a wheel, from its rising, when it burned like the flower of the poppy, to its setting, when it glowed like the fruit of the orange tree. Grandfather Amithai made time pass all too swiftly: he would whittle a toy for me, he would teach me a psalm, he would tell me family stories and sad proverbs meant for sons and grandsons, and more often than not he would make me laugh. And all of a sudden, evening would descend on us, when, regretfully, I would have to go to bed.

So, it had been ten days since I learned that death can take from you whatever it wants, and that what it wants is what you think is yours for life. Time itself then grows old from one day to the next. My own time, once so fleet, now lay as still as a puddle. For as long as Father was down in the black hole of the well and I was up above, I hadn't known what to do with myself, I could only crane my head over the lip of the well, like a foolish girl, and in a faint voice cry down to him, 'Father, Father!', and I was terrified that Death had arrived yet again to take somebody from our family. And in a flash, I imagined that it would take my father Jonah away from me, too, leaving me with only my grandmother and no men in the family. I started to cry when I saw all this so clearly in my mind. But even though the day the dead girl was brought back to life I ran to the well with all the other children, my memories of it are now rather confused. Let me think: I must have been about twelve years old. That evening there was a celebration at the mother's of the little girl from the well—the woman had no husband—with a meal in joint honour of the two men who saved her daughter, nephew and uncle. It was impossible to say which of them had done the most, as the one couldn't have saved her without the other, and in that respect, things had worked out perfectly. Grandmother said it was God who made them work out that way. Only men were seated at the table, and the women mostly stood behind and served them, while we children also found ways to keep ourselves busy there. Father didn't stay with them for long, he rose from the table and left, and having praised him so highly, those present were now quick to find fault with him.

The next day they told me that Uncle Jacob had come to take my father with him to Tarshish, to the farthermost shore of the great sea. In the meantime, I would have to stay with my grandmother, who, though old, was still beautiful, so said the guest. It's an example of how good people can be like death: if they take away someone you love, how are they any different? Any person who takes away someone dear to you, who makes someone vanish from your life, is Death. In Tarshish, a city at the mouth of a big river, whose name I don't know, the old man no longer had anybody, but instead, he had houses, servants, cattle and land, gold and silver, and a good trade. There, all the men are talkers, and they are singers too, not like here, in our land, where they sing only at weddings. They say that Father had to go there to dispose of Jacob's fortune, because Jacob was too old to deal with such things by himself any more. The old man said that Father would stay with him two or three years and then return here to us, a man forever freed of poverty, and Father would no longer have to care whether or not it rained, whether the plague struck, whether his back ached and he had nobody to till his soil and his vineyard, or whether the locusts came or the other such swarms of misfortunes that descend on us in this land of ours. But it did not turn out that way ...

From nearby came the song of a turtle dove calling to his mate. The woman's skilful hands had woven the girl's thick black locks into six plaits.

'All done, little girl!'

'What about the girl from the well?' asked the girl with the plaited hair, looking up at her grandmother, who was fleshy, and trying to imagine her small and thin.

'After she was born the second time, as they say, she was renamed Milkah, or 'Queen', because God's grace was with her. I can't remember what her name was before that, nobody remembers it. Milkah grew up, and folk called her "the girl from the well". Everybody knew her because she died and was reborn. She married at the age of thirteen and had a great many children!'

Now I'm forty, which is as old as my grandmother was then, although I'm not as beautiful as she was at this age, despite my name being Esther, which means Star. And you, my darling girl, are thirteen, which is a little older than I was when all that happened at the well. Your cheeks are as pink as roses and your hips are well rounded, and through the linen of your dress can be seen your little horns, as the poet so aptly calls them. Now that I am as old as my grandmother was then, I don't know whether imagination and forgetting twine together and play tricks on me, but as you'll see, it's only now that all the wonderful things Father experienced begin in earnest! They're things that might seem unbelievable, like something out of a story. But I know they're true. I'm going to tell you them exactly as I heard them from him when he returned home, by which time I'd grown and every woman's monthly lot had first come to me two months earlier. Father told the whole story in very few words, for he was niggardly of speech, but for me it wasn't hard to reconstruct step by step the journey he made with the skilled healer Jacob, who also had other miraculous powers. You could never imagine two men so different by nature, and maybe that's why they loved each other so much. But even so, they didn't get along together very well at all. When push came to shove, however, it was as if they were united as one. Would you like me to tell you the story? Your neck and that wee muzzle of yours, as you sit listening so intently, live up to your name, my little Weasel ...

That lad worries me greatly

'The world is like a bunch of grapes, which you eat one by one, my dear Huldah. You know, I don't feel old at all! But long ago there were years when time crawled along slowly and the sun barely seemed to move across the sky, and back then, I thought a lot about what it means to grow old. It's very simple. When you're born, there's a first time for doing all the things in the world, absolutely all of them, both the important and the unimportant ones. The more important and unimportant things you do for the first time, the fewer completely new things remain, and this is what's called growing old. It's as if that bunch of thousands and thousands of separate grapes keeps getting smaller until there's nothing left for you to pop in your mouth for the first time. The first yawn, the first smile on tiny lips that haven't yet learned to smile, lips that droop slightly on one side—oh, I remember when you first smiled at me, my little girl: you bathed my face in the radiance of it. Now you smile just like your grandmother and father ... The first step. The first one means everything, it contains all your future steps. Life goes on and, at the age of twelve or thirteen, the age you yourself have now reached, you start wondering what will it be like when you wear silk garments and a necklace of pearls at your wedding. And once a small drop of blood shows you're no longer a maid, then even that is something you'll never do for the first time again. But only after that is it good, not the first time, let me tell you, because soon you'll marry and you need to know. Then there's the first journey, the first time you see the sea, if you ever see it. As for me, I've never seen the sea, although sometimes I dream I do. Nobody from our land willingly makes a voyage across the sea, but I've often wondered what it would be like to be afloat on a ship. I'd so much have liked to find out! And then you give birth to your first child. When I knew for the first time that I was heavy with child, it was as if everything was given meaning, as if I were already enclosed in a different life. But once you've had ten children and a swarm of grandchildren, among which you were the first, my dear little weasel, you don't pay much attention to it any more.

And all these things waiting for you to do them for the first time are wrapped in great trepidation, and curiosity, and excitement, and impatience. That's what it means to be young. At first you don't see the gaps in the bunch of grapes, but halfway through life the by now grapeless and withered stem becomes all too plain. Men in particular suffer when they see what's no longer there, the emptiness of it drives them mad. Far sooner than you'd think, it's illness alone that provides you with your only new experiences, illness and people's gossip, if you care to listen to it, or even if you don't, but both illness and people's gossip age you. And then, finally, there's only one thing left to be done for the first time. You are old in truth, Huldah, when the only new thing left for you is your death. It's the first time in your life that you die! Just think of the newness of that!

It was the night of a full moon when Father and Uncle Jacob set off on their journey to Tarshish. I stayed behind with just Grandmother, your great-great-grandmother, in other words, and she stayed behind with just Esther, with me, in other words. The gaze of the guest from the ends of the earth lit up my grandmother's face, and each of us wore one of his rings on our fingers. The silver ring he gave me. Look, here it is! It will be yours.

*

31

The mules went slowly, stumbling on the rocks in the road. The son of Benjamin was cheerful, the son of Amithai, not at all.

'To tell the truth, my little Dove, I'd rather have been travelling with your mother, and I suspect that she wouldn't have been adverse either, given how often she showed her beautiful teeth while I was staying as your guest in your house. To make a woman laugh is a joy greater than you can imagine, and it's less selfish than the other joy that a man gives to a woman and takes from her. Obviously, making a woman laugh is harder than that other business, and not everybody can do it, as well you know. You're not exactly the most pleasant travelling companion, forgive an old man for saying so, an old man who is your blood relative on your father's side. If you're not poor in spirit, then letting the other man do all the talking is usually proof of indifference. "The preparations of the heart belong to man, but the answer of the tongue is from the Lord." That's how the proverb goes, at any rate. And goodwill is more precious than gold. Far be it from me to speak harsher words to you, since it is to you and you alone that I shall leave the wealth I have amassed over a lifetime. I don't wish to aggrieve the son of my cousin's beautiful wife, she who speaks as much as is required and laughs so beautifully and with such pleasure.'

Jonah made no answer even to this reproach, which couldn't have been blunter.

'I see very well that something is worrying you. Don't be annoyed at me: "Like an earring of gold or an ornament of fine gold is the rebuke of a wise judge to a listening ear," forgive me for talking in proverbs, but that's my way, as you'll see. Whenever you feel the urge, know that I'm here ready to listen and help you.'

And unconsciously fingering his earrings, old man Jacob fell into disconsolate silence, even though he wasn't usually prone to gloom. He would drive away his sorrow with some saying whose pith was audacious or ambiguous, causing those around him to marvel or smile when they discovered its meaning. He was always ready to help anybody in need and he could make himself liked in an instant. The two servants who tended to him listened to nobody else. One was lanky, with a body as wavy as seaweed, the other was short and stocky, as thick as the trunk of an oak tree. They would chatter among themselves, but to Jacob, and to him alone, did they display boundless respect.

Jacob's nephew didn't ask for his help and didn't say what it was that was troubling him, his ear remained without ornament of fine gold, without the earring of gold that is the rebuke of a wise judge. And so, with a frown on his face, Jonah ate his supper in silence and then laid himself on the ground, with his bearded cheek resting on his arm beneath him, and fell asleep the same instant, breathing through his mouth, even though his uncle would have liked to tell him the stories he had been collecting all his life so that he could share them with both mother and son. Jacob spent a long time arranging beneath his neck a small bolster which he'd brought with him from the ends of the earth. He turned now on one side, now on the other as he lay on the hard ground. He gazed at the stars, whose patterns on the firmament he knew by heart—in particular he liked the upside-down mountain with two jagged peaks. During the journey, sometimes sleep did come to him until the stars faded one by one against the whitening sky.

After many nights of little sleep and many days on the road, a time of occasional rains that came without warning but without allaying the suffocating heat, and after one of the mules twisted its leg and the slave with the seaweed-like frame became afflicted with a terrible pain in the back, which Jacob easily healed by pressing him with his fingers at certain spots, they finally arrived in Joppa. They entered the bustling port at dusk, the old man frail and tired, but as relaxed and forthcoming to other folk as an open palm, and Jonah, large and strong, but as clenched within himself as a fist, as a prophet once said and as the old man told one of his slaves, the tall, clever one, with whom he spoke sometimes, for want of another listener.

'There's something about him that reminds me of a bandit on the run. I don't know whom that lad of mine takes after.'

'Ha,' said the slave, but he was not bold enough to grin, as he didn't know whether he was meant to understand that Jonah took after his uncle.

'That lad worries me greatly. Where there's youth there's worry, and whoever yearns for the years of his youth yearns for misfortunes!'

And as if to prove him right, after they took their supper at an inn kept by a widow, Jonah vanished. He went outside to answer a call of nature and never came back. He was nowhere to be found the next morning, or afternoon, or evening. The two slaves searched every alley, enquiring of everyone they met, of every man, woman, sailor, and porter, of every craftsman and every indigent.

A deep-voiced Galilean

A disorderly cluster of small houses, Joppa lay on a low hill above the place where the mostly sandy shore formed a small rocky bay. The same as at Akko and Dor, everything was built higgledy-piggledy, some houses were made of stone, others of pungent bricks whose straws poked here and there from the walls. Some houses stood back to back, others face to face or at an angle to each other, some were sturdy, others on the point of collapse, and all showed the blank eyes of shuttered windows. Those who lingered a while in the port before setting off to sea were almost as numerous as the permanent residents. Many made a living from fishing or small trades, or from loading and unloading the ships, and often they too went to sea in search of their fortune. Life was good in Joppa, or Jaffa, as some called it, for every ship brought goods of every kind: olives and berries, beverages and grain, cedar and pine wood from the Lebanon, oak wood from Bashan, and timber, and jewels, and woven cloth.

Jacob was worried. He too tried to track down Jonah. With his smiling eyes and words that came from the heart, he easily gained people's trust, and he read a person's soul the way he read the holy scriptures and knew how to decipher it. A lifetime's observation had taught him that what you can't get from a grown man, you'll find out from the women, children, and servants. He began his search at the inn where Jonah had gone out without coming back. Since the death of the innkeeper Achim, the establishment had been run by his niggardly, withered widow. In front, in the dust of the road, two or three small, filthy beggars languished on the ground. A passing traveller might deign to cast them a word, good or bad, or some food from his pouch, this, too, good or bad.

'Hey, you, the bigger of you, the one with long hair, come here!'

The urchin thus summoned was in no hurry. He slowly rose to his feet, straightening the dirty, tattered cloth around his hips, since he saw he might be in with a chance of earning some money and he knew that that chance improved the harder and slower he played to get. He was skinny, narrow-chested, matted hair fell to his shoulders, and he limped with his right leg. He had a long neck and quite narrow eyes, with tangled eyelashes. His face had a certain melancholy charm. His toenails needed cutting.

'Were you in this place last night, child?'

The boy pondered a little, lowering his long eyelashes, as if weighing the answer most advantageous to him.

'Yes,' he finally said, with the utmost conviction.

'Even after night fell and it was completely dark?'

'Yes!'

'Did you see a sturdy man, a Galilean with a black curly beard, who came outside late last night, after everybody had left the yard of the inn. A man with a deep voice, if he happened to speak to you.'

'The bloke with a mug on him like a bandit's?'

Jacob, who had been sure the urchin was stringing him along, took heart at that.

'That's the one! If you tell me where he went, there'll be something in it for you, I'll pay you,' he said, but for the time being, he didn't show him his money.

'I'll tell you.'

The boy had a clever face and if he hadn't been so filthy, he might even have been comely. He stretched out his hand. But Jacob placed no faith in mere comeliness.

'First of all, tell me.'

'I saw him when he came out. He had one of those looks about him, he kept peering up and down the street, now right, now left. He pissed up against the wall.' Here, he turned his head slightly to indicate the spot. 'After that some woman came up to him, they talked about something, I couldn't hear what, and then they went off together.'

'Together? Do you know her? Have you seen this woman before?'

The little vagabond pondered for a short space once more, then held out his hand. This time, he spoke only once his hand had something to clasp.

'I know her. A whore.'

The old man dissimulated his amazement.

'She came here from Akko last year, been here ever since. Killed a man in Akko.'

It was plain that the urchin was pleased with what he had said.

'She killed a man?'

Anxiety now made itself heard in Jacob's voice. Jonah had left carrying gold in a pouch fastened to his girdle, under his coat.

'Yes, that's what folk say. If you want, I'll show you where she lives, but give us something to eat, me and the little 'uns, they're me brothers. We ain't eaten since yesterday, we're starving, I can barely stand up, that's how hungry I am.'

An expert at pulling the wool
over people's eyes

After the three children, who were very much alike as to their comely skin, their bodies that were nothing but bags of bones, and above all their hunger, eagerly chewed and swallowed their fill, Jacob set off with the limping vagabond. Despite raising his hip at every step so as not to put too much weight on his right foot, the urchin nonetheless advanced very quickly, stopping from time to time, where the road made a sudden turn, to wait for the old man to catch up. Finally, they came to a squat cottage that had tasselled strings hanging in the open doorway. There were hens and geese outside trying to get in past the string curtain. The boy aimed a kick at a hen, but missed. He did it only to make the hen squawk and flap its wings, after which, without wasting words, Jacob's guide ran back downhill. A seagull gave a shrill squawk and swooped down near the hens. Jacob watched as the boy ran off, his hopping gait not unlike that of the seagull.

Dusk was falling. The old man heaved a sigh and went to a small grated window.

'Is anybody home?'

To judge by the silence, there wasn't. He went back to the doorway. He took a hesitant step within, moving aside the string curtain. In the half-darkness he saw a curvaceous woman asleep on a low bench covered with a rumpled sheet. She had long hair and her coverlet had slipped onto the floor. There was a thick smell of food and sweat in the room.

'Is anybody home?' repeated Jacob, in growing embarrassment.

The woman raised herself on one elbow and looked him up and down. Once she had completed this preliminary, in a languid voice, drawling the words, she said as if reciting a prayer:

'Come hither, come hither, I have a bed made with linen from Egypt, sprinkled with aloe and cinnamon! Gifts of joy shall I give you, caresses and great pleasure, such as your senses have never experienced ...' She then added quickly, in a normal, slightly worried tone of voice, 'But it's going to cost you, you know, and you don't half look sickly. But you lot never pack it in, do you?'

Jacob gave a laugh so abrupt that he choked and then coughed at length before regaining his voice.

'You certainly do know how to tempt, you're the epitome of enticement ... I can't smell any cinnamon, though. Maybe my nose is to blame, it's not what it used to be ... Believe me, I wouldn't be adverse. But right now, I have other business and I'm in a hurry, a big hurry.'

Previously as languid as a fat, drowsy cat, the woman now tensed, her eyes darting suspiciously.

Sure of himself, Jacob went on, 'Last night you came home with a sturdy young man, a tall man, that is, with a black curly beard, whom you picked up at the inn. A man with a deep voice, if he spoke to you at all, since he's rather taciturn. His name is Jonah, I don't know whether he told you. He's my nephew. But what can I say? It's as if he were my own son, since I don't have any other children. Nobody has seen him since. I'm hoping you might be able to tell me where to find him, because we have to board ship soon. We're going to Tarshish, a town at the ends of the earth, beyond the strait that runs between the rock of Abyla and Mount Calpe.'

The woman gazed at him pensively in the half-darkness and burst out laughing. A nasty laugh it was. Then in a normal tone of voice she said:

'Oh, forgive me, grandfather. Really, you're completely un-like any of the men who visit me, and I was worried you might croak while between my legs, which is what happened to me in Akko, and he was a lot younger man than you. I had to scarper like a murderess. But even here I'm still forced to turn tricks as long as I'm able and as long as somebody still wants me, and that's why I don't turn away any customers.'

'I much preferred the way you talked to me before ... This isn't anything to do with ... I'm not like I used to be, when my passion blinded me like fury blinds a bull. Women usually can't even imagine the torment young men endure. But I'm skilful in my own way, even at my age, a lot more than other men less stooped under the burden of years. And don't forget, you charming thing, that my ancestor Abraham, praised be his name, sired Isaac at the age of a hundred, and I still have a long way to go before I'm that old. But right now, I really am in a hurry, so tell me already, I implore you—' here he looked deep into her eyes '—where my nephew went ...'

'I've no idea who you're talking about! Unfortunately, there wasn't anybody here at my house last night, granddad, somebody must have tricked you. I'd have liked to meet this Jonah of yours. Down at the inn, there's a rascal of an urchin, Elisha, or Eli for short, who every now and then sends travellers up here to me, making them believe all kinds of tall tales. He's an expert at pulling the wool over people's eyes ... He's got two or three ready-made stories, he rolls the same ones out whatever the occasion, he never tires of telling them. Like all liars, a lot of the time he hits the mark. I've never scolded him for it because by the time we clear things up, the men stay the night, which means we all profit.'

She gave another cracked laugh. From somewhere a kind of piteous whine made itself heard above her laughter and all the callous disregard on the woman's face instantly turned to alarm. Her face suddenly looked deeply lined, and only now did Jacob realise that she was far from young. His eyes had by now grown accustomed to the dark and he saw grey strands of hair at her temples. Along with the whine there entered the room a girl of perhaps eighteen, heavy with overflowing rolls of flesh, but it was not her corpulence that alarmed the visitor. Her eyes were like those of a hunted wild animal and the sounds she made had perhaps never coalesced into words. When she set eyes on Jacob, she took fright and crouched down with her head between her hands, like a beast of burden waiting to be beaten. It was plain to see that she was not in her right mind. The yelps she was making grew more rapid and began to choke her.

'There, there, mammy's little girl, everything's all right, nobody's going to do you any harm, come to mammy!' said the woman in a sweet, gentle voice that the old man would never have thought her capable of, a voice completely different from the one in which she had spoken when she had been weighing him up as a potential customer and when she had been afraid of him, a voice that was for her unfortunate daughter alone, one also able to quell the fury and the demons within.

I don't believe you!

When they arrived in front of the inn, the two servants did not have good news. Actually, they had no news at all. But there was no one there for them to give the news to, or rather, not to give any news, because like Jonah, Jacob had also disappeared. They went inside to see whether he might be in the rectangular courtyard, but there were only three or four men chattering together. They went back outside and looked up and down the street in alarm. The lanky servant found himself tugged from the right by the skirt of his coat, which was split on both sides, revealing his hairy thighs.

'Are you waiting for somebody?'

'What do you want, eh? Who are you?'

'I'm Elisha. We haven't eaten for a whole day, me and me brothers.' Here, he jutted his head in the direction of two almost naked urchins. 'If you give us something—' he now addressed the short, stocky servant, who he thought looked the stupider of the two '—I'll help you out. I know the comings and goings of everybody in Joppa.'

The short servant looked up at the tall one, silently asking what he should do. He received permission.

'Here's the thing, we're looking for our master, who's called Jacob ben Benjamin.'

'The one with a face like a bandit's? I know him, I saw him!'

'That's not him, that's not right, he's an old man, his hair is white with age, and he has a face you can trust. He likes to make jokes. And he doesn't look down on you, even if you're a servant, not like the others do, or rather not like everybody else does.'

He uttered a Phoenician curse. The boy grew animated:

'I know this Jacob of yours. I took him to see a whore. I'll take you where I took him.' Here, he held out his hand. 'But you'll have to pay me, and give us something to eat, because I haven't got the strength to walk, not one morsel has passed my lips since yesterday, not mine, not these little brothers' of mine, we're dying of hunger.'

'Hold on a minute, you sly cripple, don't you go thinking we were born yesterday,' the tall servant broke in. 'I don't believe you took the old man to see any harlot!'

'Elisha is my name. You can't have forgotten. You can also call me Eli. I'm telling you I spoke to this Jacob of yours. He's the old man with a white beard and gold earrings who was looking for that Galilean with the black beard, the one who left here yesterday and didn't come back, a tall bloke with a deep voice. That's why I took the old codger to see the whore.'

The two servants were left open-mouthed in astonishment. So, the urchin wasn't lying. In any case, he had such a knack of persuasion that you couldn't help but give in to him. He was no ordinary child.

'Jonah,' said the tall servant.

'Yes, he was looking for Jonah,' confirmed Eli, who could grasp the nub of the matter on the fly, raising his bowed eyelashes to reveal the most earnest eyes in the world. 'And that old man of yours is really worried,' he added in a downcast voice.

They gave him some green figs from their pouch. Elisha shared them with the other children. He wolfed his down in an instant. He quickly wiped his hands on the cloth he wore around his thighs and which seemed to serve that purpose alone, and led the two servants up the hill, treading on his right foot in that hopping manner of his. They made their way up the lane that Elisha had only recently come back down, but barely had they turned the first corner when Jacob himself appeared in front of them. He was coming slowly down the hill. He didn't seem at all happy. Elisha weighed the chances of his running away, but finally decided to stay put.

Kissing, weeping, laughing

Like a fugitive had Jonah quit the port, sought by so many, heedless of all. He had always been in the habit of running away from the world and into the wilderness. He never knew who or what drove him to it. All he wanted now was to be alone with the sky, the earth, the water, and the God he lost in crowded places like Joppa. His uncle, as wise as a serpent, had sensed it all too well: Jonah needed help. Jacob, as gentle as a turtledove, was ready to give him it. But Jonah could not receive it, or in any event, not from him. Moreover, Jonah knew that there was great sorrow in store for him, and knew that he would betray his uncle very soon. He kept spinning the thoughts around and around in his head, like the clay on a potter's wheel, moulding them, kneading them hard, and always they took a different turn, the pot wouldn't take shape in his mind, he couldn't finish it, because he couldn't decide the final shape he should give it, and this endless spinning of the clay dizzied him, for which reason he was very surly and sullen.

Even as a small child he'd been incapable of weeping, of complaining, of asking for help or forgiveness. When others wronged him, he never said it hurt him, nor did he say it hurt him when he wronged others. And when it so happened that he was the one who wronged others, it hurt him most of all. And happen it did. Jonah must have been around nine years old when one day Amithai beat him with a hazel switch in an attempt to nip in the bud what he saw as his son's obstinacy. For, as the proverb says, he who spares the rod spoils his son. Other children were used to it, they would howl and then forget, but Amithai's son did not cry out, he ran away from home and for three days ate nothing but wild fruit and bitter roots. He tried to eat olives straight from the tree, but they were so sour he had to spit them out. Instead, he chewed the petals of flowers and sucked sap from the stems of grasses and drank water from a stagnant pond, but his stomach wouldn't hold it down and he threw it back up. The next day, his body felt light and his head heavy, and as the sun slowly sank, in air that was still red and soft he saw the voice of God for the first time. It happened at the foot of a mountain. It all lasted only a few seconds. The voice sprang up in front of him and he wouldn't have been able to say what it looked like, but it was there, something solid in the emptiness of the air. All it said to him was, 'Jonah, Jonah, Jonah!' but thereby it comforted him, and scolded him, and encouraged him, and the boy understood very well the comfort and the scolding and the encouragement that came through the air and filled it. On the third evening, he went back home, his mother kissed him and wept and then laughed, and his father frowned, rejoiced, and spoke almost in the same way as the voice of God, shaking his head and gazing at him with velvety, tear-filled eyes: 'Jonah, Jonah, Jonah!' And much later he understood that his mother's kissing, weeping and laughing were also like the voice of God: a comfort, a reproach, an encouragement. Thereafter, Amithai never beat him again. Before he set out with his uncle, Jonah had seen the voice of God but once.

*

From the way Elisha greeted Jacob you would have thought they were friends or relatives. He didn't seem at all embar-rassed at having tricked him earlier.

'Look here, I've brought you these two!' he said, pointing at the servants. 'I'm not going to charge you anything for it, because you were good to me and I like you. But if you want me to find Jonah for you—remember, I know every coming and going in this port, and what I don't know, I know where to find out—then you'll have to pay me better ...' He then added, with a note of reproach: 'Since you can afford it!'.

He held out a hand still sticky from the green figs. Jacob marvelled at how Elisha knew the name of his nephew, but he left him with palm outstretched and gave the tall servant a certain look. With a severity you would not have expected of him, the servant felt among Elisha's tangled locks and clenched his ear between his fingernails. He tugged the ear until he forced Elisha to stand on tiptoes and berated him:

'You've got some cheek wanting to get paid too, you villain! If you don't find him—and you can search all night long, wherever you want—we'll beat you black and blue for all the lies you've told today.'

None of which bothered Elisha, who, hardened to both beatings and yelling, simply ignored it. He addressed himself to Jacob alone:

'Don't you worry, old man, I'll find him for you this very evening, if he's still alive. He's in Joppa. He can't have left by sea, because no ships have set sail. But I'll need some money, not for myself, but to loosen people's tongues.'

'You'd do well to call the master "master", you chucklehead!' yelled the servant once more, but Jacob interposed:

'Maybe I'll take you with me as a servant if you prove you're capable and rid yourself of your lice. I saw straight away that you've got rich flocks in your head, which graze like sheep and goats in a meadow. I could teach you many things, some of them wonderful. A word fitly spoken is like apples of gold in pictures of silver. You'll find us at the inn where we spent last night, at that rather unpleasant woman's, Achim's widow.'

'Go on, scram!' added the other servant for what it was worth.

Elisha left immediately, not for fear of the servants' threats, but because he was sure that with a little luck he could make a tidy sum, more than he'd ever earned in his life. The old man's feet were clean! His coat was the most expensive he'd ever seen, the slit at the neck was sewn with two threads like the purple drawn with sharp needles from inside the shellfish that fishermen call the rock snail, and his sandals were made of calf's leather: it was obvious he wore them all the time, so soft was the skin of his toes and heels. He'd never seen apples of gold in pictures of silver, but gold, silver, and bronze in the old man's pouch, yes, he'd seen them with his own two eyes. The old man could feed many people, if he had a mind. Or he could at least feed him.

If you come before Adonai …

It was already pitch dark, but Elisha knew the port even with his eyes closed. He headed for the docks, where only four ships stood at anchor. It would soon be autumn, when ships did not set out on long journeys across the sea, lest they be wrecked in a storm. The nearest ship had a broad deck and prow like a thick snake with two heads looking right and left. Next to it was a long vessel shaped like a barracuda, the kind that slips through the water with ease and can reach high speeds. The third, with a jutting bird's-head prow and fish-tail stern, seemed very solid and had a round hull that immediately drew the eye. Finally, the most magnificent was a Phoenician vessel that had arrived with goods from Sidon and Tyre. It had taken two days to unload and was probably waiting to take on another cargo before setting out to sea once more.

But there was no movement on the decks of the ships, and in the port the hustle and bustle of the day had died down, which meant Elisha had to go around and around in search of somebody from whom to glean tidings of the sturdy Galilean with the black curly beard, Jonah by name. He was just about to give up when he came across a young man seated idly, propped up against some stacked timber unloaded from a ship. Next to him lay a staff whose knob was shaped like a fist. Although he seemed to be dozing, he couldn't have been, since when Eli approached, he immediately clasped the fist-shaped knob of his staff. Eli sat down cross-legged in front of the young man and gave him a hearty handshake.

'Glad to see you, Abiel.'

The young man laughed.

'Glad to hear you, Elisha!'

'Oh, yes, well ... Are you hungry? I think I can cadge some food for you, if you want ... How's it been going?'

The young man, whose face was handsome, thanks mainly to the almost feminine lips that showed through his bronze-coloured beard, shrugged.

'The same as usual. No, there's no need, I've eaten today. But what luck brings you here?'

'There's a foreigner who's disappeared, the name's Jonah. He arrived here with some codger, who's looking for him. He's as rich as a king, the old man, I mean: I've never seen the like. Says he'll take me to sea with him if I find the bloke! Have you heard anything about him? If nobody's cut his throat to steal his pouch, since he's probably rich too, then he has to be around here somewhere.'

'I swear by the light of my eyes that he's alive,' Abiel laughed.

Only a slight start betrayed Elisha's interest. His voice retained its reserve, its almost sad tone.

'Are you sure, Abiel?'

'He paid for his passage right here, next to me. But he told the captain to be ready to sail in any direction at all, be it north, be it west. Said he'd tell him tomorrow where the voyage would take them.'

'The bloke I'm looking for will be travelling west, the old man told me so, over the sea to a place called Tarshish.'

'I think I've heard of a Tarse or a Tarsus in Anatolia, north of here. A villain came from there once, I remember him well, because he knocked me out and robbed me. Take a look: count them, it's the third ship along, a very sturdy craft, the one with the rounded hull, that's what I heard, a ship with a bird's-head prow. Your man, who had a deep voice, I heard it clearly, said that he'd spend the night on deck. They want to leave without delay, as soon as the sun comes up, that's what they settled on.

He must be the one, although I don't think he mentioned his own name.'

'Abiel, your ears see very well, nothing escapes them. I too think he must be the one, it can't be anybody else. And you ought to know that if I were the God of Abraham, I'd give you back the light of your eyes.'

'If you come before Adonai, don't forget to tell him!'

Rising to his feet, Elisha smiled at him without showing his teeth, and a dimple formed at the right corner of his mouth. Abiel sensed his smile and returned it. He then heard Elisha's footfalls receding at a run, the jerky run of those who do not tread with equal weight on each foot. He knew that Elisha was lame, but he had never asked him why. Nor had Elisha ever asked him why he was blind, or how long he had been blind.

They're not my brothers

It took him no more than a quarter of an hour to reach the yard of Achim's widow, where in the shade of the low, ramshackle arches he found the two servants fast asleep alongside other travellers, all in a heap. Snores of every pitch and tone could be heard. Taking care not to wake them, he climbed the outside stair to the flat roof, where he found the old man pacing up and down. As the moon was almost full, Jacob espied him straight away.

'Stop, wait, if you have news, don't tell me! You might compare me with a night bird, because just as an owl cannot abide the light, I cannot abide to hear news even when it's good. Oh, but I can tell you have good news, tell me this instant, come on, what are you waiting for!'

As usual, Elisha was in no hurry. He didn't pass on any information free of charge.

'Will you take me with you? I've never left Joppa before.'

'So what if you haven't? What, do you think things are better at sea, when you're a helpless passenger at the mercy of the storms? As fish are caught in the net, so sea voyagers are caught in the coming of the evil hour. The sea is deceptive. How could I take you? What if we both die? It's highly likely. And what about your brothers, what will you do with them? I can't allow it! Impossible to take you all, and if I take you, who will take care of them? I'll be doing them a wrong.'

'No, grandda- ... master,' he said, smoothly correcting himself, 'they're not my brothers, and they do have somebody to look after them. I just call them my brothers in front of strangers, so that they'll give all of us food, because I'm a better talker than they are.'

'You certainly are, I'll give you that! Don't you have parents?'

'I never knew my father. My mother was taken away.'

'By whom?'

But Elisha made no reply to that. He moved on to the news:

'He made an agreement with some sailors. He's leaving tomorrow at dawn, but they don't know the destination, he told them to be ready to sail north, or south, and if not north or south, then west, apparently ... He's already on board, I think. I'll take you there.'

Jacob's face fell, he began to totter, and Elisha quickly added:

'He's well, in good health, nobody's cut his throat.'

'Why would anybody cut his throat? What kind of talk is that? Why would he do a thing like this to me? I don't understand it! I never was able to understand that child, no more than a hen can understand a duckling.'

Elisha couldn't understand what was with the child, the hen and the duckling, and he thought the old man was talking about him. He was accustomed to always being to blame. His eyes narrowed even more.

'I told you that just because you was upset. Anyways, there's no hurry! I don't think they'll be sailing tomorrow, they haven't taken any cargo on board, and it'll take at least a day to do that, two days, definite. The captain strung him along to get him to cough up more money. They have to take victuals and drink on board. We can go there in the morning.'

'No, we'll go now!'

*

The water glinted grey, sliced by a silver strip of molten moon-light. The four ships stood black against the starry sky. On board the medium-sized ship with the bird's-head prow, nobody was moving on deck, there was nothing to be seen.

Going down to the shore, Jacob and Elisha climbed into a boat. Elisha had never rowed before, nor had Jacob, and, at first, he poked the oars in the water as if he were trying to cut meat with a knife, which meant the boat remained stationary. After a while, more by accident than anything else, one of the oars made a sweeping motion, and the boat rocked slightly and moved a little way. After that, it didn't take long for Elisha to work out how to advance over the water: he'd often seen grown men row, although he probably wasn't doing it quite like them. His arms were unexpectedly strong, despite his being thin. It made Jacob wonder how old he really was. Children who grow up on the street are either older or younger than they look. The boat rocked and the old man gripped the gunwales on both sides, but little by little they neared the ship. When they hove to, they were lucky enough to find that the rope ladder to the deck was still lowered. The well-travelled Jacob was accustomed to climbing such ladders unaided, albeit slowly, and as for Elisha, although lame, he was nimble. They walked around the deck. After a while, Eli came across something large and dark, rather like a heap, hidden next to a barrel. Stepping up to it he saw that it was a man asleep with his head resting on his crooked arm and breathing hoarsely through his mouth. He suspected it was the man they were looking for, although he himself had never seen him. In his tales about the man he had lied from start to finish. He showed Jacob the sleeping man as if he recognised him and they planted themselves on either side of him. Eli saw from Jacob's face that he had not been mistaken.

'Look at him,' said the old man in a low voice, but not in a whisper, 'he was fast asleep while I was at the end of my tether worrying about him! How can this be?'

He nudged him with his sandal. Jonah stirred, but did not awake. Elisha realised that Jacob had been talking to himself and wasn't dead set on an answer.

'Maybe he's drunk,' Eli nonetheless opined, 'because you can't wake a drunk no matter what you do, it happened to me once with—'

'No, he's not drunk. Shake him!'

Elisha stooped and with both hands grasped Jonah's free arm. He moved him back and forth, heaving on him like a sack. With a murmur that sounded like 'lo, lo!' the sleeping man sat up and looking around him in confusion. At first, he made no answer to his uncle's questions, then he said curtly and clearly:

'The captain is taking me. Anywhere. I paid him a lot. Leave tomorrow. Fine. Let it be Tarshish.'

'Tartessos!' Jacob joyfully confirmed, but he elicited no further explanations from Jonah, as he had gone back to sleep.

The voices

As if it had grown with him, feeding on him like a foal in a mare's belly, when it showed itself to him the next time, the second, the voice of God was louder and clearer, and it took place just after the episode at the well.

While all the others banqueted beneath the open sky, while old man Jacob sat proudly at the table and the still beautiful widow of Amithai stood behind to serve him, while all the others ate and laughed, some of them having grown tipsy and talking loudly, forgetting that a husband and father in the family had died not long before, Jonah ran away again, he fled towards the light of the stars and the waxing moon, farther than the last house in the village. Although the others had been toasting him as a hero, along with his uncle from far away, although they had tried to outdo each other in their praises of the two men who, acting as one, had saved the little girl from the bottom of the well, Jonah felt guilty and was gnawed by remorse. He couldn't remember exactly, but he suspected that it was he himself who had left the lid of the well open, the lid he usually pushed back into place. And he wouldn't have forgotten to do it if it hadn't been for his uncle. On the other hand, if it hadn't been for his uncle, maybe he would now have had the death of an innocent child and a distraught mother to feel guilty about. These bad thoughts pierced him from within and with every word of praise heaped upon him by the guests, with every shout of laughter, his burden grew. He wanted to cry out and beg their forgiveness, but the strong voice within him would not emerge. It pounded him in his guts. He'd been drinking wine, and at the lewd words of one of the men at the table, his member had stiffened in lust for a woman. I shouldn't wonder if you yourself got married tomorrow or the day after, and it's high time you knew about such things. Jonah was thinking of visiting Hannah. She lived near us, and although I was only little, even I knew that she had become Father's paramour after Mother's death or, who knows, even before that. Once, Grandfather told me the secret of how her name was the same when you read it from right to left, the way our nation reads, or left to right, the way other nations read. And he traced the letters with a stick for me in the dust. Hannah was beautiful and she was the only woman in Gat-Hefer with blue eyes. She had been widowed at a young age, when some nameless disease snatched away her three small children and her husband within the space of just a few days. She wished she could have died with them, but the disease, which comes only unsummoned, passed her by. After a year of grief and mourning, she met an unknown widower, who stayed at her house on certain nights and he entered her with a skill such as her poor husband had never possessed. But as for him, he was able. After he left, she would lie there, a state of well-being pervading her body, her soul at peace, as laden with fruit as a vineyard. After a few days, the stranger, her lover, told her that his name was Jonah. Nothing more. That he had a daughter, whose name was Esther, she discovered for herself. For a time, I hated her. It felt as if she were taking my father away from me. What a good thing that you've fallen asleep, my darling, otherwise I wouldn't have been able to tell you all this!

*

I was asleep, dreaming, but my heart kept watch. It is night and I am waiting for you, my love, in my sheer silk shirt, through which my body shows, soft and white. Come quickly, my dark love, come, let us grow drunk on love at midnight, I long for your impetuous touch, come, seek me, be my master, let us take delight in each other, awake me, guide me, plough my furrow and sow your seed in me that I might make children for you in the summer, children who will multiply like blades of wheat and fill the face of the earth, that I might make children to replace those that death took from me and are down below in the ground, who will never more show themselves to me, like barren seeds. May you drink the wine of my love and grow drunk, endlessly repeating my name, Hannah, Hannah, my love, my pomegranate, I sicken for love of you! Your voice troubles me, it calls to me, and I hear you even in my dream, and in my dream, I see you, I see your voice.

*

He walked bewildered and, in his ears, there was a droning sound like the buzzing of flies and the rippling of water. He reached her house, but at the last moment he came to a halt, turned, and walked away on tiptoes. The house was still visible in the distance when he thought to see her outline standing by the door, white, ripe, but with a wondrously narrow waist, and his heart broke for pity. When dawn began to glimmer and a healthy breeze scattered the heat of the night and the mist in his mind, his eyes and his ears, Jonah saw the voice once more, for the second time.

The solidity within the air's emptiness all but vibrated, and although it was of a texture different than that of light, an all-pervading radiance enveloped Jonah, who had not slept for a single moment or stopped walking. Now he stopped. Everything God told him, he saw with his own eyes: he arose, he boarded a ship and went north, and he disembarked and travelled with a caravan to Nineveh, the largest city in the world, in Aram-Nacharaim, the warlike land, the land of Ashur, where there were broad streets unnumbered, so many that you lost your way, there were plazas shaped like flowers and stars, and tall, broad palaces, bathed in the abundant blue shade of lapis lazuli, surrounded with crenelated walls, and there were merchants as numerous as the stars in the heavens, folk whose hearts were uncircumcised, everything was terrifying and you could not find your way, you wandered lost among houses as tall as the cedars of the Lebanon. Evil rulers, corrupt to the marrow of their bones. Executioners who tore out the tongues and eyes of the vanquished and hung severed heads around the necks of their prisoners that they might serve as a warning to all those who beheld them. Their king had sickly eyes, he had debauched slaves and beasts that sinned with mankind, and as soon as he entered that city, Jonah began to prophesy its perdition due to the evils of its inhabitants, who were like unto those of Sodom and Gomorrah. After which Jonah was not sure whether the words were still God's, but he could see, as if from a great height, how the sickly city, its body consumed with black plague, crumbled and collapsed in on itself, and it was reduced to dust and rubble, and dust and flames rose as high as the clouds amid the cries and the ruins, and they were like a huge crown from which then sprang up another city, a city as good and beautiful and white and delicate as a dove.

Full of the voice of God and troubled with happiness, he turned back, and now he spent the night at Hannah's. After he made love to her and heard her moan become shriller and shriller, as if in pain, although he knew that it was for joy that she moaned, he found the courage to tell her he was leaving. She burst into tears. And she angrily reproached him, for the first time like a wife, and not like his bashful secret lover: 'Now? Now? Now of all times you find to leave?'

Then she added in a soft, joyful voice: 'We're going to have a child.'

But the child inside her could not be seen, he did not see it, it was as if it did not exist. Jonah still felt full of the voice he had seen and which also had seen him. He left the woman in the doorway, her eyes red, her hair dishevelled.

In the village, the celebration had come to an end, all were sleeping, and the birds were pecking the leftovers on the table. He immediately wanted to tell the guest from afar that he could only accompany him as far as Joppa, whence, however, his uncle would voyage west, while he would take another ship north, before travelling by caravan to Nineveh. He lay down with this thought and slept deeply until evening. When he awoke, the world manifested itself to him differently and he was no longer even sure of the voice's command, whereas his uncle, who gazed on him with love and tenderness, was close to him and placed all his hope in him. How could he do such a thing? How could he do such a thing to his mother, who had only just lost her husband? And perhaps he also thought a little of me, his star, and of how I would be left an orphan ... Who would believe that he had spoken to God, or, to be more exact, that God had spoken to him? He was caught between two betrayals: either yesterday's voice or his family. No, if he was to go to Nineveh, he could only do so covertly, without saying anything about it. But he would hurt the others, and Jacob would be thrown into despair, since his life and wealth would then be scattered like clouds in the wind.

Although Jonah was unable to show it, Jacob had forevermore become very dear to him. In any event, my dear, Father never said he loved anyone, he never said it even to me, even though at the time I was his only child and I'm absolutely certain that he did love me in his way. And as for him, he was afraid that if he went to Nineveh, they might burn him alive or place him in the hands of the executioners and hang his severed head around someone's neck. Or that they might hammer a ring through his nose, which was how they kept their prisoners chained. Jonah's thoughts span around and around, like the potter's clay, in an uncontrollable whirl. He abruptly decided to put a stop to it: he would go to the rotten city of Nineveh and never see Jacob again. He had good grounds to do so. No matter how close and how dear to him he might be, his uncle was not God.

He therefore went back to Joppa and came to the shore. He looked in his pouch of gold once more. He knew what he had to do. And like any act of treachery, he would have to do it quickly, lest he change his mind and be caught. He had good luck straight away and he took it to be a sign. He lay himself down to sleep with his mind at peace. But he was woken by the very man he hoped never again to see, for the sole reason that he felt ashamed in his presence. Which is why, like almost every fugitive, he betrayed once again. He betrayed what he held most dear in his heart: he betrayed the voice.

'Then Tarshish it shall be!'

'Tartessos!' came the joyful reply.

It won't be any worse than here

The ship bobbed over the waves like a seagull, the beak of its prow sundering the horizon and its fishtail stern leaving a white-fringed trail behind. The final destination was very far away, at the ends of the Great Sea. But for the time being the wind was not favourable. A stray gust would fill the dirty white sail, puffing it out like the round cheek of a hale and hearty young man, giving the vessel a shove, before leaving it to sag like the wrinkled face of an old man, at which they would be left becalmed. The oarsmen, at their benches, their oars at the ready in their rowlocks, would then await the order.

Two days had passed since Jacob had found Jonah again. The captain, a short man from Iberia, in constant motion, his hair a mass of ringlets that always seemed wet, had made thorough preparations, particularly given that to the money already paid over had been added an even greater sum on the part of old man Jacob. There was no reason for the captain to tell Jacob that another man had already paid, however. He had whooped for joy when he discovered the destination of the voyage, for after years of roaming the waves, he would at last have the opportunity to go home to his children, his wife Adina, and his numerous brothers and cousins. Unlike Jonah, whose frowning face somehow made him feel at a loss, even though he was sure he was a decent man, Jacob had won the captain over with the very first words he spoke. Now they would joke among themselves in the tongue of the Iberians, as if they had known each other a lifetime, and Sansón and Hernando would join in, relatives of the captain who had set off from home with him and on whom he relied in difficult moments. Sansón had six fingers on his left hand, the one he used for eating, and was a trusty lad, always ready to leap into the fire or rather the water for the captain's sake. Hernando had a round face and an overbite, which gave him a slight impediment in his tongue.

The captain had sought, found and hired another two sturdy oarsmen, besides his own, who were of various nations, four on each side. But the thing that consumed the greatest part of his time was taking on board supplies, an operation that stretched over a few days. The main thing was the water, stored in barrels and amphorae on the deck of the deeply scooped hold. Next in importance was the olive oil, in its fat-bellied clay pots. To the joy of Jacob, the captain ordered a few jugs of honey from a bee-keeper, a very expensive commodity, as precious as gold, since it never spoiled, and procured cakes of unleavened dough from the bakers' lane. Few had tasted honey like that, as most were familiar only with wild honey. And then, of course, there was also what they would fish for themselves during the journey, and besides, for the first few days, they also had a supply of fruit and vegetables. In every port, the replenishment of this supply was the captain's first concern: he knew from experience that without fruit and peas or other legumes, the sailors would be struck down by an illness that was like an invisible beast devouring their muscles, they would have terrifying hallucinations, their speech would become garbled, and they would lose control of their arms and legs, without having drunk strong liquor. He had once lost half his crew this way. To a nameless disease that filled the mariners with the same terror as the plague itself. The captain ordered that a sack of dried lentils be brought on board for soup and a few pouches of spices, including the bay leaves that the old beekeeper had given him in gratitude for his purchase. A tub of salted sheep's cheese completed the provisions, and for the good cheer of the passengers and himself he had set aside skins of red wine, while the crew had to make do with a slightly stronger white wine. But the thing of which the captain was especially proud was a goat, on which he had spent a small fortune. They would have milk both fresh and sour, or at least the captain and his two notable guests would. Obviously, he had to buy barley and bran and broom for the goat to munch all day long. And once the goat's feed ran out, he would slaughter it. Siran, an Armenian as withered as a raisin, who, besides his other duties, cooked for the captain and the captain alone, would then make a series of tasty suppers from the goat. And after all this expenditure, the payment he had received from the two travellers, the young man and the old, was not even visibly diminished. The captain could not have been more content.

*

The sailors and the oarsmen were of different nations. They communicated among themselves in few words, in a mixed language whose expressions were familiar to all those who travelled the waves. Besides the captain's relatives and the small Armenian, there was also an extremely knowledgeable Phoenician—the last time there was a storm, he had been every-where at once, wherever he was needed, as if under a magic spell that allowed him to pop up in more than one place simul-taneously—who was loved by all. There were two sons of Amon, Nubians as strong as bulls, one old, one young, perhaps even father and son, and there were two Greeks, perhaps brothers, one with a large saddle-like nose, the other with a nose long and straight, who spoke only among themselves. Certainly, there were also others, but who can remember them now? In the hard trials that are never far away when you spend a long time with the same men aboard a rolling and pitching timber, with death always lurking ahead and to right and left, and only ever vanquished in your wake, Siran knew how to hearten the crew with his contagious laugh and his zither. Often when he played it he would accompany the notes of the sheep-gut strings with a voice which, although not deep, was so beautiful that all at once it quelled the fury of the men, albeit not the waves. During storms, Siran was good for nothing, however, and would start to tremble and vomit as if he had yellow fever.

While Jonah, to all appearances, was asleep with his eyes open—he saw fit to leave the ship only once, to attend to some business or other at the inn, where he spoke a few stern words to Achim's widow, also calling the woman from next door to be present—and the captain and crew were occupied now on deck, now in the hold, now on the docks, Jacob had been making his own preparations. The first thing he did was order the short servant to shave Elisha's head and thereby rid him of his lice. He had by now informed the boy that he was taking him on the journey with him and would keep him by his side until his dying day, for he sensed that Death now moved beside him, buzzing like a wasp. He needed somebody agile and quick-witted to assist him in an increasing number of tasks, as each of them became harder and harder for him. When he saw the gleaming razor as it swooped down on his head, Eli tried to flee. They held him on both sides to stop him struggling, but even so, he still came away with a few gashes on his scalp. He looked strange like that, without his long hair, and now revealed, the skin beneath shone white in comparison with his brass-coloured face. The other two children in front of the inn laughed at him and pointed their fingers. But when he told them he was going far away, the little one began to sob inconsolably and threw his thin little arms around his legs, pressing his unnaturally distended belly to his brother's knees and trying in vain to hold him back.

'It's all right, I'll be coming right back,' he said, 'and I'll bring you something. What do you want me to bring you when I come back?'

'My mammy,' whined the child, wiping away the snot from his nose with the back of his hand.

'No, ask for something else,' Eli quickly said. 'I'll bring you a toy ship, with sails and oars, and you'll be able to float it on the water.' Then he said to the older of the two, 'And I'm going to leave you my catapult to look after. So you can defend yourselves. But you'll give me it back when I return!'

Eli left the two children, their faces crumpled with sadness, and tried not to look back. He went to say farewell to Abiel, and found him in the spot where he sat most often to beg, on the corner between two usually crowded lanes.

'Abiel, I've come to say goodbye. I'm going to sea. The old man's taking me with him as a servant. It won't be any worse than it is here. My old gaffer's name is Jacob. He's a healer, and I heard he brought back to life a girl who fell down a well. He knows how to read and write like them priests up in the temple. Says he's going to teach me to write. You think he'll be able to pull off witchcraft like that?'

Abiel lifted his face to Eli's, but made no answer. A few tears welled from his almost closed eyelids with their tiny eyelashes. Eli tried to feign joy, although he knew not the meaning of joy:

'He left me without a single hair on my head, go on, feel my head to see how smooth and pointy it is.'

Eli knew that Abiel saw with his fingers. He took one of his hands to place it on his scalp, but Abiel could not suppress a cry of pain. It was only then that Eli saw that his friend's left hand was red and swollen.

Abiel had had a bad day. He was inured to humiliations, but this time they had been worse than ever. The trouble had been due to an innkeeper's son. The innkeeper had been kind to the blind man, he used to give him jobs to do, sometimes difficult ones, but he would then pay him fairly, although never too much. A rumour had spread that the innkeeper was Abiel's father, although this was mere idle talk. After the old man died and his son took over the inn, things had changed. The inn-keeper's son gave Abiel nasty tasks and more often than not failed to pay him afterwards. This time, he had made him feel through a heap of garbage in the port, offloaded from the ships, telling him that when a servant dumped the trash from the inn there, he had probably also thrown out the only knife. He had promised him a copious meal if he found it. After feeling his way through ordure, dead rats and birds, peelings, rotten fish, and shells, on which he had lacerated his hands, and after enduring the putrid stench, which would have made him throw up had he not had an empty belly, the innkeeper returned and mockingly said: 'Well, you looked for it like a fool! I found the knife almost straight away, but then I got side-tracked, what with one thing and another, you know how busy I am, and I forgot to come and tell you.' He'd then objurgated him in a growing fury: 'You scrounged off my father more than long enough, you ought to toil as my slave your whole life to make up for it, except you're good for nothing. You're not going to get any free meals from me! Your mother was a wretched strumpet, and that's why she gave birth to you the way you are, like a blind mole!' As he left, he'd given a cackle of coarse laughter, well pleased with himself.

Feeling his way with his staff, Abiel had gone to where the shore was flat and bathed in the sea to cleanse himself of the stench of the garbage and the innkeeper's laughter, but on his way back some men who spoke a language he could not understand had hit him on the hand with something that might have been a plank or an oar and taken his staff with the knob carved in the shape of a fist. It had been a precious gift from his sister, Zahra, a gentle creature and, so folk said, a beauty, who for as long as she had lived had taken care of him like a mother, although she was only four years older than he. When he held the wooden fist in his own, it was as if she were still there, helping him. When she fell ill with a disease of the lungs, he was with her and listened to her rattling breath until he heard no more. He felt her face, coming to the soft, moist ball of an eye and an open lid that no longer blinked, and he had closed it with trembling fingers before feeling for the other. He had closed the other eyelid, stroking the lashes in despair. When, after an interval during which he knew not whether it was day or night, he ran his hands over her face once more, he felt something cold and hard, as if his sister had been turned into a block of stone. He had kissed the stony brow and rent his garments.

'You were my only friend. And now even you ...' but he could not finish the words.

Tears welled once more from the slits of his eyes. He felt warm breath on his hand: Eli was kissing his wounds.

'Wait for me here, Abiel. I'll be back.'

'When?' he said in a choking voice, but Eli did not hear him.

As Eli's jerky footsteps swiftly receded, Abiel opened the floodgates of his tears and for the first time he wished never to have been born. Or else to die then and there. But the God who had brought Jonah to Joppa and put him on the ship had other plans for Abiel and, without a doubt, other trials.

Dinner is ready

Both ship and wind drifted to a standstill. The shore was no longer visible, but they knew they were still close to port. Seagulls were swarming above them. The goat had been tethered to the deck and, digging in its four legs, bleated piteously whenever a bored sailor tugged its beard for amusement. A ginger cat, who seemed right at home on board, was dozing in the sun. Astern, Abiel seemed to be looking back towards Joppa. The captain regarded him grimly. An old mariners' superstition had it that a blind man aboard brought misfortune, but Jacob had forced the captain's hand both in word and deed, with silver above the price he had already paid. The captain loved his ship like a woman and often, particularly in difficult moments, he spoke to it aloud, and nobody was surprised to hear him. He would tell her, 'My brave little girl,' and praise her or scold her, or he would urge her on, depending on the circumstances. Now, he was consoling her, putting on airs in front of her, the way some men do with their mistresses:

'Don't be afraid, little girl, I'll take as good care of you as I do of the eyes in my head. We'll come through! Just let him try to harm you, for the sea is the sea and it has a place for him, and as for my men, they know how to get rid of a jinx ...'

Instead of his two servants, who had remained in port, the old man had set off to sea with a child and a blind man, his only helpmeets for the whole of the voyage, which might even last two years, the same as the outward journey. But it was as plain as could be that he was not sorry. He had called Eli and Abiel astern to join him—they were the only ones there—and he addressed them both in a curt voice, like a master demanding complete obedience:

'Elisha, you will be busy day and night: you have to keep an eye on my nephew, Jonah. Make sure he doesn't forget to eat, or throw himself in the sea, or get into a brawl with anybody, or whatever else. Look at him standing there at the prow, next to the wooden bird's head, looking out to sea, but let me tell you, he sees nothing, so that you might even think his eyes were as wooden as the bird's. The instant you sense any danger, come and tell me. It fills me with alarm, that face of his, and there's been something eating away at him inside ever since he saddled his mule and we set out from Gat-Hefer, but I can't understand what. I can't get a word out of him. He's pining away. I'm very afraid that he might be assailed by the noonday sickness, as the psalmist calls it, the noonday demon, which is the worst demon of all.'

'Yes, grandda- ... yes, master, I'll not let him out of my sight. It won't even be hard, when you think how little room there is here on this ship, because you can see everybody else all the time, and everybody else can see you all the time ... And who are these others? These demons, I mean.'

'Never mind them, you'll have time enough to get to know them ... Actually, you're wrong, it's harder keeping an eye on them here, believe me! Once you grow accustomed to people, you stop seeing them. And if two or three men go below deck to sleep or if they go to visit the black tub, who'll notice? Keep your eyes peeled! Besides that, my boy, for the time being you also have to take care of my second servant, here present, whom I owe to you, because I thought you were going to give up the ghost when you came to offer him to me. You have the gift of persuasion, no doubt about it, and in that you resemble me a little ... Be his guide until he learns the layout of the ship, take care lest he fall and let none of those men do him in. As one skilled in reading the future, I tell you that they'll try to do it.'

Both Elisha and Abiel gave a shudder.

'But they won't succeed, will they?' Eli asked faintly.

The old man made no reply, but went on:

'For those men, I'm sorry to say, are nothing but savages, even the captain, and they start thinking evil thoughts if somebody has an infirmity, convinced that he's a jinx. Look at that tomcat, he's got more brains.'

The ginger tomcat, ignoring Eli and Jacob, was rubbing up against Abiel's legs, and Abiel was stroking him with his sound hand. Jacob had tended to Abiel's wounded hand: in his travelling bag he had all kinds of herbs and coloured powders. Eli had gazed at the remedies in fascination, and Jacob had opened the soft stoppers, made of something called cork, which could be found in abundance at Tartessos, and let him smell them one by one: there were simples for open wounds, infected wounds, contusions, pustules, ringing and rattling in the ears, an irregular heartbeat, sore throats, jaundice, children's ailments, concussion, fainting, and many more. The only one Eli was familiar with was sea salt, which he now learned could be placed on a wound to absorb the blood and prevent pus from forming. The old man also showed him saltpetre, wild privet, tinctures of every variety, syrup of green pine cones, sachets of ground willow leaves and asafoetida, which the Persians called 'the food of the gods', while simple folk called it the 'devil's dung'. First, he had cleansed Abiel's wound with a liquid that smelled as sharp as raki and which stung, after which he wrapped the injured hand in clean cloths. The swelling had receded and now Abiel's hand barely hurt at all. Uncle Jacob was truly a healer.

As if he had seen the gist of the words that came from the old man's mouth, Abiel turned his face towards him and asked:

'What about me? I'm just in the way here. The sea is like land that tilts in every direction. I'm trying to learn to keep my balance. And I constantly feel as if I've eaten food that is off.'

The old man's reply sounded harsh:

'You too have a lot of work to do, and it's harder work, since you're a grown man.'

He saw Abiel's face relax, and so he smiled and frowned at the same time, putting on an even sterner voice:

'I didn't bring you along to sit twiddling your thumbs! First of all, once your hand has healed, you will have to help me with my arms and legs, and my back, which lose their strength after so many days of sitting down and I can feel the flesh melting off them. So, every morning and every evening, you'll take care of my body so that I don't grow stiff. I'll teach you how. You can start today, with just your right hand, which is sound, and, so I see, strong. Well then ... And another thing, given your hearing must be sharper than that of anyone else on this ship, you will also have to lend a sharp ear and tell me whether they're planning anything harmful against us. When you're not poor, there are lots of people who harbour ill intentions towards you, and thank the God of Abraham, I'm not at all poor.'

'You're the richest man I've ever seen,' put in Elisha.

His eyes shone with joy.

'That's right, my boy shout it out loud, let everybody know! I thought you were cleverer than that! I haven't finished with you yet: every day, you'll come to me so that I can teach you to read and to do arithmetic. Wisdom is power. It is with wisdom not gold that you buy the world. I hope your head works as well as that big, insatiable mouth of yours. And now, enough, you've worn me out already!'

Two tall mariners, who both looked alike, had come up and one of them cast a strange glance at the group in the stern, after which they exchanged a look that escaped neither Elisha nor Jacob.

Abiel sniffed the air. He did not feel safe on board, but he had no way of leaving the ship now. He would have to be more careful than ever he had been on land.

*

Father set out on the voyage without a single white hair on his head. When he came back, four full moons later by my count, he had not a single black hair on his head. And his skin was strangely bleached, as if the sun could no longer darken it. Only his eyes now gleamed darkly, in contrast with his white face and his beard, which was white and crinkly. His hair had grown down to his shoulders. I remembered him as swarthy. But he wasn't any more. He must have been about thirty-four at the time. Grandmother ran out to meet a caravan that was slowly approaching our house, and I immediately went after her. He rode in front, his legs hanging almost to the ground. When I saw him dismount his mule, I didn't recognise him. He hugged us both at the same time, but at me he gazed for a long moment: I had grown taller and my body was fuller, and so our embrace was like that of two strangers—'Father, Father!' 'Esther! Is it you?'—even though I had waited for him day after day and every morning and every evening I had prayed with Grandmother for him to come home. That he returned is a miracle, and you yourself will be amazed when I tell you the story of what he went through, but for the time being, we've only reached the first day aboard ship. Let's put some bread on the hearth to bake and then I'll tell you what happened next.

Like most other sensitive men in the grip of strong passions, my dear Huldah, with your little weasel eyes, my father Jonah instantly took to his heart anyone who said a good word, and he hated anyone who hurled abuse or even only contradicted him. But sometimes the two would come from one and the same man, whom he would now love, now hate. Jacob, whom he loved, now seemed to have struck him with the rod of Amithai. He felt judged, weighed up, watched over. Jonah would have fled far away, the way he always did, but he had nowhere to flee, since he couldn't walk on water. So, he hid away in the bowels of the ship, where not a ray of sunlight could pierce. When he climbed down through the wooden trapdoor, he felt as if he were descending into the well once more. He hadn't asked for a rushlight and only now did he realise that his fear of the dark and of deep places had never left him since what happened at the well. But even so, he managed to lap himself in the waters of sleep, rocked by the waters of the sea, the same as he had once taken refuge in the land of Zebulon, far from the house of his parents in Gat-Hefer.

As for Jacob, his nephew had given him a number of surprises, although he now regarded him as his sole heir and was therefore inclined to close his eyes to his faults. For example, he had seen that Jonah had a tendency to ogle the two shapely Nubians—despite the age difference between them, both were of consummate beauty, with almond-shaped eyes, high foreheads, fleshy lips, and glossy skin as if carved from ebony—and that he avoided them only because of their black skin. Jonah didn't go anywhere near the other men either, and his uncle wondered whether he regarded all those who worshipped unknown gods as beneath him. Jacob, who had lived a lifetime among foreigners, judged a man by different tokens. The way a man looked you in the eye and the way he laughed spoke louder than his skin or his features. Amithai, 'The True', had judged others in exactly the same way as Jacob, and they had spoken of this before Jacob set off into the world, immediately after the boy's circumcision, and consequently Jacob couldn't understand why Jonah, who had been raised by his cousin, didn't take after him in his way of thinking. But nature has secrets that are not easily discovered during the course of a lifetime, even a long one, like Jacob's.

At the captain's order, the hired men began to pull their oars and the ship now moved forward slowly and smoothly. That evening, the captain invited the two paying travellers, and them alone, to take their supper with him and his cousins. A sailor went to wake Jonah, who was still asleep, telling him that the meal was ready. The tomcat wove in and out among their legs, mewling to be fed. When he saw Sansón's six-fingered hand, Jonah turned red in the face and stared in a manner that could not be ignored. Sansón withdrew his hand and clenched his eleven fingers into two fists ready to strike, for he was as hotblooded as all young men, and Iberian young men in particular, but Jacob quickly intervened to save the situation and turned the thoughts of those at the table to other things:

'Where have you hidden the women? Captain, tell us the truth, which of your men is a woman disguised in man's clothing? I've heard that this is what sailors do so that they won't get bored for such a bitterly long time!'

The rest of the meal went well. The captain revealed that he was a religious man who fulfilled his duties to the gods. That he had a house in Tartessos. That he had two sons and some daughters. And that for a few years he had had no news of his family.

'If we ride out the storms, I'll see my wife again. She's full of sultry charm, she's got plump, silky knees, she's shapely, although to go by her name, she ought to be delicate, as she's called Adina.'

'Speaking for myself, I'm afraid of pirates,' said Jacob.

'Piracy's a minor misfortune, not a major disaster!'

The captain gave an odd smile as he said this, which didn't escape Jacob. Then, after taking yet another cup of wine, he spluttered:

'I'm not at all happy that you brought a blind man on board!'

Sansón immediately seconded this.

'It's stupid of you to say so, forgive me for telling you to your face!' barked Jacob, who, according to his custom, had not touched a drop of water. 'Only bad, greedy men bring bad luck, whereas good men—and Abiel is a good as freshly baked bread—bring the good will of both your gods and my God. What's more, captain, I shall even ask you to protect him from your men and to ensure that nothing bad happens to him, and then, if he arrives safely in Tartessos, I shall count out as much as I paid over to you on our departure. What do you say?'

Warmed by the prospect and the wine, the captain seemed to be in agreement. He asked Jacob whether it was true that he did not drink water.

'It's all too true, captain. At least not when I'm on a voyage, since I drink water at home. Water can be dirty and it causes many diseases. But not wine, even if it makes you light-headed and finally bites like a snake, as they say.'

The captain laughed.

'And are you the same?' he asked Jonah, tempting him.

'No. It's never bitten me. Ever.'

His voice evinced neither pride nor scorn. Jonah was a strange man.

'A good death to you, captain!' said old man Jacob, in token of the highest friendship, before he withdrew.

It was late. He had drunk rather a lot.

'What did you say?'

'A good night to you, although as for myself, I say that men ought to wish each other a good death rather than a good night, it's very important ...'

The captain made no reply. He laid his head on the table and instantly fell asleep. The snake had bitten him too in the end. It was as if Jacob's wish had been fulfilled.

Good people!

Like the tomcat toying with the mice on board, fate plays with a man's greatest fears. It does not rest until he drops his guard and then it grabs his neck in its jaws and lets him writhe. It was as if fate now wished to plunge Jacob into misfortune and to prove right the crew, which believed that a blind man on board brought bad luck. The very next day, the Phoenician, the best and dearest crewman began to tremble with a fever, the sweat poured off him and beaded his gentle, trusting face, he kept begging for water, and finally, he began to babble in a delirium. The captain immediately asked the old man to examine him. Somehow, while taking on board provisions at Joppa, the captain had learned of Jacob's renown as a healer. Jacob covered his nose and mouth with a cloth and went to the sick man, who was lying on the deck. He had long ago adopted this habit, since most sick people smelled badly and the air around them was tainted. With a polished blade of wood, he prised open the large, chattering, yellow teeth and saw bleeding pustules on his tongue and in his throat. His mouth reeked. Without wishing to, Jacob took a step back. He washed himself well with a solution that smelled of raki, ordered nobody to approach the sick man, and took the captain to one side, so that the others wouldn't hear:

'I have seen this only once before, captain, it is an unknown but deadly plague. Nobody knows the cure.'

'A plague?'

The captain tried to speak bluffly, but Jacob could sense his terror: he knew how to control a ship, but the human body is harder to control, harder even than a ship in a storm. The sickness had put fear into him.

'Yes, a plague, one that can easily be caught. You must somehow keep him apart, get the men to build a screen around him, and whoever goes near him should wear a cloth over his face, the same as I did. But better let there be a single man to give him water as often as possible, as he'll neither ask for food nor be able to take it.'

'Hadn't we better throw him overboard?' said the sorely tried captain, but then he looked aside in shame, at the barely ruffled waves. In the last storm, the Phoenician had saved him, and the captain feared the gods.

Jacob pretended not to have heard.

'I'll examine him a few times a day. If the sickness progresses to looseness of the bowels, then there is no hope for him.'

The captain and Jacob had conferred in a whisper, but aboard a ship there is no room for great secrets. So, the news swiftly spread and a gust of madness blew among the men. Not one of them would tend to the sick man, and Jacob could hardly blame them for it. So long a voyage was a battle of life and death, and to survive you had to dispense with reckless gestures, which is to say, you didn't pick up your enemy's spear for him when he dropped it so that he could then stab you in the belly.

Abiel sensed the danger almost at the same time as Elisha did, and long before Jacob. They had grown up on the street, in a port teeming with all kinds of people, and their senses had been honed. Abiel's nostrils twitched as if snuffling for air as he sat cross-legged on the poop deck, and Eli went and stood in front of him, as if by chance.

'Him!' exclaimed one of the rowers, prodding the air with his finger. The finger pointed at Eli's legs, but all the sailors knew that he was pointing past him and at the man sitting behind him.

'The blind man,' shouted the two Greeks almost both at once, a cry that was at once taken up by the Nubians and went from man to man, before finally they fell to repeating it in a muttered hiss, their eyes flashing daggers.

'Let the blind man tend him, or better still, let us throw him in the sea, for then our sick comrade will be cured by himself,' said a voice. 'He's the one who brought the sickness.'

They were now yelling all at once, while the captain looked on, unwilling to interfere. Even Siran, otherwise so cheerful and gentle, cast angry glances at the blind man. They all seemed genuinely convinced that Abiel alone was to blame for the fact that the Phoenician, their best comrade, was suffering. They wished to avenge their comrade, to sentence the blind man without trial.

'Good people! Good people, what do you want to do? Think more carefully! He is in no way to blame, the sickness doesn't choose, he must have caught it in port. If Abiel were in any way at fault, he would be the one who was sick, wouldn't he?' Jacob tried to tell them, but his clear voice was straight away smothered in the slime of the general discontent and a few sailors now threateningly approached Abiel, who could not see them, but sensed them, as animals sense an approaching fire. He began to shiver slightly, guarded by Elisha, who had planted himself in front of him to stop the tide of men, even though he knew that they would waft him aside like a seagull's feather.

*

The next instant, a large shadow fell across Elisha, cast by a massive body that had sprung up as if from nowhere. It was Jonah, his back to Elisha and facing the sailors. He was smiling. It was the smile he had had when he saw the girl from the well cradled in the arms of her mother, the smile that had astonished his uncle at the time, and which astonished him all the more so now. Be that as it may, the last thing that Jacob would have expected in the midst of a crowd of furious men, who were as unstoppable as a force of nature—and furious men are one of the most savage forces of nature—was for somebody to get it into his head to stand in their way, with folded arms, smiling as if about to play a prank. Besides, where had he sprung up from? And when? He had seemed absent, wholly wrapped up in himself, he had not even acknowledged Abiel and Elisha, as if he didn't know what dangers lurked around him, but now here he was, with that smile of his, the one that resembled the smile of cousin Amithai's beautiful wife.

'I'll do it. Just me. I'll take care of him. The sick man. Illness doesn't affect me. Not a bit. Not ever. Leave the lads alone. My friends. Under my protection. From now on.'

He didn't raise his voice. But his deep, firm voice was a bronze shield against which the sailor's shouts snapped like twigs. The splinters lay scattered on the deck around Jonah, who did not deign even to tread them underfoot, and the silence, after the uproar of a moment ago, seemed endless.

He had spoken to them in the voice of the voice. He realised that he had unwittingly projected the depth of the voice. And only after he saw what happened to his simple, unsought words, for he was not at all fleet of tongue, as Jacob was well aware, only then did he understand that henceforward it would be his weapon. Always and in all places, it would be enough for him to speak in the voice of the voice that had shown itself to him. It was through this that he was different from everybody else. His words possessed power.

Elisha embraced Jonah in mad joy. Abiel, who had stood up, embraced Eli, then with his uninjured hand he groped for the face of his saviour, to know what he looked like. He felt the cheekbones, the curliness and silkiness of the beard, the strong nose, then the fleshy lips, he felt the moist teeth, for his saviour was still smiling. Jacob stared at his nephew for a long moment. He was unable to get over his astonishment. The sailors had grown calm as if by magic and went about their business, as if their eyes had not been bulging with fury a moment ago. Jonah went and without haste crafted a screen to place around the sick man. He gave him water to drink from a wooden cup which was later to be thrown into the sea and, in his presence, the Phoenician's suffering eased. When he saw that the sick man had fallen asleep, Jonah withdrew. Jacob then rubbed his nephew with his strong-smelling liquor.

The captain decided it was important that he tell his ship about Jonah. In the end, the man had quelled a mutiny by speaking just two or three words and now he was risking his life for one of the captain's men, without anybody demanding it of him. 'My little girl, who would have thought that that silent man was possessed of so much vigour? He doesn't know the meaning of the word 'death'! It's the first time I've ever seen anything like it. Just you be calm, and we'll be home dry!' And he emphasised his words by waving his hand in the air and giving a determined nod, as if the ship could not only hear but also see him.

By the smell

That evening, while Abiel was massaging Jacob's muscles with his uninjured hand, in fulfilment of the duties laid down from the very start, the old man decided to ask him about his blindness. But he approached the matter from a distance, taking a very roundabout way. He thought Abiel had had enough excitement for one day and didn't want to disturb him even more, but the curiosity that had driven him his whole life nudged him on. So, he asked him about his family and found out that the only person he'd had in the world was his sister, Zahra, who died in his arms. He found out that she had given him a staff with a knob shaped like a fist, which Abiel regarded as his magical adjunct and without which everything went badly for him, as was now plain, because it had been stolen from him the day before he boarded the ship thanks to Jacob's generosity.

'Who took it from you?'

'There were two men. I think they were tall. I would recognise them by their smell.'

'Tall? By their smell?' Jacob asked, taking an interest.

'Yes, I can sense the height from which a man's voice comes from and that's how I gauge how tall he is, and the men in question were talking, although I couldn't make sense of the words. It might have been Greek, I don't know. Also, every man has his own unique smell. The same as plants. Grass smells one way, every flower another way, every kind of tree, bush, or palm yet another way. It's as if I have a second nose to make up for my eyes, and I recognise a man by his smell. For example, you, master, smell fresh and clean in the morning, the way only my Zahra used to smell, and that does me good, later, in the middle of the day, after you have been working with your powders, sharp odours are added, which sometimes make me sneeze, and in the evening, they combine with the sweet smell of wine. And the captain smells like a tanned goat skin.'

'And what about that cussed lad of ours?'

'Eli used to smell of green figs and dust. Since he's been aboard ship, he's suddenly grown taller and smells of sweat and raisins.'

'The rascal eats my raisins every day. And what about Jonah?'

'I can't catch Jonah's smell. But his voice thrums even when he whispers, even when he's silent. I recognise him by that rumble, like a cart's as it rolls across small stones or shells.'

'How about that, my boy, I'm finding out lots of things from you and I'm delighted that we're together. You may call me "uncle" from now on. We Jews are all related in the end!'

'I humbly thank you! Uncle!'

'And perhaps I can help you. Have your eyes been like this since birth?'

There it was, he had dared to ask. A while passed before Abiel answered. He had not spoken of it to anybody since Zahra's death.

'I don't know. A long time ago, I thought to remember some ... I don't know what to call the...'

Abiel lifted his uninjured hand from Jacob's arm, which he had been massaging, and swiftly made all kinds of shapes in the air. When Jacob turned his head towards him, he thought to see angles, creatures, trees, loops, all in a series of unstoppable movements.

'And my oldest memory is connected with what might have been colours, but it's a very vague memory, engulfed by the manifold darkness that exists inside me. Zahra used to say they must be colours, the white of my mother's garment, she would say, and the blue of her head covering, when I was very small.'

'So, you haven't been like this from birth,' Jacob cautiously put forward. 'But how then did it happen? Where were you born? How old are you?'

'I don't know. Nobody has counted the years. I'm probably twenty-something, but I could be older. In any event, they have been long years. The first few years were good and, in comparison with those that came afterward, they were wonderful. I was born here, or rather there, in the port, at Joppa. My father was a fisherman, my mother the daughter of a quite wealthy merchant, and very beautiful they say. They loved us, and especially Zahra, who looked like Mother, with an aquiline nose, a mouth the colour of pomegranate flowers, but I was also very dear to them the way I was, because I was a boy and they used to tell me I was handsome, they would hold me in their arms whenever they held her too. We grew up without a care. I almost didn't realise I was different from everybody else. But one day, Father never came home from sea. At the time there were many pirates, or maybe he drowned or ran away. Nobody was ever able to tell me. Soon after that, my mother lost her mind. One night I dreamed differently than usual, something that I think was colours. I was overjoyed. But the next day, Mother hanged herself from a beam. Zahra found her. It was Zahra who raised me after that, husbanding the little we had. I don't know how she managed. When she died, I didn't have anything to eat and I went out to beg. I never went back home. This has been my life.'

'My dear boy!' said Jacob and then fell silent for a long time. 'God wants something from you. Otherwise you wouldn't have reached the age you have, however old you might be, and I must tell you that you look very handsome, despite ... but anyway. The fact that Eli begged me to take you with us and that I agreed to it straight away, not to mention the many other observations that an old and experienced man such as myself makes without even thinking, all lead me to the clear belief that Adonai wants something from you ... You still haven't told me about your eyes ... enough, stop, my muscles are hurting, you have firm and skilful fingers, and when you're able to use your left hand too, you'll be flawless.'

'My eyes cleaved together soon after I was born, my mother told me. I've often wondered whether somebody might be able to cut open this hardened skin and restore my eyes to the light. But I don't believe in miracles.'

'If you don't call them miracles, you can easily believe in them,' said Jacob, looking at him closely, but Abiel did not know what he meant. Sensing Jacob's gaze, he covered his face with his hand.

'No need for that,' said Jacob, 'there's nothing for you to be ashamed of there. We'll see ... even though that's not the appropriate word ... or on the contrary, maybe it is. In any event, my nephew will protect you and nobody will throw you in the water.'

'My father taught me to swim when I was little,' said Abiel. 'He bathed me in the sea many times. I'm not afraid of water.'

Ox, house, camel, sword

Elisha still hadn't got used to the narrow confines of the ship. True, when they set sail, he had stood leaning beneath the polished bird's head and watched the prow cleaving the water, and the gliding of the ship had filled him with good cheer, it had finally released him from the all the evils and cares of the world that he'd left behind in Joppa. He told Abiel that he'd never felt that way before, the smooth, effortless forward motion filled him with wonder, and if he closed his eyes he could even believe he had grown wings, like a seagull's. To advance without moving your legs or without cart wheels trundling beneath you was a novelty to him. Whenever he'd gone from one place to another before, it had demanded a physical effort, one that had been all the more painful since he injured the sole of his foot. But now he stood still and could feel the wind in his face as if he were running. On the other hand, he was used to moving around, to being busy, to hoodwinking people to come by food, to struggling for his own and others' survival, and then to sleeping like a log after a full day. Now he was idle most of the day, he was happy when he was given something to do, no matter how hard it might be, and the sailors set him to perform every task that happened along. Although he would fall asleep straight away, rocked by the ship and listening to the lapping of the water, he slept lightly, waking up at every footfall or creak, after which he would lie with his eyes open, filled with confused presentiments.

He had noticed that the two Greek rowers, Deimos and Zeuxidamos, didn't sleep much either. They were athletic in stature, they resembled each other, and they didn't care about anybody else, not even the captain, whom they obeyed only for the sake of form, smirking at him when his back was turned. They talked in a whisper a great deal, but Eli, whose hearing was almost as sharp as Abiel's, could hear them very well, even if he couldn't understand what they were saying. Unlike most of the crew, he didn't know an iota of Greek. The old man, who amazed him every day with some new thing, had promised to teach him the language, and the lad thought it would be as simple as learning any other skill, the matter of a few days. Eli kept his eyes on the two and found something to keep himself busy with nearby whenever they strayed too close to Jacob or Abiel. Deimos paid no attention to him, but one night he caught Zeuxidamos, the one whose nose was like a saddle, looking at him in a way that only murderers look: cruelly. Eli knew that some men needed no reason to kill. It was enough for somebody not to like your face. Zeuxidamos followed him everywhere with his eyes. Eli felt he was never out of his shadow.

From the day after the incident with the Phoenician, things nonetheless seemed to settle into a rhythm lacking in surprises, but with an instinct honed by the uncontrollable torrent of events in port, Eli sensed that this was not really so. He played a waiting game, keeping watch over all the crew, as he had been asked. The passing days were monotonous. In the morning, Jacob would teach him the alphabet, explaining to him the meaning of each letter and how they combined. They would study five letters a day, on a wax tablet. These were mysteries known only to a select few, and Eli was almost afraid to approach them, as if they were a magic that might bring about his doom. At the same time, Jacob taught him to count on the fingers of his two hands. After they filled the wax tablet, the old man would hold it to the flame of a rushlight and watch the letters melt and vanish. When the wax cooled, he would once more conjure them into being. Pure sorcery. It was difficult, the most difficult thing to which Eli had ever applied his brain, but it didn't bore him. So far he had learned *alef*, *beth*, *gimel*, *daleth*, *he*, which meant *ox*, *house*, *camel*, *door*, *window*, and *1, 2, 3, 4, 5*. When he had nothing better to do, Elisha would repeat the letters to himself, making himself a house with a door and window, with an ox and a camel to the right and left, then on his fingers he would add a door and a window to equal nine or an ox and a camel to equal four. He would then feel his scalp, on which the thick brush of a clean head of hair was sprouting, as if making sure that the ox and the house and all the rest were still inside and weren't trying to get out. He liked the ticklish feeling under his fingertips as he ran them up and down his scalp, against the grain of that brush. He would go to Abiel and tell him everything he had learned, everything he had seen aboard ship, he would tell him his new sea thoughts, so different from his land thoughts.

'You're growing up, Elisha, you're already a different you than the one I knew in Joppa. How old are you, in fact?'

'Maybe about fifteen.'

'What? That old?'

'Yes, maybe older, I don't know for sure. I always pretended I was younger, so that people would treat me better, because people are very bad. It wasn't even hard to fool them, given how I look.'

Abiel could sense his disconsolation, but not finding the words to hearten him, he said nothing. Sadder than usual, Eli added:

'If I die, please take that little brother of mine a wooden ship, a toy one, but make sure it's like this one, with a mast and a sail. I'll ask one of the men to make it for him. I promised him.'

'Don't talk nonsense! Why would you die? How could you die? If I'm the one who dies, then you won't have to do anything. I don't have anybody,' he laughed.

'Yes, you do, you have me. You're my older brother now.'

Eli then told him his suspicions regarding the Greeks and about the way Zeuxidamos looked at him.

'Well, I didn't want to tell you,' Abiel confessed, 'so as not to make you worry or say something reckless, but I think they're the ones who hit me and stole the staff Zahra gave me. I sensed them by their smell. They both smell of wet camel hair.'

'Ha! That's right,' exclaimed Elisha in triumph, 'they both wear a camel-hair girdle, Abiel! You don't even need eyes to be able to see… A good thing you told me. It means your staff is around here somewhere and I swear I'll find it for you. And it will bring you good luck once more, and maybe we'll reach Tartessos, and we'll both go back home rich.'

But there was neither hope nor joy in his voice. When Jacob came to the letter *zain*, 'sword', ז, he found out about Eli's presentiment. Eli narrowed his eyes even more than usual, drew the letter that did indeed look like a sword, and said:

'With this sword, *zain*, Zeuxidamos will cut my throat. He's been dogging me and it makes me worry about my brothers, because I left them all by themselves. They were used to me getting food for them and protecting them. I beat them myself a lot of times, true, but mostly I protected them so that others wouldn't beat them. I'm afraid the little one won't live till I get back. I told him that I'd …' but he couldn't go on.

'I can't believe it!' exclaimed the old man. His face turned red with fury and his beard all of a sudden looked like it was being ruffled by a wind. You lied to me and lied to me again, you said you didn't have any brothers, you said they weren't your brothers, shame on you! There are six things that the Lord hates, even seven, and a lying tongue is the second! I would send you back this instant if I were able. You ought to be thrown overboard. You're dreadful! You're incapable of uttering a word of truth! I'm not going to teach you another thing, you don't deserve it!'

He threw the wax tablet on the deck and Eli saw that he had tears in his hazel eyes, sunk deep beneath his bushy grey eyebrows, they too awry. The old man was in tears, genuine tears. Eli wouldn't have believed the gentle Jacob capable of such wrath, nor could he understand what there was to weep about. Eli had lied his whole life, and had only gained thereby: it was how he got food, how he survived. He couldn't see what there was to be so distraught about, but he sensed that the old man's anger had a different cause. He expected the worst, to be left to his own devices, not to have a master any more, to be left to the mercy of the sailors and thrown into the sea as a sacrifice, but that very moment, Jonah appeared next to him, as if from nowhere. His face was peaceful and he spoke only to Jacob:

'I went down. Once. You: each of you getting ready. You know, don't you? I went to the inn. Paid her. The woman. Achim's widow. For his brothers. To take care of them. Let's have faith!'

His stony mode of speech calmed Jacob as if by magic. He trembled briefly, as if he were cold. There was no point in his asking Jonah the tide of questions that swelled on his tongue. And anyway, the next moment, Jonah turned around and vanished, probably into the belly of the ship once more, which was where he'd kept himself ever since they set sail. But from then on, both Jacob and Elisha, each for his own different reasons, was convinced that Jonah was a man possessed of powers. They both felt relieved that they could rely on him. Almost as much as they could on the one who gave him those powers.

Something else, just as bad

The plague did not seem to be spreading for the time being, but nor did the Phoenician seem to be any better. He was given water a few times a day, not being able to swallow anything else, and his flesh, once so taut and rounded, was melting away like wax from a candle. It even made you ill to see him possessed by the demon of the sickness that tortured him and which left his skin hanging loose from his ever more visibly protruding bones, even though Jacob and Jonah were the only ones who saw him behind the screen. Sometimes the captain went to look at him too, covering his face with a large cloth, like a Bedouin in a sandstorm, and then he would stare at him in amazement for an instant before turning around and rushing to give the crew surly orders, as if he were pressed by some task that would brook no delay.

As for the crew, they had started giving Abiel evil looks once more. The blind man had found a nook for himself on the poop deck, where he was in nobody's way, and he sat there the same as he had once sat at the crossroads of Joppa's crowded streets, except that here he didn't beg for alms. Most of the time, the tomcat curled up in Abiel's lap. Both had russet hair. Elisha saw to Abiel's meals, and sometimes Siran brought him leftovers from the captain's supper and exchanged a few words with him, albeit quickly and making sure none of the others saw him. In the Armenian there was great compassion, but in him too there was even greater fear. Probably it was this unseen battle raging within his heart that lent his face its air of permanent disquiet. Eli, on the other hand, as Jacob demanded of him, walked Abiel all over the ship to accustom him to his new, floating home, he led him to the black tub and nannied him as if he were the older of the two, oblivious to the sidelong glances of the crew. Zeuxidamos had begun to linger around Abiel, but it was at Eli that he mostly looked, never letting him out of his sight. Once, he brought Abiel a jug of milk, which he himself had milked from the captain's goat. Eli cast him a harsh, suspicious look, and Zeuxidamos lowered his eyes, like a beaten dog. Eli was sure that there was something sinister behind it and told Abiel not to drink the milk, but the blind man paid him no heed. Abiel, too, sensed something strange in the Greek's behaviour.

One day, when Jacob opened the Phoenician's mouth with his polished wooden spatula, and Jonah poured him a few drops of water from a small bladder—he had thrown away the wooden cup because the water he poured from it would spill from the sides of the dying man's mouth and be wasted—the bleeding wounds could be seen to have vanished. The sick man now asked for food in a faint voice. There followed a week that gave rise to fresh hope: the wind was blowing in the right direction, the ship advanced without the help of the oarsmen, and the Phoenician was gaining strength as quickly as he had formerly wasted away. But when Jacob moved aside the screen and announced that the danger had passed and the Phoenician could resume his place among the others, the savagery of the crew once more showed its face. Most of them had inured themselves to the thought that the sick man was going to die, and in their minds they had as good as thrown him overboard. Now they were obliged to welcome him back on deck, alive, and since all were as afraid of sickness as much as they were of evil spells, sea monsters, bad luck, and the abodes of the dead, they didn't want to have him anywhere near them. The wind had changed direction again, it was thrusting them back the way they had come, and the captain had had to give the order to lower the yellowish-white sail. The oarsmen toiled to the point of exhaustion and they hated the rest of the crew, who didn't have so much hard work to do. The Phoenician, once so well loved, who had helped each and every one of them in difficult moments during storms, was now barely tolerated. Gratitude and remembrance of good deeds were not qualities possessed by the men of the ship with the bird's head and fish's tail. His recovery was painful to him, since on the one hand, he had once been in ten places at once and worked as hard as ten men, but now he was no longer good for anything much, and on the other, he could see how none of his old comrades wanted anything to do with him, and how none but the two strangers, Jonah and the old healer, had the courage to come into close contact with him. Enmities swelled to bursting point among the crew members, and mutiny threatened once more. But something else entirely was to happen, something just as bad.

*

Jacob had barely fallen asleep, at dawn, as was his habit, when he felt a hand shaking him and a voice speaking precipitously in his ear. It was the captain. It took the old man a while to understand that what the captain was telling him was really happening: the crew were about to hang Abiel from the mast. Something had happened during the night to enrage them, but Jacob couldn't understand what. This time, they wanted to get rid of the jinx once and for all. The captain, who had promised Jacob he would look after Abiel and hadn't forgotten that he would be paid in gold for doing so, as much gold as he had received when they set sail, had kept his promise, warning him of what was about to happen, garbling the words in his haste.

Once he had his wits about him, Jacob saw the captain's cousins, Hernando, with his round face and overbite, and Sansón, holding a rope in which he had tied a noose. Sansón was holding it in his six-fingered hand. Hernando's eyes were bulging out of his head, almost as if on stalks, so furious was he. The old man asked what the matter was in a voice that could not have been firmer. He learned that Abiel wandered the ship at night, like a ghost, and stared at the men with his sightless eyes. It was a known fact that before the new moon death would take whichever man his blind gaze fell upon. Hernando had caught him standing over him during the night and if he was to escape with his life, the blind man himself must be given over to death.

Men don't need much more reason than that to kill somebody, my dear Dorcas. And things on board ship were not going well at all: from the very first, somebody had brought them bad luck, although it wasn't the blind man. There was not a word of truth in what they said. It was Elisha who had told them that Zeuxidamos kept coming to look at him in the night, and after that, they insanely twisted it to make it the blind man who was looking. Even now I tremble to think of the scene, which my grandmother Huldah, who was named after the weasel and even looked like one, heard straight from her grandmother Esther. You know who Esther was, don't you?

The listener's little face showed her dissatisfaction at the storyteller having interrupted the story with this question just as it reached the most terrifying and most interesting part, and the girl answered in jest:

'No, I don't!'

But the woman telling the story, her face furrowed with old age, didn't pick up on the sarcasm and exclaimed in alarm:

'How can you not know, when you're a descendant of the Prophet Jonah! You should be happy you were born into the family of a man filled with the holy spirit and that you're of the seventh generation. You should remember that all your life! Come now, you, who has the name and the ankles of a gazelle, repeat to me quickly all the people who inherited the ring, since I've told you so many times before.'

'Including Jonah, or just the women?'

'It's up to you.'

'Jonah, who was a man, sired Esther, but it was her mother gave birth to her. We don't know what her mother's name was, because she died not long after that and she never possessed the ring. Esther, who received the silver ring from Jacob, gave birth to Dinah, Dinah gave birth to Huldah, Huldah gave birth to Rebecca, Rebecca gave birth to ... well, she gave birth to Ruth, meaning you. You gave birth to my mother Edna and she gave birth to me, Dorcas. And when I grow up, I'll give birth to Sara, God willing, because that's what I want to call her, and I'll also give her lots of brothers and sisters, but of all of them, only to Sara, the firstborn, only to her will I leave the silver ring that my mother is going give me when I get married... . Isn't it true that great-great-great-umpteen times great-grandfather Jonah saved the blind man's life?'

'No, no, he didn't show himself right then. Abiel, who wasn't feeling well and had gone to the black tub many times in the night was now on his feet. He couldn't see what was in front of him, of course. He didn't know that next to him stood a man with bulging eyes and a noose for his neck. But he had heard a murmur and had backed up against the gunwale, and he was holding his hands up as if to fend off something. Unfortunately, Elisha, his friend, was asleep. You have to remember that more often than not all kinds of adventurers end up on a ship, including thieves and murderers, none but men, and none but merciless men, as delicacy is reserved only for us women, my dear, and even then, not all women, but only some of us. On a ship, it's a life and death struggle. And from time to time, those men need to see horrors, since only afterward can they rest easy, for a time. They need a victim to torture. The more innocent the victim, the better. They all wanted to see the young blind man hanged. They bound his legs and tied his hands behind his back, all the while mocking him and slapping him, especially across the eyes. Zeuxidamos didn't take any part in it, but watched the victim without blinking.

Jacob, who had arrived in a hurry, his shirt and his beard awry, weighed the situation. He knew that either he must find a solution on the spot or he must watch helpless as Abiel, his servant, was slaughtered like a gentle lamb. First of all, the old man raised his hand, the gesture of a king demanding silence before making an important announcement. And silence fell.

Nearby, terrifying

He knew all too well that he had nothing with which to fill that silence. He thought of promising them things, of promising them gold and silver if they let Abiel go. But the state they were in, like a pack of wild animals, they would have been capable of killing him too, just so that they could take everything for themselves, without being obligated. Maybe it would have been better to frighten them with something. Men of their ilk have three gods: greed, fear, and cruelty. But nothing came to Jacob's mind with which he might frighten them. He prayed to God to smite them with a thunderbolt. In vain! The morning sky showed rosy blue and cloudless. So, long moments of silence passed and when one of the men raised a cry, the old man was certain that the end had come for Abiel and perhaps even for himself. But once again, the God of Jonah, of Jacob, and of their ancestor Abraham had other plans.

A sailor standing on the left, his hand resting on the gunwale, let out a thick roar, as if it were him they were about to kill. Snatching his fingers from the gunwale as if they had been burnt with hot coals, he pointed trembling at the sea. The rest of the men rushed to the port side so suddenly that they tilted the vessel, as if righting it in a storm. Jacob looked too, and even Abiel turned his bruised face in that direction.

About fifty paces away, Jacob first saw a long, deep trench in the water, aslant from him, whose edges were just closing over something huge but only briefly glimpsed. For a long moment nobody said a word. They had neither tongues nor mouths, but only eyes. Then the sailors espied emerging from the waves, slowly, you might even have said leisurely, which made it all the more terrifying, a glistening mountain of solid flesh, a back as round as the wheel of a gigantic cart, which for a while rose ever higher, black, appalling, before rolling back down with a cruel whistling noise in its wake. The trench in the water closed above it once more. The boundlessly large creature vanished for a few instants, then the whole of its body burst from the water, a cumbersome, gigantic thunderbolt of flesh, twisting its whitish belly upward, and from every mouth at once there erupted a shout as it opened its maw, as huge as a deep cavern, and they saw the spikes that guarded its entrance. The waves set in motion by the monster rocked the ship perilously, and the bound Abiel toppled to the deck. All the men unthinkingly took a few steps backward, but straight away, as if drawn by a power greater than fear, they leaned over the gunwales once more. The captain spoke the word that was in all the others' minds:

'Leviathan!'

Jacob rushed over to Abiel and untied him:

'A monster, or I don't know what. Not a hundred paces away from us, very close, terrifying. It's been sent from heaven, it came in answer to my prayers: glory be to God, He has saved you!'

The creature sank once more and, even though the men stood frozen all day watching, it did not reappear. They had escaped this time, but terror could be read on every face. The next day, nobody avoided the Phoenician any more, who had seen the horror along with all the others. On the contrary, they were now friendly towards him. And none of them were at odds with Abiel any more, whose face was covered in bruises, particularly around the eyes. Fear had united them for the first time and made them treat each other well. Of those on board, only Elisha, Jonah, and Siran had not seen the creature, and of course Abiel, but he at least had seen it with his ears. The other three had been asleep in the belly of the ship and even though they had rushed on deck when it had started to rock, they had seen nothing, but heard only the sailors talking all at once. Eli could not forgive himself for having slept so deeply when so many things had been happening, he was dying of pique and envy, and he would have given anything to see the Leviathan, as all the others called it. He was not afraid. Zeuxidamos stroked his hair to console him, but Eli furiously shook him off. For a number of days afterwards, the only talk was of the prodigy of the dragon from the deeps or whatever it might have been. Each remembered it differently and they took pleasure in telling and retelling the details they had seen, particularly in front of the three who had not been there:

'Some five times longer than the ship.'

'And twice as wide.'

'As black as coal, only the eyes were white.'

'No, the eyes were as red as fire and gave off sparks.'

'It had no eyes, I didn't see any eye, just a hole in the top of its head.'

'And it had shcales like iron shields on itsh back,' remembered Hernando.

'Where did you come up with scales?' his cousin contradicted him. 'I was amazed at how smooth it was, like an eel gleaming in the water. But on its head, it had prongs of flesh, like the little horns of a kid.'

'Try casting a hundred iron spears in it and you'll see it turn to mush, like melting wax.'

'My father, who was a fisherman and vanished at sea, told me that you can't hook Leviathan with a rod and you can't snare its tongue on a line. He was afraid of it, and I think that it was what killed him, because one day he never came back.'

'But what about that maw, which was big enough to swallow our ship, raised mast and all? It could have drunk us all up in one gulp, along with this little girl of mine, if it had wanted, and it could have crushed us like grapes in a press.'

'And there was something white on its belly, and it was ridged as if furrowed by a plough.'

'And it was swollen from all the men and the ships it must have swallowed.'

'The teeth, those fangsh of shtone, I can shee them before me even now.'

'And the nostril on the top of its head, which spurted water and brimstone.'

'What about the tail? Didn't you see its tail? Who's ever seen the like? You'd have thought they were the spread wings of a black demon. Just the tip of that tail could have smashed our ship to smithereens.'

Abiel caught the men's attention when he told Elisha about the shrill whistling he heard. And he imitated the monster: yooooooooooooooo, fffyoooooooooo, yyyoooooooooooo, making the sound go up and down in a tone no mortal ear had heard before. They made Abiel repeat it countless times, and it was obvious that the blind man, overjoyed at the men talking to him for the first time, remembered with the greatest precision what he had heard and could reproduce the monster's terrifying music as if playing a whistle. Zeuxidamos remembered that he had heard the sounds too, but because of what he had been seeing and because of his amazement—he didn't call it fear—he had forgotten it. And he cast a shy smile at where Abiel and Eli were sitting. Deimos couldn't remember it at all. The captain had heard the sounds, too, but not the others. Hernando opened the lips of his round face in a kind of smile, showing his teeth with their overbite, and in a lisping voice he told what he could remember, only because he now felt he had to take the blind man's side in every matter, ashamed of what he had done before Leviathan appeared, or whatever it might have been. In short, the captain now commanded a different crew than the one with which he had set sail and he shared the news with his ship: 'My brave little girl, you ought to know that a miracle has happened!' Jonah alone remained the same, turned in on himself and his own thoughts. The story of the monster moved him not at all. He had his own monster. And he was possessed of the spirit.

BOOK TWO

The Storm

The goat

The wind now drove the ship from behind, its beak pecking the swathe of diamonds that glittered all the way from the western horizon. Before every sundown, Eli spend long periods at the prow and his eyes never tired of the flashes, the glimmers, the flurry of the soft-edged beads, first yellow, then orange, then red, which the sun scattered over the water. Jacob, who never missed an occasion to pronounce a proverb, reminded him that three things left no traces in the world, or even four things: the eagle in the sky, the snake on the rock, and the ship on the sea. Elisha wanted to know what the fourth one was, but the old man said that it was too soon for him to learn of it and anyway he would find out not from him but from a woman. One evening, the lad listened, without budging from the spot where he stood, as the men talked about how it was necessary that they make an important sacrifice in thanks for both plague and monster having spared their lives.

They decided to sacrifice the goat, which would be all the easier now that they had nothing more to feed it and it was growing emaciated. Apart from the old man, who was well familiar with the ritual of sacrifice and the various methods of immolation, albeit only according to the Jewish rite, the others had never troubled their heads over such things. The captain made them pray each to his own god that Leviathan not approach the ship again. Then, because Jacob refused to act as priest for the whole company, the honour fell upon the Phoenician, who had the soundest reasons to give thanks and make sacrifice. He was fully recovered. He chose to proceed as a butcher rather than a priest, without paying attention to the fine details, although it was true that the place where they found themselves justified certain shortcuts and simplifications. The goat gave a prolonged and terrible bleat, and three cups of its blood were poured into the sea, while the Phoenician mumbled some words. Elisha understood those words quite well, since they resembled the words of his own language. It was only then that the lad turned towards the men, regarding them with obvious curiosity.

Since they left Joppa, Eli was the one who had changed the most, and so too had his life. He was now unrecognisable. His hair was clean and wavy, even if the salt wind made it stiff, and Jacob had made him cut his long toenails with a large pair of scissors from one of his bags. His infirm foot had healed (the old man had tended it daily) and now he barely limped at all. The real metamorphosis was that over the course of a few weeks he had been transformed from a child into a young man. He had exchanged one body for another. His chest was broader, his Adam's apple bobbed up and down on his long throat when he swallowed, down darkened his upper lip. His eyelashes were still curly, his eyes still narrow, but they were livelier. Jacob had taught him the final letters *shin* 'tooth', *s*, 300, and *tav*, 'sign', *t*, 400. He knew how to combine them now. He could count to a thousand. And his voice was fuller. He was waiting impatiently for something, without knowing what, and a lot of the time he was excited without reason, or angry, or, most often, sad. He was sick of life on board ship and wanted to be free again to do what he pleased, as he had been before Jacob found him.

The others too had noticed the change in Elisha. At first, although he was Jacob's servant, he had served all and been beaten by all alike. Accustomed as he was to all this, he hadn't much cared. But lately, he had refused to let himself be beaten or to take orders, obeying only the captain and Jacob. He would answer the men back, impertinently or spitefully, sometimes dolefully and begging their compassion. But the more he learned, which happened during the day, in the sight of them all, and quickly too, since he was fleet of understanding, the men began to look at him with greater attention and with a kind of intimidation. The Greek with the saddle-like nose would seek his eyes under the deep shade of their lashes, he would seek to be near him, and it was as if he were begging him for something, although what exactly remained obscure. Eli, who had at first feared that Zeuxidamos wanted to murder him, now sensed that the Greek was under his power, that the situation between them had been reversed and servant was now master, although this was as yet murky, and since nothing ever turns out for the best, it was now Deimos who regarded him with enmity.

That evening they all ate goat meat and cast a fatty morsel into the waves to appease the sea monsters. There were also fresh vegetables and wine. A week before, the ship had landed for the first time since setting sail, in Azza, and they had procured from the Philistines everything they needed. It seemed that the voyage was now going well. The captain felt the blood seething in his veins in gratitude when he prayed to the great gods of the Iberian heaven, Endovelico, Nabia and Trebaruna, thanking them because peace reigned on his vessel, nobody had died, either of sickness or ill feeling or any other cause, the plague had not spread, the monster had spared them, and the terror of it had brought only good. And at the end of the voyage he could glimpse a handsome payment, although it was not fitting that he should speak of this to the gods, and instead he shared his elation with his little girl. The night of the sacrifice, all of them had lain down to sleep with full bellies and at peace.

It was then that Zeuxidamos lay down next to Elisha for the first time, and, as if by chance, he draped a protective arm over the boy's slender waist. Thinking the boy was asleep, with infinite delicacy he slipped his hand beneath his shirt and lightly stroked his chest, making him shiver. He then slid his hand down over Elisha's belly, he gently turned him over and caressed his firm buttocks, he twisted him back around, grasping the tender snake between his legs, he rubbed its tip with soft fingers until, as swiftly as could be, he felt it harden in his ever-greedier palm. In his astonishment, Elisha made no move to resist.

For the first time since they left Gat-Hefer, Jonah felt happy and free. Perhaps he had chosen the best course after all in deciding to help Jacob ben Benjamin, his father's cousin. He fell asleep with his mind at rest. The same as every night, Abiel had curled up in the poop, but this time he dreamed of colours, as he had only once before, not knowing what colours were. When he awoke, he was certain that that day something very bad was going to happen.

The immortals are angry

Like a man put to torment did the timbers groan and shriek. The sun had just passed its zenith when Abiel, huddled in the prow, heard the creaking and cracking and realised that the deck was shuddering. He felt suddenly cold and a nameless fear laid hold of him. He could not understand what was happening, it was as if somebody had all of a sudden cast him into a whirlwind. Some of the rowers found their little stone dice snatched from their hands into the air as they played, as if the gods had deprived them of their game so that they could keep it all to themselves.

Elisha had languished as if sick beneath the relentless sun all morning, not far away from Abiel, but when the darkness of night descended on them in the middle of the day, he leapt to his feet with the same swiftness as he had once possessed on dry land whenever he sensed danger. A huge gust of wind tilted the deck and sent him sprawling. Old man Jacob, who had experienced something similar on the outward voyage, immediately sought shelter in the storeroom for food and water, calling his servants to him, but nobody heard him in the moaning and the roaring that had been unleashed. The heavy black udders of the clouds weighed down on each other, massed at the outer edges of the sea, scuttled back and forth, and as they neared the ship, they swelled until they all but came crashing down on the men, while the winds, released from their storerooms, joined forces to ram the starboard obliquely. The ship lifted its prow to the heavens, as if the winged creature at its tip were trying to take flight, but then miraculously righted itself. The men, who, at the captain's order, were toiling without success to lower the sail, saw birds of flame fleeting above them, bright against the heavens on every side, and thunderclaps boomed in their ears, first one, then another, then another. Abiel hid his head in his hands, at every boom thinking a thunderbolt had struck him. Elisha led him from the stern, which was almost in the water. They fell to the deck, now one, now the other, now both at once, but finally he managed to lead him midships and get him inside the confined space where the old man had taken shelter. There, Jacob embraced him like a father. A tempest had blown up, and it was raining not buckets but enormous waves, which crashed down from above to swell the waves from below. All was now water, fire in the sky, howling wind. After an endless time, the sailors managed to lower the sail and roll it into a bale. They then tethered themselves together in pairs, with lengths of rope around their waists, fastened with the knot of Herakles, so as not to be hurled overboard by the raging storm. Waves were already crashing over the parapet onto the deck and over the men.

'She's too heavy!' shouted the captain. 'We'll throw cargo overboard to make her lighter. Little girl, don't give up! Don't let us down, little girl!'

The fresh, wholesome food they'd only just taken on board and many amphorae of water and wine were thrown overboard, with pangs of misgiving. They also jettisoned the black tub, which in ordinary weather nobody emptied into the sea lest they anger the gods of the deep with their filth. The slippery deck, wrenched up and down, back and forth like a swing, tortured their every step, and the ropes hindered them so badly that the Nubians and the Phoenician untied themselves, grabbing onto whatever they could to steady themselves. The mast swayed in the wind like a reed. For a time, the waves stopped crashing over the deck, although they still struck the black sides of the ship with the horns of their battering rams. In terror, the men endured the savage waves and the threat of death. The captain yelled first at the men, then at the ship herself: 'Hold firm, little girl, brace yourself, save us!'

The depths churned and unknown powers harrowed the heavens.

'We're taking on water again, we've started to take on water again,' shouted the Phoenician and quickly started baling with a large bowl.

The others helped, at the captain's order. Then, just as the winds seemed to relent a little, even though anyone familiar with the sea knew that the lull wouldn't last, the captain told them to gather around him in a circle. He spoke loudly and firmly:

'The immortals are angry with us. Somebody has a grave sin on his conscience, or maybe more than one of you do. Here's the thing: you'll each confess to your god or gods, right here and now, you'll beg their forgiveness for whatever you have done and pray that our ship will hold together and keep us alive! It's the only thing left to be done! I'm going to do it myself! We'll make it through this alive!'

The men were instantly filled with hope. They began to pray, some standing, some seated, some kneeling, some aloud, some in a whisper, and a few silently. Deimos prayed to Poseidon, the son of Chronos: 'Thou, who art master of all the waves of the sea and whom every wave, no matter how tiny, and every creature of the deep, no matter how lowly, obeys, thou, Poseidon, who dwellest on the unseen bottom of the sea with thy chosen consort and who dost lift islands to the surface with thy trident or sink them like stones, I pray thee, end the madness and the tumult that overwhelms our ship, lest we perish to the last man, and save me and my life, for I do not wish to die before my time. Thou, who didst build the walls of Troy together with the radiant Apollo, let me see my city once again, let me at least see the place where I was born. And let me see my mother, the poor, feeble woman, whose heart is wracked with worry.

Let me bring rejoicing to her old age one more time, when I rush to meet her embrace. Forgive me, powerful one, for thou alone knowest what thou must forgive me, for nothing that happens in thy watery kingdom escapes you, and I swear that I will no longer envy the blind man or the boy, I will no longer bear Zeuxidamos a grudge and I will sacrifice thee a fatted ram as soon as I set foot on dry land.'

Next to him, on his knees, the captain invoked his gods once more: 'I have erred against you in your goodness, Endovelico, Nabia and Trebaruna! From the start of the journey I've thought about nothing but the old man's fortune and wanted him to give me more of it. The unworthy thought of stealing it has even passed my mind. Forgive me, forgive me, forgive me, it was only out of worry for my numerous family, and out of a desire to make Adina happy. And the reassuring thought that the old man has plenty more where this came from! But now maybe nobody on this ship will escape alive, because of me and my greed. If we live, I won't take another penny from him, even if he willingly offers it, I swear!'

The Phoenician, who was on the port side, was whispering in his own language: 'All-powerful Baal, master of the rain, the lightning and the thunder, who dost raise and quell the storm as thou pleasest, and thou, laurel-wreathed Melkart, ruler of Tyre, whom I fled like a thief, pursued by the curses of that wench, forgive me, for I am a villain. Astarte, cruel and beautiful goddess of love, just was thine anger! But already thou hast punished me with the plague. Forgive me! Thou knowest that that woman tortured me like a demon and I could no longer endure her shouting and yelling, but I still shouldn't have fled like that. Baal, Astarte, and Melkart, I know that I have not thanked either the healer who tended me or the Jew that gave me water and did not leave me to die, for I deemed myself somehow above them. As soon as the storm dies down, I will do everything necessary, but I won't go back to that mad woman, even if it means dying right here and now, swallowed by the waves.' After which he resumed baling water.

Hernando was babbling in a voice made lisping by his over-bite, but it was hard to say how the words were connected with each other, since they formed more a litany without beginning or end: cousin, I, the blind man, waves, home, storm, forgive-ness, and so on, with frequent repetitions and long pauses.

Zeuxidamos undid the knot of Herakles, took off the rope te-thering him, and went down into the belly of the ship. Thence he returned, to the Captain's surprise, holding a staff with a knob shaped like a clenched fist and put it in Abiel's hand without saying a word. He did not know how to beg forgiveness. But thinking that the hour of his death was nigh, he prayed to Apollo: 'Show thyself, Phoebus Apollo, illumine our hearts, lu-minous one, with thy smile and ask Aeolus to call back his chil-dren, who are playing a terribly cruel game with us and wish to empty us into the sea like slops thrown to the animals. Save us, thou for whose birth Poseidon raised an island from the sea on which thou might rest, ask him to lead us to a tranquil island. Bring us ashore, beautiful god ... I gave back the staff, I was going to do it anyway, but I was ashamed to do so in front of that boy with the black curls, whom I love like a madman. Forgive me!'

Abiel grasped the staff firmly in his hand. He was as cer-tain that he would escape with his life as he had been certain that something bad was going to happen after he dreamed the dream of the two colours or whatever they might have been. To Zahra alone would he have known how to pray, but he felt no need to beg forgiveness for anything. He knew that she was watching over him no matter what.

Of the Nubians, only the father prayed, but he prayed also on behalf of his son, and it took him a long time to decide on whom he should call for aid. In the end, he began with Amon Ra, the Hidden One, the overlord of the gods, then he cried out to Bisu and Beset, who were as deformed in body and hideous in visage as they were benevolent, the protectors of families, and therefore of the Nubians' family too. He called also on Shu, the god of the air, who does not let the sun perish, and he prayed to him not to abandon them, since they bore no blame. Albeit reluctantly, he also mentioned Inpu, the jackal-headed god, whom the Greeks call Anubis and who guides souls on their journey to the other world, and he prayed that he not make any haste. He didn't have much for which to ask forgiveness, nor did his son, except perhaps for the incident with the blind man, they themselves hadn't done anything, but the fact was they had been there and looked on as he was humiliated. He knew who was guilty for that. It was Hernando and Sansón, but they had absolved themselves of their guilt, since the first had then striven to enter into Abiel's graces and the second had fashioned the boy a beautiful toy ship, a task in which his extra finger hadn't hindered him but quite the opposite. So, Amon Ru was asked to forgive them both and to preserve the lives of all on board.

Jacob did not think he had anything to reproach himself for, except perhaps a smidgen of pride. He assured the God who had delivered His people from bondage in Egypt that his slight tendency to pride was a good thing, since without it he wouldn't be able to heal people and assist them. He also assured Him that a lot of the time he was very afraid of failure. He then recited a short, solemn prayer for aid in the time of tribulation in which they found themselves.

As for Elisha, he had never prayed before and had no idea how to do it, and as for the concept of guilt, in his brief life he had not encountered it theretofore. Had he encountered it, he wouldn't have understood it. He had seen beatings and thefts, he had even seen men killed and women violently subjected to the strength of a man, he had seen fear in the perpetrators, but nobody had ever repented for what they had done. He wanted to live to see his brothers again and to feel the youngest hugging his legs as he had done before he went away. Then his thoughts turned to his wretched fate and before his eyes there flashed everything that had happened to him up to that cursed day, as happens only in the moment of death, so they say.

Throw me!

Despite the sailors confessing so many sins and, for better or worse, praying for absolution, albeit in great haste, the rain still came down in torrents and the deck was increasingly swamped by waves. The ship was slowly sinking, though all the men, even Jacob and Abiel, were now tethered to each other and toiling to bail water overboard. The captain, an experienced mariner, sensed the imminence of death.

'Not everybody has prayed!' he cried. 'Somebody has a sin so grave that it's dragging us down into the deep. Let him confess it now and beg absolution!'

It was Zeuxidamos who remembered Jonah. Like all the others, he was accustomed to seeing him only seldom, and so much was he out of sight that he was out of mind among the crew. But when Zeuxidamos had gone down into the impenetrable dark of the ship's belly to fetch the staff, he had stumbled over the sleeping man. Jonah had not woken up, and Zeuxidamos, beset by other worries, left him where he lay. The captain ordered that Zeuxidamos wake him and quickly bring him up on deck.

After an interval that seemed long and unbearable, Jonah showed himself on deck, followed by Zeuxidamos, acting as his guard. A sudden wave crashed over the gunwale and soaked Jonah, like a barrel of water poured over his head, giving his black beard and hair an oily sheen.

'We all prayed while you were asleep, but the raging elements didn't abate. Tell us who you are and where you come from. Why did you want to sail north but then suddenly changed your mind as if it were all one to you?"

Before Jonah, who was awkward of speech, could reply, the captain questioned him further:

'To which god do you pray? What are your sins? It's you who brought this misfortune down on us, isn't it? What is your trade? Whom did you kill? Speak!'

Jacob realised, with some amazement, that the crew of the ship didn't know that Jonah was his nephew and had made no connection between them. True, at supper the first evening, when the captain invited both of them to eat at his table, nobody had treated them as relatives, but merely as two travellers who had each paid separately from his own purse and who seemed merely acquaintances. The men did not need to know any more than that. Nor had there been any occasion after that for Jacob to mention Jonah was his nephew. They had not received any more invitations to eat at the captain's table. As for Jonah, he never opened his mouth. You couldn't get anything out of him. Elisha was the only one who knew exactly who Jonah was, and he had also told Abiel, but anyway, before the appearance of the monster brought about a complete change of heart in them, the sailors wouldn't have dreamed of talking to either of them. The old man quickly answered on his nephew's behalf. But no sooner did he open his mouth than the captain gave him a shove, impatient as he was to let the other man speak. And Jonah's voice, which was now none other than the voice of the voice, spoke to them, without haste or fear, drowning out the all-enveloping din of the storm:

'Jew. Fled. From before the face of the Lord God. He made the heavens, the earth, the sea. Didn't obey.'

'But why? Why did you do such a thing?'

'Fear. Maybe. Don't know.'

'Fear of what? Of whom?' the captain asked yet again.

'Of prophesying. Afraid. In Nineveh. Forty days till destruction.'

'The destruction of Nineveh? A city so illustrious, the biggest in the world, is to be destroyed?' interposed Jacob, who was beginning to understand what had made Jonah act so strangely ever since they left Gat-Hefer.

'The voice!' said Jonah in the voice of the voice. 'Saw it. My God. He commanded me.'

While he spoke, the roar of the tempest couldn't be heard, as if some unseen hand had locked up the winds in their storerooms at the edge of the sky, and the rain, although it still fell, made not a sound. It was as if somebody had placed a huge beaker over them as he spoke, isolating them from the fury of the waters. But now the tumult of the storm made itself heard once more, and the wind blew with redoubled strength. The captain, caught up in the turmoil of the elements and gripped by terror for the first time, shouted to make himself heard:

'What am I to do with you so that I can save my men and my little girl? How am I to quell the waves enraged at your reckless deed? You're the one to blame!'

When Jonah spoke, the storm fell silent once more, and in the silence the voice made itself heard:

'Yes, I am. Into the sea! Throw me! Can't swim. You'll stop the rain. The waves. You'll escape.'

Before the captain could answer, Jacob interrupted, in fright:

'No, no! He has confessed his sin. Remember the seven things that the Lord hates above all others. The third is hands that spill innocent blood! And know ye that righteousness is more pleasing than blood sacrifice! Let us not sin yet again, as we did with Abiel!' he said, generously including himself among those who had sinned.

As none of the men made any move, as none of them spoke a word, Jacob went on:

'Let us all pray to his God, who is also mine, let us pray that He forgive him. He's my nephew. I've never committed any major sin in my life, I've saved the lives of children and men and women, even recently, in Get-Hefer, which is where Jonah is from, a poor little child fell down a ... but now is not the time ... God will hear me and perhaps He will listen to me. Let us not make ourselves sinners by killing him!'

The old man was overjoyed that he had persuaded them, he himself almost unable to believe it. None of them now wished to make himself guilty of the death of a man. The captain went to the prow and let out a whoop.

'I can see mountains through the mists. The storm's driven the ship from out to sea closer to shore. To the oars! We'll try to reach the shore! Maybe it's a sign! Come on, little girl, come on, we're home free!'

The rowers took their places and began to pull the oars with all their might. But the sea rose up against them and no matter how hard the rowers strained, the ship made no headway, as if tethered to the seabed. The mountains that had appeared to the captain through thick curtains of mist were no longer visible. The storm was bellowing once more, the rain lashed the men, and the waves, which for a while had not risen above the gunwales, were washing over the deck.

'Lord God of the People of Israel,' cried out the captain in despair, 'let us not perish for the sake of the man who did not obey You and fled from Your commandment. And if You have forgiven him, let us not be his murderers. Do not suffer us, Lord of the Jews, to spill the blood of an innocent man, quell the storm, so that we will know that you have forgiven him and us along with him. It will be according to your will and commandment, O Lord, captain of the ship of the world, the ship of all things seen and unseen!'

In reply, the storm and the sea roared louder than ever and the ship suddenly lurched to starboard, then to stern, flinging them all to the deck. Jacob shouted something, but the others could see only his open mouth, and his words were lost in the din. Instead, they heard the voice of Jonah, which boomed louder than thunder.

'Throw me.'

The captain made a sign to a few of the rowers. They grasped Jonah by the arms and legs, and from the sagging prow, they laid him on the water, almost without needing to lift him.

He saw only darkness

Jonah flapped his arms helplessly and it was obvious he really didn't know how to swim. The same instant, the water from the sky stopped coming down and the water of the sea subsided into smoothness. Soft little waves with fluffy white crests caressed the ship and they were the sole trace of the raging elements of only a short while before. The waters were sluggish, sleepy, as if resting after great exertion. The hollows of ears that had been filled with roaring were now soothed by silence, and a sweet spring-like breeze was blowing. The time was sunset. Through a crack in clouds that was as large as their ship appeared the marvellous rosy-blue of the sky and against it a horned moon, thinner than a pared fingernail, was beginning to glint. It was as if they had glided into a different realm and they gazed in amazement, not daring to utter a word. It was as if they had seen God, and He was good and He was merciful. Some wept. Others prayed or swore to become better men. To make sacrifice. The captain knelt and prayed to the God of Jonah. For Jonah. And for them all. Jacob stood stock still, and his face was like the wax of a writing tablet. The Phoenician looked disconsolate. Abiel, having risen to his feet, leaned on his staff, and from how intent he was on the spot where Jonah had been standing but moments ago, you would have sworn he could see. Elisha was so disturbed by it all that he burst into laughter.

The ship once more stood upright in the water and even without the sail being hoisted on the mast, it slipped slowly across the waves towards the shore that shimmered in the distance. A few of the men, among them the captain, rushed to the prow to see what had become of Jonah, to know whether he was still floundering in the water or whether he had drowned. They espied him some two hundred paces in their wake. The tiny head still bobbed above the water, the mouth open, probably swallowing water, closing and then opening again to gasp for air, the arms still flapping helplessly. It crossed the captain's mind that he should try to save him, even though he didn't know how such a thing would be possible, but it was plain that the God of Israel was heedless of the captain's intention since that very instant behind Jonah there yawned the roof of a cave from which hung huge stony teeth. A shout went up from all the mouths of those gathered at the prow: they recognised that maw. Eli, who hadn't seen the monster till now, was filled with both joy and fear, but his joy was the stronger. Like the torrent of a river rushing downhill, the water filled the cavity, sucked in by unseen depths, and on the swell Jonah was borne into that cavern of flesh. The overarching firmament of the mouth snapped shut, a spout of water spurted through the hole in the creature's head, and then all sank like a ship snatched down into a whirlpool, vanishing into the depths. A moment later, Elisha saw the black back turning like a wheel, smooth and glossy, then the waves that seethed white all around were instantly stilled and the monster was gone, as if it had been nothing but a phantasm. And the strange thought came to him that perhaps the storm waves had been unleashed by the monster itself as it rose in search of its prey.

*

Jonah told Esther, Esther told her daughter Dinah and Dinah's daughter Hulda, Hulda her daughter Rebecca and Rebecca's daughter Ruth, Ruth her daughter Edna and Edna's daughter Dorcas. Dorcas named her daughter Sarah, as was her wish, and

God was kind to her. She told her daughter Sarah and Sarah's daughter Adah, Adah her son Athaliah and Athaliah's daughter Edidah, Edidah her son Jokebed and Jokebed's daughter Rahab, Rahab her daughter Rhoda and Rhoda's daughter Safira, and Safira, fearing she would not have a child to whom she could pass down the story (she was already thirty-four years old), told the story to a man who wrote it down four centuries after the death of Jonah. But notwithstanding, she then gave birth to Ayala, her little foal, and she read to her what had been written, but adding a wealth of details, so that now there were two stories, one short, set down in writing, the other long. Ayala gave birth to Eva, and Eva told the story to Hagar and Hagar's daughter Iesha. Iesha told it to Naomi and she told it to her daughter Rachel. Rachel told Suzannah and she her daughter Miriam. Miriam told it to my mother Atarah, whose name means 'crown' and who was born almost at the same time as Jesus of Naztrat or Nazareth, and she told it to me.

All our names are the names of God, my dear daughter, both the men's names and the women's. He has lent them to us for the space of our short lives, so said Jacob. His silver ring, with the sapphire stone, is your mother's now, and when you marry, it will be passed down to you. In this way, with the story constantly reinforced, always told twice, passed down from daughter to daughter, we can be sure that our ancestor will never be forgotten. I don't like my name, which is Dalila, but I named my daughter, your mother, Esther, the same as the star at the dawn of our family, from whom our story set out. And you, Phoebe, my dear granddaughter, we love you like the sun that Jonah lost when he sat in the monster's mouth or merely took shelter beneath its fin, since I don't really believe that he ended up in the belly of the creature, *dag gadol*, the giant fish, as some of the preservers of the story call it, so that they could fill their children with awe and see their mouths agape, like yours is now. And nobody actually knows how long he was there.

The truth is that it was then and there, wherever it was and for however long, that Jonah regained his power of speech. Whereas before he had spoken grudgingly, articulating only the pith of the matter, and had not prayed during the tempest like the others, now he spoke a harrowing three-part prayer (maybe this is where the idea of the three days came from), which I learned from my mother and grandmother, and which I'm going to tell you, so that it won't be forgotten. The prayer was so beautiful that God heard it and answered it, which is to say, he filled the empty shell of the words with the living kernel of the spirit. For words have no value unless God fill their husk with His spirit.

So, as the ship glided shoreward, all the men aboard, apart from Jacob, were overjoyed at having escaped. The miracle of the waters subsiding was the most majestic thing that had happened in their wretched, sorely tried lives. The fact that one of them had been thrown overboard was hardly uppermost in their minds, not least because the Galilean himself had urged them to do it, in that deep voice of his, a voice you couldn't disobey. Nobody had been able to befriend him, not even Eli, who got on well with everybody. The Phoenician alone was aggrieved. He'd promised his gods that he would thank the Jewish man who had slaked his thirst when he was ill and now he would never be able to. He felt sorry for the man cast into the jaws of death. He thought that he would bear the guilt for it all his life.

Jonah was floundering, losing strength. In Gat-Hefer, nobody knew how to swim. He thrashed all four limbs like a paddling dog, to thrust away the water below him, and he was still somehow at the surface. But it was almost as if he were like somebody falling into a deep chasm and flapping his arms to thrust the air below him and stay aloft. He remembered the well. That day, in his village, he had braced himself against the wall of the well shaft with both arms outstretched until they turned numb. A few times, when he could no longer take the strain, he had sunk into the water and swallowed it, but the water was good, it was drinking water, water from a well. Now he swallowed salt water and he was drowning, and his eyes stung, he kept them closed, and when he was no longer capable of moving his limbs, he felt himself borne away on a current like a woodchip carried downstream on a river. It was then that he opened his eyes, but all around he saw nothing but darkness. He thought he had entered the realm of the dead. He was greeted by a fearsome warm stench of decay.

Once, during one of his long retreats from the humankind, he had descended into a cave in the side of Mount Carmel. There were a few steps carved into the rock, which he had trodden at first, but then he had stumbled and fallen, sliding down for a long way, into the nethermost reaches of the mountain, far from any other human being. He had lain inert for a long period, all around him there was blackness and silence, and he had thought that that place would be his tomb, that he would be buried alive forevermore. That this would be his death! His mother, the beautiful wife of Amithai, had told him that every man tried on many deaths, like girdles or sandals, before he found the one that fit. But that untimely death did not fit him, to be buried alive in the nethermost reaches of a mountain, without anybody knowing what had happened to him. He lay there with his thoughts and he felt terribly alone and helpless. Then, somehow or other, he remembered God. How can you feel alone when God is with you, no matter how insignificant you might be, and all the more so when He has chosen you to see His voice? He rose to his feet and groped his way along the rock walls, realising he was in a tunnel. A tunnel ought to lead somewhere, and if it came to a dead end, he would turn back, go in a different direction, carry on until God, Who was with him, even if He didn't speak or show Himself to him, brought him out into the light once more. His will be done. Time stood still there, but he walked on and on, groping along the tunnel, like a huge mole. Sometimes he descended, sometimes he climbed, he felt the ground before him with his foot, with his knees, with the palms of his hands, even with his chest. And after steps unnumbered, the darkness gradually began to alter in density, it thinned, greyed, his mole eyes gradually became human eyes once more, the walls on either side began to acquire an outline, and then all of a sudden, after a bend, a disk of light appeared to him: the egress on the other side of the mountain. He was now on a completely different slope than the one by which he had entered, and his passage had changed him, as if he had been born again, born another.

For Jonah, it was the same now as when he fell into the cave, although he couldn't understand how you could fall from water into water, into a hollow within the water, into a belly within the water. He didn't know what had happened to him. He couldn't see, he had become a mole again, as he had been then, in his early youth, but he could breathe and at least he no longer swallowed brine, even though his tongue was stinging and his nose was itching and the stench was beyond endurance. He had sunk into something soft and harsh at the same time, a slime that was here springy, there tough. But unlike during the episode inside Mount Carmel, God was no longer at his side, since Jonah had fled from Him.

His head had turned into a soft cave. There was no sight in his eyes, but his ears were full of hearing. He listened. A continuous snorting, a muffled thumping. From time to time, sticky, slimy creatures or objects struck up against him, frightening him. He tried to rise to his feet, but he tottered like a child that had yet to learn to walk and he fell back down, to his knees. He would have liked to set off walking, as he had done then, in the belly of the mountain, but he didn't know where he was—unless, which was likely, in spite of it all, he was in the realm of the dead—or which way to go. As helpless as a shackled prisoner, buffered by sharp objects, by slobbering fists, his eyes deprived of light, his ears deprived of silence, his mind on all those who would never, ever see him again, he began to sob loudly, and his sobs were as large as himself, and he swallowed tears as salty as the brine in which he had drowned without dying. Much later, after his weeping ebbed away without any time having elapsed along with it, after he slept his restless sleep, without thought, without hope, without faith, he nonetheless began to pray, and his prayer possessed a power that he, who knew a thing or two about praying, had never before experienced. His body became so heavy that it was as if God Himself were hanging from it while holding the entire world in His hand.

Forgive me!

He prayed three times. The first time he prayed for the sake of the voice:

I turn my face to you like the flower! Why do you not come to me when I call you from the nethermost reaches of my being, from its very roots that are planted in the darkness as in soft, good soil? You are all I have, I have been wrenched from space and time, you alone remain to me, you alone know me. You alone do I love. You alone would I wish to see here, my beloved voice ...

The skin of my heart has burst like a grape, and the spirit within it has been crushed.

With my fists I cannot strike the darkness. With my fingers I cannot pick the sightlessness from my eyes that I might see you. With my fingers I cannot pick the booming hearing from my ears that I might hear only you. You are within me and you are outside me, but I cannot grasp you.

Lord, you have cast me into a dungeon whose door is bolted with water. There is no seeing in my eyes. There is no walking in my tread. There is no living in my life now.

If not you, who are both father and mother, who are both life and death, then who shall give birth to me now that I am hidden away within walls of flesh like an infant in the womb, as blind and powerless as an unborn child? Who will comfort me in my comfortlessness? Who will find me, a grain of sand in the middle of the wide sea, if not you?

You cannot flee from me, for I remember you and I ceaselessly imagine you, I who was imagined by you.

Draw nigh, be not afraid of me, I am not afraid of you, for love knows not fear, and fear knows not love! I call to you from the depths of my despair. You, who listen to nightingale's trill and frog's croak alike, listen to my trill and my croak. From the abyss into which I have tumbled I seek your loftiness. I am here! From the darkness in which I am swaddled, unswaddle me!

*

The second time, he prayed very briefly for forgiveness: Can you forgive me? Do you forgive me? You can do anything.

*

The third time, he prayed for himself and his own life:

There is no day and there is no night. Time does not reveal itself in the whiteness of the dawn that comes not. The black sun that is not does not roll across the black sky that is not.

My soul was once filled with soul, it gave birth to my host of blossoming souls, to your meadow, but now all of them are rotting. My soul is now rotting, before the death of my body—do not allow it, Lord! Once you forgive me, they will all blossom anew, there will be verdure and flowers in the dry husk of the heart and each fragrant shoot will return to life. At your touch my sorrows blossom like joys.

Let me cry out to you from my depths, for only in the great sea of my soul have I drowned, only the waves of my heart have swallowed me up: I need you! Come! Deliver me! Heal me! Heal me of myself, I am the sickness, you are my cure!

I don't know how to swim inside myself, I am drowning in myself. I cannot reach the shore of myself.

I hear you. You cry out to me. And the first Jonah is for soothing and the second is for admonishing and the third is for encouraging. Jonah! Jonah! Jonah! The same as formerly, the same as the first time.

And the voice of my mother is the echo of you. She cries out to me, Lord. Might my earthly mother still be alive? Rather than she not be able to see me, better that she no longer be. But better that she be, and that she see me, and that she pray for me. If you do not hear me, then may You hear her. Hear her, heavenly father, hear my earthly mother!

Free me from the black belly. Outside, where the eyes have sight, where it is day, where the sky is blue, where the sun is. Or where night is speckled with myriad stars. Nobody can count the stars, nobody knows their number, only you, my Lord.

Help me, You! Have mercy, You! Save me, You!

I am crushed like a grape beneath the sole of Your foot and the sweet juice of my life seeps from the skin of my heart. Lord, clarify me like the drop of wine, clarify me, Lord!

I sinned. I fled. Draw the watery bolt of this watery cage in which you have shut me, that I might run to you. Lift me up! Forgive me!

To be born again!

In Gat-Hefer, the grape harvest had just come to an end. Early that morning, the sky was covered with clouds whose white, curly crests were like the crests of waves. The wind rustled gently among the vine leaves, which had begun to lose their green softness, to wither and change colour. A few bunches of grapes had been deliberately left on the vines to shrivel to raisins, which people called the Lord's grapes, although nobody knew why. The women had gathered to separate the hard stalks from the elongated, golden grapes and the grapes with clean skins from those blotched with mould.

In the circle of women that had formed at random, Jonah's mother happened to be sitting between her son's lover, Hannah, she of the blue eyes, and the mother of the girl who fell down the well. Esther, her granddaughter, was sitting on the opposite side of the circle. Looking at her, as she sat beside the largest number of wicker baskets emptied of their grapes, since she worked faster than any of the other women, Amithai's widow could not help but sigh: her granddaughter was plain-looking, with a rather long humped nose, a protruding chin, a neck too short. But if God willed, she would find her a good husband, after her son returned home with the money cousin Jacob had saved up at the other end of the world. The little thing lacked neither industriousness nor cleverness. Perhaps she was too clever for a girl? She knew very well the reason why: between her husband and the girl an unusual friendship had sprung up. Amithai had treated her like a boy, since Jonah had not yet sired a son.

'How is Milkah?' somebody asked the mother of the girl from the well, naming the little girl by her new name.

'She's growing. She's happy. I don't think she remembers anything of what happened. Fortunately, she didn't realise. Had it not been for Jonah ben Amithai—' she cast a look of gratitude at Amithai's widow, who was by her side, knowing it would gladden her '—she would have been dead. And I would have thrown myself down the well after her, to be with her.'

She had said it countless times before, but the women never tired of hearing it, and she never tired of saying it.

'Not him,' said Jonah's mother, showing her beautiful smile, 'I mean, not only him! But also, above all, my cousin Jacob. My son got her out, but Jacob raised her back to life.'

Esther joined the woman's conversation, although she knew it was not fitting at her age. Amithai had indeed educated her badly: 'He didn't raise her back to life, he's not God. Uncle Jacob told me what he did and he taught me to do it too. It's something that only sailors know. When a man swallows too much water, you press your hands on his chest and if that still doesn't work, you place your lips on the drowned man's and drink the water out of his body, through his mouth.'

'Yes, that's right, that's right,' remembered the beautiful, slender neighbour who had been with Milkah's mother at the time, 'it had looked to me as if he was kissing her!'

And she flushed with excitement, as if reliving the whole thing.

'As you press down on the chest, you recite these words, slowly, but without drawing them out too long: "Black water, bad water, none wants thee, none drinks thee, wash away to sea, perish in the sea, from the innards flee, may thou a raincloud be. May thou a raincloud be ... Pour thy seawater rain down on the plain. May heaven—and here you say the name of the drowned man—keep and raise him from death's sleep." You say all that so that you know how long to press down. When you finish speaking those words, if he hasn't spat out the water, it means the man is dead.'

'I dreamed of Jonah,' said Hannah almost in a whisper, and Esther looked her up and down with a look wholly unlike that of a child. She had noticed that Hannah had been wearing baggier clothes lately.

The women abruptly fell silent. They all knew that Jonah had visited Hannah by night, they all knew that she had lost her husband and children, but even so, it was not fitting that she utter his name like that, for all to hear, or that she involve them in her dreams.

'A very bad dream, a terribly lucid dream. It's lodged in my mind. I'm very afraid it might foretell some misfortune,' she said, lowering her luminous eyes.

Probably this was the reason why she had dared to speak. Her fear of an evil omen was greater than her fear of the gossiping mouths of the women of Gat-Hefer. She had made them party to it, made them a wall between her and the dream.

'What did you dream about Father?' demanded Esther peremptorily. Curiosity conquered both her resentment and that of the other women.

Hannah barely dared speak and she grimly went on plucking stalks from the grapes: 'I couldn't see his face, it was as if his face had been torn away, and he was swimming in pitch darkness with that faceless head, but I knew it was him. He was drowning. That's why I told you, since you were talking about drowning and black water. But he wasn't drowning in water, he was drowning in darkness. And in the dream, I heard his despairing voice crying out to ...' she pointed her head at Jonah's mother. 'I awoke with the sound of his cry in my ears.'

As Hannah spoke, Amithai's widow was transfigured. She was now trembling.

'Stop!' yelled Milkah's mother, to whom Amithai's widow was now a tender sister to be protected. 'Aren't you ashamed? What business do you have dreaming of Jonah?'

'I didn't mean to,' said Hannah, and her blue eyes filled with tears. She didn't tell them that in the dream she had groped for the faceless face to kiss it, but she had felt no face. The women had finished and since night had not yet fallen, they decided to tread the grapes. They all went to the trough and washed their feet. Then, two by two, they went to the small stone presses that were scooped from the ground and began to crush the grapes with the soles of their feet, treading with all their weight, hopping, slipping, feeling the taut skins pop and the sticky juice squirt out. The bulging grapes became softer and softer underfoot, and the sticky juice more and more watery. The juice now came to their ankles. They were all laughing, even Hannah and Esther.

I don't know why, but when I was your age and Grand-mother Phoebe told me the story about cleaning the grapes in Gat-Hefer hundreds of years ago and about Hannah's dream, this is how I imagined her, my darling: I imagined our ancestor with the luminous name as clever, and surly, and plain-looking. People are very unjust when they tell stories. Maybe Jonah's daughter didn't have a nose like I told you, and maybe she wasn't at all harsh, or even clever, but gentle and silly, or maybe she was good-looking and bad. There are things that I know for sure, for example that Jonah's mother had an enchanting smile and that he inherited her smile, the smile that you too have, but other things are as cloudy as the grape juice, you cannot help but try to clarify them by yourself, to decant them, to turn them into wine using your imagination, because otherwise what would be the good of telling any story? And when I see you, Avigail, when I see your joy when I tell you stories about our family, since joy lies hidden in your very name, and your name is borrowed from God, when I see you, I cannot help but spin out the tale for you as if I had been there myself. But the truth is that Esther really must have been very clever: it is from her that the whole story comes down, from her who was the first storyteller.

Jonah's mother, who was your great-great-great- (I don't know how many greats) grandmother, did not wish to join in the women's general rejoicing. She went home and looked for the beakers her departed son had whittled. With the utmost love, she took one, filled it with the last year's wine, and then poured it on the ground, drop by drop, praying ceaselessly that her son return safely. The wine seeped into the ground, but the spirit of the grapes rose to the heavens with the mother's prayer, like a sacrifice. And God heard the prayer.

I'm joking, my dear!

... Like a grape beneath the sole of your foot, the sweet juice of my life is crushed from the skin of my heart. Lord, clarify me like a drop of wine and give me strength!

Lift me outside once more. Where the eyes can see and there is daylight and blue sky and sunshine. Or where there is cool star-spangled night. Nobody can number the stars but You alone, O Lord! Here, whether I close my eyes or open them it is all one. How I would like to see your numberless stars even if only once.

Yes, God heard him, my dear, as he repeated those words to himself. Was it him that He heard, the man in the cage of flesh enclosed by the huge wall of water, or, more likely, did He hear his mother, among the vine-clad hills of Gat-Hefer? Nobody but God can know. But after he finished his prayer, which probably he recited at the same time as that spoken by his mother, Jonah grew very dizzy and felt he was falling backward into emptiness, looking through eyes in which there was no wide-eyed seeing. And all of a sudden, the seeing returned to his eyes and his sight filled with stars, some so close that you could catch them in your hand, stars that were in motion, others so high above that they were but specks of silver dust which none could number but God. It was as if he were floating in the waters of the sky. He grew drunk on the sky the way you would grow drunk on the spirit of wine; he took voluptuous delight in the sky. It was a good thing it was night, otherwise he might have been blinded. He heard his own voice chortling and babbling words of gratitude. He laughed, he wept, he spoke, he saw. Then he flapped his arms again, as he had before he entered the place where there was no time and no sight, but only the stench of decay. He couldn't understand whence and by what means he came to be outside, like a child released into the world by its mother. It was as if a cave of flesh had yawned open and then closed back up. The creature, if creature it had been, was gone, it hadn't bidden Jonah farewell, it hadn't been waiting for him to thank it or to pay it for the lodging—I'm joking, my dear, so glad am I at the unexpected twist in the story.

Only much later did Jonah think that the monster the sailors had talked about but which he alone had not seen was the same one that took him prisoner just as he was about to drown. He didn't know how long he had remained in its mouth or in its belly, since time did not exist in that cage of darkness and he had no idea where he was. Up until the moment he prayed, he was caught between worlds. The monster could have been anything at all. Once he prayed, however, things became clear, and it was plain that God had sent the creature not to kill him, but to save him from drowning. It often happens that after a time things change their meaning completely, and prayer possesses the quality of instantly clarifying every kind of water, even seawater. He was forgiven.

But now that time had returned to the world with the appearance of the stars in the firmament, he was forced to fight for his life and to reach the shore. He knew that he would not drown, unless the Lord became angry with him again—but it never even occurred to him to make Him angry again. He found that by lying on his back with his eyes fixed on the sky, slowly moving his arms and legs up and down, the sea would keep him afloat, as if he were resting on a soft bed. Each passing moment drained his strength, since now the moments were passing once more, and their passing was good, it was comforting. He felt as if he were about to lose consciousness, but he was overjoyed, he was filled with gratitude, and not a hint of fear or mistrust now existed in the starry firmament, beneath which someone took care that he should reach the shore.

With the body of a man
and the tail of a fish

The boy let out a long whine. He was six or seven, thin, his arms and legs like twigs. His face was swarthy, grimy, framed by very curly hair made stiff by the salt breeze. On hearing the boy's cry, the girl, five years or so older than he, and as thin and dirty as he was, knew that something bad had happened. She had been left far behind, but now she broke into a run, hindered by her long garments, which she rolled up in her haste to save her brother. The same as every morning, their father had gone fishing very early, and their mother, always alone, always tired, always aggrieved, was giving suck to a ceaselessly whimpering infant. Only when she held it to her breast, stopping its mouth, did she have a moment's peace. In a rough-hewn wooden trough slept another baby. Three infants were buried at the side of the house. In the dark room in which lived the parents, four children, and, over winter, a sheep and a ram, the air was always thick.

The girl and the boy were overjoyed at being sent to gather shellfish. The previous dawn, their father had not gone out to fish since a storm was raging, and it continued all day, subsiding only after the sun set. The wind that had blown all through the night and the waves that had heaved and crashed one after the other would certainly have brought a fresh harvest to quell their hunger until their father's return. All around them were rusty-red rocks, which the sea had carved into a flight of pocked, irregular steps. On the shore there was only a single large spit of sand. The children had to compete with the seagulls that had arrived in straggling flocks, and which, as famished as they were, more often than not left them with nothing.

In a short space, the girl reached her brother, who, using a grey feather he'd picked up, was pointing at a large white creature that the sea had washed ashore, like a fish lying belly up, laved at intervals by the waves. They were about to run back the way they had come, but curiosity got the better of their fear, as is usually the case. They approached gingerly, lest they waken the beast, the man, the god, the demon, whatever it might be. The little boy gave a start whenever a bigger wave seemed to shift the creature. Once they were close enough, they saw that it was nothing to be frightened of: merely a man with no clothes on. They circled him without knowing what to do, examining him closely. He seemed to be dead. His mouth was open and his skin had a preternatural luminosity, such as they had never seen before, but it was also full of scratches. Although the body looked young and vigorous, the hair and beard were those of an old man, white, full of shells, and only at the armpits and below the belly was his hair black, growing in large, thick tufts. The seagulls wheeled above them echoing each other's cries.

'He's drowned,' the girl ventured to say, but she spoke softly, as if fearful she might wake the dead man. 'He's not from here.'

'Maybe his ship sank.'

'A pirate,' whispered the girl.

'Or Marid, the spirit of the sea,' whispered the little boy.

'How can he be a spirit? Don't you see?' said the girl, pointing at the black tuft between the creature's legs.

The boy laughed. His sister laughed too. Their fear of the dead man had passed.

'Let's go farther up the shore, maybe we'll find something ...'

'Treasure!' said the boy, his eyes agleam.

'Yes, we'll leave the dead man here and go looking for treasure!' decided the girl, but then almost immediately let out a cry: 'Look, look, he closed his mouth! He's not dead!'

They ran a little way away, but keeping their eyes fastened on the prone man. To their horror, a horror that the boy voiced with a gasp, oooh, the man opened his eyes. The children now barely dared to breathe. Having awoken from the dead, the man looked at the sky and then clenched his eyes shut as if they hurt. He seemed unable to move. After a long while, the boy moved a step closer to the recumbent creature, which made not the slightest twitch. Another step closer. Still nothing. The girl followed him, resting her hands on his shoulders. The man had by now noticed them and was trying to say something, but his tongue refused to obey him. He made a few gurgles, then fell silent, and his eyes closed, as if now he were well and truly dead. Strangely, the waves held back, no longer lapping up against his face. The boy ventured to touch the man's nose with his seagull feather, but nothing happened.

'Let's collect some shellfish. Maybe he's hungry.'

Within moments, they harvested a good few oysters. The girl broke open the shells with a rock, and her brother held the soft slippery body of an oyster to the man's lips. The man opened his eyes, but not his mouth.

'Eat,' commanded the boy, in the same voice as his father used when speaking to him.

The man seemed to understand him. He took the soft body of the shellfish in his quivering lips and swallowed it. It took a while before the children fed him everything they had collected. Then the man croaked as if he wished to say something.

'He's telling us who he is,' the girl supposed. 'I'm Yerusha,' she said, then added, as if not seeing fit to utter his name, 'This is my brother. Are you a pirate?'

'I'm Dodai,' the little one put in, since he copied almost everything his sister did.

The man mumbled something again, but the children couldn't understand what. They grasped his arms and tried to drag him farther away from the water. He was tall and heavy and there was no chance of their budging him. It was strange that the sea had cast him up on the only spit of sand along that coast and that the waves had retreated, no longer lapping against him. The children set about collecting more shells and filled the hems of their smocks. Then they sat down next to the man and ate. They were famished all the time and their bellies were distended.

At intervals they gave the man another oyster, as if they were feeding one of their animals. In a way, he was their animal. It occurred to the girl that he might also be thirsty. But for that, one of them would have to run home to fetch water. They were afraid of their mother's tongue and the back of her hand, which fell even more heavily than their father's. In the end, Yerusha decided to go herself, but not before collecting some shellfish for her mother. She told Dodai not to budge from the spot and to take great care of the pirate. When he recovered his strength, they would ask him about treasure, without fail.

At home, the girl was happy to see that her mother had fallen asleep with the infant at her breast. At her throat, threaded on a leather thong, hung a small, rudely carved, striated olive-wood figurine: Dagon, worshipped by all the Philistines, which is to say the people of the sea. Dagon, the god with the torso of a man and the tail of a fish. The infant in the trough, frail and silent, was awake. Yerusha left a pile of shellfish next to her mother, for her to eat when she woke up. She then quickly took a deep clay bowl and filled it with water from the jug next to the door. On her way back, although she tried hard to tread softly and hold the bowl steady, she spilled about half of the water.

She found her little brother busy picking the shells caught in the man's white hair and beard. Dodai was babbling away, the way children talk, without caring if anybody heard or answered him, but in any event, the man seemed not to understand what he said.

'Hold his head up so that we can give him water to drink.'

The little boy, who by now was not at all afraid of the man cast up by the sea, took his large head in his small hands. The head on its own was heavy, but the boy braced himself and held it upright. Struggling and straining, the girl managed to give the man all the water left in the bowl. The man looked at her in gratitude and said something. Dodai thought he was saying his name, *Doda, Doda*, but to the girl he seemed to be saying *Toda, Toda*.

'Maybe he wants some more,' said the boy.

'He's glad,' observed Yerusha.

The man moved, making a great effort. He managed to prop himself up with his hands and sit up. He sat shivering.

'Let's bring him some clothes to put on.'

'Where from?'

'You go get them,' decided Yerusha, 'because I'm the one who brought him the water. Get the sheet. If Mother's awake, tell her what we found,' she told him, with a trace of doubt.

It was obvious that Dodai was not at all pleased at what he'd been asked to do, but looking at his catch—after all, he was the one who'd found him—he set off at a run. On the way, a thought occurred to him as to what he should tell his mother in order to get off lightly. An astonishing thought, which made him marvel. When he got there, his mother was indeed awake and in a bad mood as always.

Unbelievable

In a lifetime spent at sea, the captain had never seen the like: not only was his ship unscathed, having ridden out the wildest storm he'd ever experienced, but now a ripe breeze bore it gently along the coast and it slipped through the waves almost gaily, without any need of oars or tiller. They sailed like this for a week. The men were once more filled with anxiety, since their drinking water would last them another day at most, if they drank in moderation, but from the prow, where he kept an uninterrupted watch, the captain said over and over again:

'No doubt about it, that Jew knew it all from the very start. The way he kept saying, "Throw me, throw me, only then will the waters subside." And his God did his bidding. From now on I'm going to pray to Him, which doesn't mean I'll forget our own gods up there above, my little girl. We got away! We got away! You were terrific! A good girl, a brave girl ... Just a little farther and you'll have your rest. We'll pull through!'

Hernando came up to him and placed his hand on his shoulder. Probably he'd heard the captain, because he reinforced what he'd just said, lisping the words as usual because of his overbite:

'Jonah hash, I mean, he had, because now he's part of the monshter that shwallowed him, he had a powerful God. And a jusht one: He punished him because he didn't obey his command, but he didn't let ush perish along with him, because we weren't to blame in any way for him running away. Look,' he cried, almost in desperation, 'aren't those the rocksh off Joppa?'

A number of the sailors heard him and crowded together at the prow. They all recognised the rocks that were about a day's sail from Joppa. It was unbelievable: they'd sailed from port for weeks but now they back where they started. The storm had sent them flying back over the sea, but the crew, who had witnessed so many marvels since they set sail, no longer marvelled at anything. They hugged the captain in their sinewy arms, as if he was the one who had performed the miracle. They couldn't hug the gods. Nor could they hug the new God.

Jacob came to look too, and the men respectfully made way for him, for they now knew that Jonah had been his nephew. The old man had grown even older over the last week. He didn't smile any more, or joke, or speak in parables. He was almost as silent as his nephew had been before the monster swallowed him. Elisha constantly kept him company, trying to cheer him up. He was still learning new things every day, things trickier and trickier, but for all that he was keener and more diligent than ever, Jacob no longer praised him or paid him any mind. It was only now that the boy realised how much he needed the old man's praise, but it was as if Jacob no longer saw him.

'Abiel, what are we going to do with the old gaffer, 'cause he's not going to live much longer if he carries on like this. We'll be out on our ear again, the both of us. Just when I'd got used to him.'

'Let our luck fall where it may,' said Abiel calmly, gripping the knob of his staff, from which he was now inseparable.

The ginger tomcat was curled up in Abiel's lap, blinking its narrowed eyes in the sun, eyes as narrow as Eli's. Jacob had scratched Abiel's name on the staff, although it was pointless since none but the captain could read it. True, Elisha could now read it too, and he often stroked the scored letters of Abiel's name, as if marvelling that a name could be stroked.

'Jonah had special powers, even I get that,' Elisha continued, 'when he went inside the monster's gob, I froze, I couldn't move for terror. A good thing you can't see, Abiel, because you can't unsee a thing like that once you've seen it. Every night, it's like I'm seeing it again before my very eyes: Jonah going inside the monster's mouth, and then the mouth closing and him vanishing into the depths, and sometimes it's like I'm the one it's swallowing ... But he was the one who wanted them to throw him in the sea, wasn't he? When the water stopped, the rain and the waves, all at once, in an instant, it was the most, the most—'

'Beautiful?'

'Yes, the most beautiful thing that ever happened to me in my life. And he saved us all! The bloke didn't die for nothing! Everybody I'd ever seen die before that died for nothing.'

'Zahra would have done the same. She would have sacrificed herself. After all that, I started believing in God too, you know.'

'He was brave, and no mistake. Like when he took care of that Phoenician. But he was guilty, wasn't he?' said Elisha, in an attempt to console himself. 'He was punished.'

'Guilty? Punished? Would you go and prophesy the destruction of the greatest, the most powerful, the cruellest city on earth? Wouldn't you be afraid? Wouldn't you run away? Blood springs in that city like water springs from the wells where we live.'

'I'd have run away too, and really, really quick,' admitted Elisha.

A few moments later, Elisha leapt to his feet and went to the bird's head, where a rumour could be heard. He quickly returned to the stern and told his friend the big news: they were nearing Joppa.

'And when you think of how much we've suffered and all the things we've been through, for us now to be back where we started! And without any gain!'

Resembling none of the others

'On the shore a god's been washed up by the waves,' cried Dodai to his mother as he grabbed the only sheet from the only mattress in the room where they all slept. 'It's Dagon and he's stark naked! Come quick!' At which he ran off again.

In all her life, the mother of Dodai and Yerusha had seen no more than a dozen men, and only four of them close to: her husband, a surly man good at fishing and harsh of speech, who had sired seven children with her without ever caressing her, and the three fishermen from the next houses, at great distances from each other down the shore, all three small, thin, sallow, with silent wives and droves of children. She now looked closely at the fifth, who was sitting with his legs crossed on the spit of sand by the shore. He resembled none of the others she knew. She thought he looked like a giant, it was as if he radiated light, and unconsciously she fingered the figurine of the god around her neck. As he sat there with his legs entwined, bare-chested, strong of arm, the man on the shore really did resemble Dagon, the god of the tribes, he of the fish tail. The infant she was holding began to whimper, but she paid it no heed. Yerusha and Dodai were telling her something, but she didn't hear them, as if they weren't even there. To her, the only person there was the man washed up by the waves, she had eyes only for him, and she had ears only for his voice, but which for the time being did not make itself heard. She had only just laid eyes on him, but already she placed all her hopes in him. She sensed that this Dagon in the flesh and blood, who had sprung from her every evening's thoughts, would bring them happiness and change their lives of uninterrupted affliction. With a deep bow, she asked whether he might deign to enter their house and bestow his blessing upon it. The god made no reply. But he gazed on her with kindness. Nobody had ever gazed on her with kindness before.

In the meantime, Dodai had given him the sheet, and he had knotted it around his waist, concealing the bottom half of his body and thereby allowing the woman to imagine that his fish tail had been restored. They helped him to his feet, after which all of them set off towards the house. Too overwhelmed to know what she was doing, the woman pressed the infant to her breast very hard and it began to scream. Dagon stroked the little head and smiled at it the way only gods know how. It was the first caress the little one had ever felt, the first smile it had ever seen, and this was the guest's first miracle. In amazement, the woman felt her little boy, who had whined constantly since the day he was born, become all of a sudden calm and she saw his little mouth spread in a tiny smile, like a face in the water answering the face looking down at it.

The god stepped inside the house, along with him entered a beam of sunlight. The woman saw that he was young and comely and that his hair and beard were silver. They sat him on the straw mattress and gave him more water to drink. He lit up the room. Yerusha and Dodai busied themselves close to him, now convinced, like their mother, that he was Dagon or some lofty emissary of the god at the very least. The woman straight away set about baking some flat cakes, and the smoke and the savoury smell tickled the guest's nostrils. None of them were surprised when, at dusk, the fisherman arrived with a basket full of fish larger and more numerous than ever before. They were still flapping their tails, probably in joyful recognition of the god. It was Dagon's second miracle.

But the man of the house regarded the stranger with glowering eyes and assailed him with a volley of questions:

'What are you doing here? Don't you think that I'm going to feed you while you sit around sunning your belly! Where did you come from? Who are you? What do you want?'

The stranger made no answer and merely gazed at him, showing no fear, the way the denizens of the deep gaze at you or those of the endless expanses above the sky, from the place called the firmament, because it's firm enough for you to stand on it and make your home there. The woman, who since the guest's arrival had been at peace, her countenance tranquil and serene, took her husband by the hand, led him outside, and explained to him, barely suppressing her excitement:

'Don't you see? His light rises like the dawn! He looks like none other than he himself!' and she pointed at the small Dagon hanging at her throat. 'Don't you know that the gods take human shape so as to put us to the test? He came in answer to my prayers. Don't you see that ever since he came, the child hasn't bawled any more, and your catch of fish is bigger than ever before? Aren't these miracles? Let us show him respect, let us sacrifice our supper to him, let us give him our bed, and from now on, our luck will change, I feel it ...'

Not her words, but the look on her face allayed the fisherman's doubts, and he too was filled with a kind of invigoration that he had seldom felt before, except when he had an unexpectedly good catch. It was a different woman who was speaking to him now than the one he had left that morning when he went out to fish, and the whole room was transformed by the large white presence sitting in the middle of it. And the infant at the woman's breast really was sleeping peacefully.

So, they cooked a copious supper and all ate their fill, and most of all the guest, in keeping with his stature in the house and in the world. The woman alone sat and looked, barely able to touch her food. But with every bite the stranger took, she felt the better, as if she herself had swallowed it. They put the stranger to bed on the straw mattress, and laid themselves down on the floor. Dodai and Yerusha had never seen their parents like this: at peace, better people, very happy. When the stranger opened his mouth and spoke in his own language, which sounded like the rippling of water, the children laughed. The gods spoke a strange language.

The third miracle occurred the next day, at dawn.

The land tricks them

It was afternoon when they sighted port and reached shore. A month had passed since their so carefully prepared departure. They had lost almost all their provisions at sea, the goat had been sacrificed, but they had kept their lives and as for the captain, he still had the gold he had been paid, while some of the men had gained a new God in their heaven. One man had perished, a common occurrence during a sea voyage. What was uncommon was the way in which he had perished, and the tale of it was one that they would never forget as long as they lived. Ashore, it would be told among the fishermen again and again, over cups of wine, during the long evenings when there was no work. And the *dag gadol* of the story, Leviathan or the monster, was constantly to change its appearance, until finally nobody knew what it had really looked like, not even the storyteller who had seen it with his own eyes.

There was not so much activity in port now, for with the coming of autumn the hustle and bustle attendant upon the loading and unloading of ships dwindled. In Joppa, the mild winters with their gentle drizzle let everyday life flow along slowly, and only the sea was capricious, always discontented, like a woman, as the sailors were wont to say. Other than fishing on boats that hugged the coastline, nothing much happened in the dreary months that lay ahead. The men from the vessel with the head of a bird and the tail of a fish didn't want to show their disconcertion and so they spoke to each other words of feigned good cheer. They tried to mask their disquiet by cracking snide malicious jokes, but neither joking nor snideness were what they were before they started the voyage. The truth was that other than taking pleasure in feeling firm, unbudging ground underfoot after being rocked on the seas for so long, they didn't know what to do. It was hard for them to part from their comrades and the captain's little girl, as even they had come to call the ship, and they would dearly have liked the captain to tell them that they were setting sail again in a few days. But only Jacob could have given the order, and without Jonah, there was no point in another voyage to Tarshish at the ends of the earth. The day before, in front of Elisha, but speaking to himself, Jacob had said that he would like to go back to Gat-Hefer, but didn't have the courage to face the widow of his cousin Amithai and give her the news that through nobody's fault but his own, her beloved son had been thrown overboard and swallowed by a terrifying fish, and that now the vast sea was his vast grave.

No, that he could not do, in no wise. He would stay in Joppa until spring, when, perhaps, he would find the courage to go to her and assure her that he was ready to atone for his sins alongside her and share her grief, even to the end of their lives, which, in his case, could not be far off. And to beg her forgiveness and console her that, just as the fish is caught in the net and the bird in the snare, her son too was caught in an evil hour, and it was the will of the Lord. He had no further need of his two servants for the time being. He would call them if he changed his mind. Such harshness was something new for him.

'Farewell, uncle,' said Abiel, making bold only now, on parting, to address him as he had been permitted.

*

When he set foot once more in the port where he had lived his whole life, Elisha found himself swaying. It was as if the ground were tricking him, defying him, rolling like the waves. He grew dizzy and without realising it he waddled like a duck.

But he no longer limped, because the sole of his foot had at long last healed. On seeing so familiar places again he was filled with a joy that was as unexpected as it was fierce. Tears came to his eyes. At the same time, fear throttled him and he felt as if he were suffocating when he thought of his little brothers. Experiences had become much harder for him to bear during the voyage. When he departed, almost nothing had moved his heart, he had seemed wise and calm, albeit sad, but now within him there was always a tempest, as if he had grown up in reverse, from old age to youth. He quickly told Abiel that he would look for him in the old places familiar to them both and ran off in the direction of the inn, taking with him the toy ship fashioned by Sansón. He gave himself courage by remembering the words of Jonah, which he thought of constantly: 'I went to the inn. I paid her. For his brothers. To take care. Let us have faith!' But Elisha knew Achim's widow better than that and had no faith in her at all. Nor in anybody else, for that matter.

My dear Yeshua, your mother and my daughter, Deborah, is the first of the line of Jonah to have borne only sons. So, you, as her first born, are duty-bound to pass down the story of our ancestor and to wear the silver and sapphire ring of Esther on your finger. I must tell you that Jonah was Amithai's only son, and if he had sisters, nobody now remembers them. If you have a daughter, you must give her the silver ring when she marries. If not, let us hope that the boys too will pass down the ring and the story.

Life is very cruel sometimes, as you yourself know by now, since your parents both died when you were little. But I am here and I intend to stay with you till you take a wife who will fill the earth with our line, the line of Jonah. Before us, of the seed of Jonah were born twenty-score and thirty sons and daughters, unless your grandfather has tallied incorrectly. But only two-score and eight have worn the ring. You are the forty-ninth, after the two-score and eight women.

In her way, Achim's widow kept the promise she made to Jonah, which is to say, in the way that anybody else from Joppa would have kept a promise. She gave the two little beggars a meal a day, not a very good one, but made them do heavy work, particularly the older of the two, and when she deemed he hadn't done it properly or hadn't done enough, she would beat both of them black and blue, indiscriminately. Nobody cared. The children decided to run away. Like a dog, the older one burrowed a hole in the earth on the other side of the wall, in which he hid a bag containing everything he'd been able to pinch from the inn. They didn't have much yet: a flint, four dried figs, and some crumbled cake, as well as the catapult from their brother.

The boy was holding his arms outstretched so that the little one could load them with firewood. The little one was standing on tiptoes as the older one bent his knees so that he could pile on as many faggots as possible. Staggering under the load, the older brother headed towards the oven in the middle of the yard, from which wafted the scent of baking bread, making you hungry. Because he was looking to the side, lest he trip, he didn't see Elisha as he raced through the arch that gave onto the courtyard. The two collided, causing the boy to drop the pile of faggots. He was about to burst into tears, but looking up he saw a face that both did and didn't resemble the one that had gone away, and he froze to the spot, not knowing what to do. The little one, on the other hand, who had watched from a distance as the two bumped into each other, went to them as quickly as he could, his bare feet slapping the ground, and pressed his head against them, as he had when Elisha left and as if for evermore. When he did nonetheless peel his head away from their legs, he saw before him a little toy ship, rather crudely fashioned, its mast lopsided. It was without doubt the most beautiful thing he had ever seen in his life. His mouth twisted and he stood for a long moment, undecided, after which he burst into sobs.

Achim's widow was at the oven, baking bread. She recognised the newcomer at a single glance. Fearful that Jonah could not be far away, instead of driving away the intruder and beating the boy for dropping the firewood, she determined to learn the news about the man who had paid her and was perhaps ready to do so again. Come what may, she had no intention of relinquishing the two boys, especially given they would become increasingly useful the more they grew. She asked the visitor about the ship and the Galilean. Caught off guard, Elisha, who right then felt happy with life and with everybody in the world, told her that they had returned safely, all except Jonah, who had drowned during a storm. The window's eyes gleamed and Elisha immediately realised what an unforgivable mistake he had made. Jacob would have known to tell her a proverb, the one about how the evil man who oppresses the innocent mocks his Creator and is finally undone by his own evil, but Eli had not yet learned this proverb, either from the old man or from life.

Making friends

Jacob busied himself with all kinds of urgent matters as a means of forgetting the disastrous voyage, during which not only the sea but also, and even more so, the heavens had been against him. Ever since he disembarked, to him the heavens were no longer above, the earth lay deep in shadow, and all people were hardened in their evil. In exchange for a gold girdle, he had bought himself a spacious house next door to the man who had sold him the honey, one of the few solid buildings in Joppa, and for the price of a ring, he hired two serving women to cook for him and keep house. From morning to evening, he was to be found in one of the rooms of the house, the smallest and dimmest, wracking his brains, while the women chattered away among themselves. Over and over he relived the events he had experienced, from his arrival in Gat-Hefer to the disappearance of his nephew, the son of his beautiful sister-in-law, into the maw of the sea creature. Hard to believe, but seeing is believing, and he had seen the horror with his own two eyes. It kept flashing through his mind that he was to blame for it all, not because he had taken Jonah from the village, away from his mother and his daughter, but because of a far older sin, from when he was young and loose of tongue and comportment, from when he was convinced that all things were his due. It was that sin which made him flee to the ends of the earth. He had taken with him a riddle, a question whose answer was as simple as yes or no, and all through his journey with Jonah, from the very first step he took, he had tried and failed to solve it. Could Jonah's terrible end have been the solution, providing the answer 'yes'? The old man's velvety eyes, shaded by his unruly eyebrows, filled with tears, and with his hand he waved the thought away, as if he could see and touch it there in front of him. He felt a little guilty towards both Elisha and Abiel, but there was nothing he could do, he had no room for them in his soul right then, when there was only room for grief. Since his departure from Gat-Hefer three months had elapsed, two months since he boarded the ship, and one month since his return to Joppa.

One day he remembered the woman from Akko, her between whose legs a man once died, and her sick daughter, and how worried he had been when he had gone to her while looking for Jonah. He remembered the spiritual powers he had still then possessed, which warmed the heavens and the earth and himself with their invisible rays of light. He had been a friend of the world, of the wide world, and the world had responded with friendship. He had hoped for, expected and received everything from the world, from people, and from God, he had been bequeathed an abundance of fruits, for it is said that a wish fulfilled is a fruitful tree. Back then he was Aaron's staff, which buds, gives leaf, flowers, and finally bears a harvest of almonds. Now, more even than his body, his soul too was stooped and there was no room in it for joy or fear or hope, for flowers or fruit. It was plain that he was afflicted by the noonday demon of the psalm, his soul slowly consumed by the destruction that wasteth at noonday. And likewise it was noon when he first vanquished his demon and managed to tear himself away from the room where he had lain idle, staring at the ceiling. He wanted to make friends with the wide world once more and to heal himself.

But as soon as he left the house he sensed that it would not be easy, that the world was not yet prepared for the friendship he once more proffered. The wind blew dust in his eyes and they watered continually, then he was attacked by starving dogs—a good thing he had a staff with him to beat them off. He eventually found the path to the house with the string curtain in the doorway, where that highly unusual boy had once led him, skilfully deceiving even him, who boasted that he could count on the fingers of one hand those who had ever fooled him and still have two fingers to spare. When he found it, the place was swarming with hens and geese as before.

The same as the last time, he asked at the barred window:

'Is anybody home?'

And the same as the last time, nobody replied. He then entered the semi-darkness of the room. But within, nothing looked the same: it was clean, the heavy reek was gone, and the woman was sitting sewing a shirt, bent low over her work. She barely looked up at Jacob. She showed no sign of recognising him.

'Don't you remember me? I came here one day, not so long since, even though to me it seems a lifetime ago. The boy Elisha sent me here, fooling me with the greatest of ease, when I was looking for my nephew Jonah.'

'Did you find him?' asked the woman evenly, without a trace of interest, and Jacob noticed how much she had changed in the time that had elapsed since he went away: she no longer anointed her face with oil to make it shine, her eyes no longer glittered, and the flesh sagged from her. She was old.

'I found him, and then lost him again.'

'And you have come to me looking for him again? Know that he hasn't been here this time either. And in any event, I'm not in that line of work anymore. I sew shirts and sell them for food. Would you like to buy one?'

'I'll buy more than one, if you make them to my instructions. But I didn't come here looking for Jonah, although obviously everything I do now is connected to him in a way. Look, I've brought you some drops to help your daughter: give her them in the morning and the evening, with her food, and she will be less agitated and she won't suffocate anymore.'

He couldn't understand the woman's reaction: she gazed at him in scorn, hatred, malice. Jacob, who had been expecting at least a modicum of joy, if not gratitude, on her part, was left bewildered. He was one who could read people's faces the way he read the holy scriptures, but now he didn't know what to think.

'Naturally, I'm not asking you for any payment!' he hastened to add.

'My daughter is in the abode of the dead,' said the woman in the same malicious voice. 'I don't think she'll be needing them there. But you can give her them when you yourself go there, which can't be far off!'

The grief-stricken can be cruel in their words and unjust, Jacob knew that.

'What was her name?'

'Anah.'

'All our names are borrowed from God. She was the answer that God gave you, for that is what her name means. Don't turn the answer into a question, and you may be sure of it: to Him has Anah returned.'

He also knew that the grief-stricken want to tell their story.

'How did it happen?'

'A man came ... he came to me, but I wasn't at home. I don't know what he said to her or what he did to her. The girl was so frightened that she suffocated. When I came back, I was able to hold her in my arms for scarcely a few moments before she gave up the ghost. The villain fled. I didn't even look at him, I had eyes only for her at the time. Fearing that he might decide to visit me again and I wouldn't even know he was my daughter's murderer, I haven't received anybody since then!'

'Do you have other children? Perhaps in Akko?'

The woman shook her head, then said bitterly:

'Other women have so many that they can count them on both their fingers and toes, but to me God gave only one sickly child and her He took back quickly! Since then I have not prayed again. Ever.'

'And He took Jonah from me,' said Jacob gently.

'But at least you didn't give birth to him, at least you didn't suckle him!'

'But probably I sired him,' said Jacob. 'Look for me at the large house next door to the man who sells honey so that I can tell you what I want you to sew for me.'

He left more cheerful than he had arrived, to the woman's amazement. For the first time, he had told somebody his secret. For the first time, God too heard it spoken aloud.

With mouth agape

The fisherman's wife, who in all her life had never experienced so many things as she had that day, couldn't sleep for happiness. As she wanted and needed to keep vigil over the sleeping god, she softly rose from the side of her snoring husband and sat down cross-legged near the straw mattress on which the guest lay. That bed for a whole family was too short for him and his feet dangled off the end. Through the doorway seeped the light of the fire left to smoulder a few steps away outside and shadows flickered on the floor. Through the hole of the window fell moonbeams in a slant, and the room was alive with lights of every kind. With a thrill, she saw that the white god was not asleep either, and his eyes gleamed in the dark, as white as he himself. When she realised that the great Dagon was slowly turning his face to her, she was gripped with fright and felt a claw snagging at her heart. But his eyes were gentle and the claw slowly released her heart, although its beating thudded in her ears for a while yet. Then something even more astounding happened: the god shifted his arm and reached out his hand towards hers. Her hand, covered in calluses and scratches, her misused hand slipped into his large warm palm, which closed around it. The woman felt pervaded by so much goodness that she almost fainted. It was the most powerful thing she had ever experienced. The god held her hand, gently but ever so long a time. She did not need anything else in the world, she did not need even the world, she could have remained like that for the rest of her life. Then, his fingers opened once more, he released her and made a sign for her to lie down to sleep. She obeyed him—how could she not obey him?—and fell asleep the same instant.

In the morning, the fisherman went out in his boat, the same as he did every day, but not before giving his guest a deep bow as a fitting mark of his family's respect. After a night's sleep, he was again unsure as to whether the guest was really Dagon, but even so, he sensed he was dealing with somebody out of the ordinary, a kind of wizard who demanded submission, and perhaps thanks to him he would make as large a catch of fish as he had the evening before. He took with him his second net, just in case. The guest did not move, he did not make a sound, he simply looked him in the eyes, but the fisherman had no idea what that look of his meant, and never in his life had he tried to understand another face. Yerusha and Dodai, who deemed the newcomer a gift that the sea had made to the two of them alone, each grasped him by the hand and led him to the seashore. To their puzzlement, their mother did not try to stop them. She was smiling as she had never smiled before, and she was silent. They went at random among the seawater-pocked shelves of the jagged rust-coloured rocks. The boy stooped to pick up things he found while the girl hopped around like the seabirds. They talked to the man as if he could understand them. He remained silent, smiling at them sometimes. After a while, he knelt facing the sea and uttered some strange words. The children were certain he was casting a magic spell. They would have been disappointed to discover it was a prayer, namely a prayer of thanks. Be that as it may, when the man stood up and turned towards them, the third miracle occurred. Before his eyes and behind the children, who turned to see what he was looking at, a cleft in the rock could be seen, an ingress the children had never noticed before.

'He cut the rock,' said the girl. 'That entrance wasn't here before, or we'd have seen it long ago. Dad would have shown us it.'

'I wouldn't be surprised if he's led us to treasure,' whispered Dodai.

'What treasure? There you go again! Can't you get it in your head he's a god, not a pirate? Can't you see he's the spitting image of the Dagon Mama wears on her necklace?'

'So what! As if the gods wouldn't know where the treasure is! They know everything, don't they?'

Yerusha had to admit that this was true. The two children went to the cleft in the rock, with the man following behind. They slipped inside the crevice, which was larger than was visible from the shore and found themselves in a huge cave: neither its roof nor its back wall were visible. Apart from the light that pierced through the entrance, the rest of the cave was plunged in darkness. Yerusha decided to run home and fetch a torch and some coals from the fire. She returned quite quickly, with the coals in a big clay pot, but she hadn't found the torch.

'Stupid!' her brother chided her.

But the man made a sign for them to wait, after which he vanished for such a long time that the children started to ask themselves whether he had left them for good.

'He must have gone down to the bottom of the sea, where he lives, to fetch some fire,' said Yerusha.

'I don't believe you. You can't live at the bottom of the sea.'

'What about the fish? Don't they live there?'

'And besides, how could you keep a fire burning underwater without it going out?'

'If he's a god, he can do anything,' concluded the girl.

It was just then that the object of their quarrel returned. Unlike the first time, he came not from the sea, but from along the shore. He didn't look wet and his fish's tail hadn't grown back, but he was carrying a thick branch around the end of which he had tightly wrapped some bark and dry grass before binding it with a strip of cloth. That strip of cloth was now missing from the man's makeshift garment, the family sheet.

All three entered the huge cavity in the rock: first the man, holding aloft the dancing light of the torch, then Yerusha, who was holding her pot of glowing coals—it gave off a drop of light and was good in case the torch went out—and behind her, Dodai. Inside it was cold and the two children began to shiver.

They advanced quite a way, the going was easy since the cave floor was of beaten earth, but the man kept turning around to see the slit of light from the entrance, to make sure he knew the way back out. To the children's disappointment, there didn't seem to be anything there. So much space, but all of it empty! They were now at the very back of the cave. The man-god then raised the torch as if he already knew: on the yellowish wall the children saw a huge fish, its open mouth revealing large fangs. The tail made up half of its body and the creature's black eye peered at the unexpected light after gazing on darkness for untold years. But what was terrible to see was that from the mouth protruded a man, feet-first and stiff as a plank, his legs splayed, presumably because the creature's prey was struggling. The children took a step back: they didn't know what a drawing was, never having seen one in their lives, nobody had taught them that such things existed in the world, and they stood as open-mouthed as the fish. A shudder passed through the god, he who had brought them there to reveal these things, and he too took a step back.

The fish was outlined in black, and beneath could be seen the remnants of a fire, dead for who knows how long, for who knows how many generations, and some rather large teeth, perhaps the leftovers of a copious meal. Could the teeth be all that was left of the very fish that was painted on the wall? The man took a few steps along the wall, leaving the children next to the sea monster and the half a man, which were now lent a terrifying reddish flicker by the glowing coals in Yerusha's clay pot. In a recess, the man came upon two skeletons. In the light of the torch they seemed small, and they were huddled together in an embrace. He quickly went back to Dodai and Yerusha, he stooped to pick up the teeth, then urged the children back towards the slit of daylight. There was nothing else for them to do in the cave. The torch went out just as they reached the entrance and the man left it there: he was certain that Yerusha and Dodai would return there many times. For a long while he worked on what he had taken from inside, from next to the cold hearth. He gave each of them a tooth as big as a finger, of the kind which, as the children knew very well, ward off evil spirits. Then he traced a sign on their foreheads with his hand and sent them back from whence they came. They were never to see him again. They were never to forget him.

Like a Mother

Like earth that soaks up water and is never sated, Achim's insatiable widow had long since swallowed up all the money Jonah had given her to feed the two children and still she wanted more. From the very start, she had treated the two little beggars as her slaves, just as Elisha had feared, and now she had learned of the terrible death of their protector, the story having travelled from mouth to mouth and reached even her ramshackle courtyard, nothing could stop her from behaving as she pleased. They were a nuisance, nothing less: two empty bellies to fill. While Achim was alive, he had been the one who was rapacious and it was she who moderated his greed, but ever since he died, it was as if she'd been possessed by his spirit. She'd bought a number of houses in Joppa, although they stood empty for the time being. She felt her conscience was clear, she'd kept her oath, by feeding them, and she fed them still, albeit only once a day now, which meant it was only fair and honest that they should work for it, the same as anybody else would have done, if it came to that. In any case, they couldn't be any great help to her, thin and sickly as they were. She was amazed the little one still lived, and she took no joy in it. She'd immediately confiscated the ship Elisha brought him. If only she'd been able to put that Elisha to work too, she thought to herself one day, standing in front of her neighbours' house, gossiping, but she had no way of catching him, even if the boy came when she wasn't around and always brought the little ones something and was always plotting some roguery or other. On the other hand, she boasted, she'd detected it straight away when one of the two stole something!

'I saw he kept going out of the yard and I couldn't understand why. But yesterday, I followed him. Can you imagine? He had a bag buried out past the wall and in it there was food and all kinds of things, all of them shamelessly stolen from me. Don't think I didn't beat him till he was black and blue, and both the one and the other kept going, 'ow! ow! stop hitting me!' You'd have thought their hour had come, and I left them both lying flat on the ground. And I didn't give them nowt to eat, so that they'd learn not to steal no more! And I reckon I'll not give them nowt to eat today, neither.'

'What were they up to with that bag?' asked an elderly neighbour.

'I got it out of them: they was planning to run away from me, the villains! After I fed them all this time! They'd have died too, if it hadn't been for me!'

The other neighbour, a younger woman, who'd witnessed it when Jonah made the agreement—he'd summoned her to do just that—ventured to say:

'But that man paid you for three years! I was amazed at how much silver you took from him. He said that if he wasn't back in three years, only then should you put them to work. I remember it like it was yesterday: "Three years. I'll be back. Maybe sooner. Take care of them. Like a mother." Aren't you afraid of God?'

Envy and pity vied in her voice, but envy was the stronger.

'Not really, no, to tell the truth. I was afraid of the man, because he looked quick to anger and had a heavy hand, but now he's gone and got himself swallowed by a fish, and the sea done swallowed that fish with him in it, so there's no reason for me to be afraid now. He'll be back to see I didn't obey him the day I see the back of my own neck.'

And pleased at herself for giving such an answer, Achim's widow went to the courtyard of the inn, where travellers on their way to Egypt were waiting: some were talking, some were sleeping, four were playing dice, having unloaded their mules and their one horse. The children were nowhere to be seen: the widow had locked them in the wine cellar and had a mind to leave them there longer. She'd ceased caring. But the God of Jonah, of whom she wasn't afraid, wished otherwise, and He was to manifest His will before the setting of the sun.

But it wasn't possible

'Listen here, Abiel, I think I can see the tip of a mast, far, far away, on the horizon. Yes, look now, I can see it better now, it really is a mast, but where could they be going, with winter just around the corner?'

'Maybe they're coming here.'

'No, hardly, what business would they have in Joppa? Nothing happens here till spring. I reckon they're on their way to Tyre, in which case, they ought to get a move on. Ah, now it's gone!'

'Must be the last goods cargo from Egypt. In this weather, when the ships lie in port, goods sell much more dearly, and there'll always be some who stake their lives to make a profit. And more often than not they lose the bet.'

The time was afternoon, and it was an unusually fine day, with only a gentle breeze off the sea. Elisha was at the side of Abiel, who was begging, the same as he used to, now at the crossroads between the two goods thoroughfares, now in the port, near where the ships rocked at anchor, the same four that were there before his sea voyage. Neither he nor Eli had eaten anything. Eli's hair had grown long again, down to his shoulders, and so had his fingernails and toenails, but he wasn't dirty any more. He bathed in the increasingly cold sea and rubbed his skin, since Jacob had taught him to wash every day, which almost nobody else in Joppa did. His longish face, with its narrow eyes and curly lashes, was full of sadness and charm. His good fortune had been short-lived, and the latest events had turned him aside from a path which previously he had neither taken stock of nor paid any mind. At the time, he'd been busy just living from day to day, he'd had bad days and good days, and ordinary days, but now he wanted to understand why this was the way of it and not otherwise. It was a question to which perhaps not even Jacob knew the answer. Every day he looked for work to do in exchange for food, but he didn't always find it. When he received more food than usual, he would first run to the inn to give his brothers some of it without the widow seeing him, after which he went to Abiel. Sometimes he would be starving when he went to the blind man, who, if he had any food, would save a mouthful for him too. He had lived this way before, without worrying about it overly much. Since their return, Abiel was neither happier nor sadder than before, and this pleased Eli: Abiel's equanimity was his anchor. He no longer saw the others from the ship except by accident at best, and to his amazement, he hadn't encountered Jacob even once, as if the old man were dead. Eli found out where he lived and often walked up and down near his house, in the hope of bumping into him, but since he didn't, he suspected that Jacob never left his chamber. He didn't have the courage to enter the house, as if he would have been committing some shameful act. Eli missed Jacob and hoped he wasn't ill. One day, however, he found himself face to face with Zeuxidamos. Both stopped short, but after their eyes met, the boy quickly went on his way without looking back. What had happened on board ship embarrassed him and wakened the demons of the body. The same thing happened to him when he saw beautiful girls, whom he now gazed at with rapt attention and different eyes, and sometimes he called out words to them.

The day before, Elisha hadn't managed to see his brothers, even though he'd stood waiting for an opportunity the whole afternoon, and he confessed to his friend that he was beside himself with worry. He got up from where he sat next to Abiel and headed back to the inn to make one more attempt to see the boys. Abiel was left sitting there, gazing out to sea with his sightless eyes. Time passed, and what Eli had thought the tip of a mast had now grown a fraction. More time elapsed, and what had seemed a point now grew to the size of an apple then a marrow and finally a bark, and a bark it remained. At twilight, the bark reached the shore, helped by a wind off the open sea. Nobody had noticed its approach, although Abiel's eyes were pointed right at it. From the bark clambered a man with a white beard and white hair, but with brawny arms and legs. Over his shoulder was slung a sack on a leather strap, and he walked slowly.

*

'Abiel!' heard the blind man, who thought himself alone and started in fright.

He knew that voice. There was only one man who spoke like that, but it couldn't be he. That voice had died. It no longer existed in the world, having been swallowed by the monster that had earlier saved Abiel. He thought constantly about that strange occurrence: the huge fish that all the men on the ship had told him about had saved him only later to kill the other. It had been good for him, bad for the other. It was sometimes like that with people too. From the creature now in front of him he picked up not a scent, as he would from any other human being, but a vibration. He gripped the staff Zahra had given him more tightly—ever since Zeuxidamos gave him it back on the day of the tempest, he had never been parted from it—he raised it in front of himself for protection and spoke in a hoarse voice:

'Who or what are you?'

The question sounded hostile. The voice was firm in its reply.

'Jonah. It's me. Don't doubt.'

A few moments later, the voice spoke once more:

'Abiel!'

The blind man was harrowed. Imagine if you can, my little Mikal ben Yeshua, who is still afraid of the dark, imagine yourself in his place, in the darkness before him there could have been anything at all, a spirit, a demon, any of the fearsome creatures that mariners tell stories about to pass the time while they're away at sea. When you have eyes to see, you may be afraid, but your fear is a single fear, it has a single face. But for him fear had countless heads, and each head filled him with a different kind of fear. You can imagine how much Abiel wished Elisha had stayed to able to tell him what was there in front of him! True, Abiel hadn't actually seen Jonah die, and I think it must have crossed his mind that they'd all been lying to him, telling him seafarers' tales. Well did he recall the episode of the sick Phoenician: when the crew had attacked him, Jonah, springing out of nowhere, had rescued him, after which, in gratitude, he had felt his face with his fingers, caressing him. The memory of it helped him now:

'Bend down! I want to feel your face.'

The man knelt down beside him. Abiel gripped his staff tightly in his right hand, but his left hand he stretched out before himself, grimacing as if the hand might suddenly be bitten, or swallowed up, or crushed, or as if it might come into contact with something repulsive. But it met a human face, and Abiel recognised the cheekbones and the silkiness of the curly beard, which his fingers remembered well, since it hadn't been long since they felt them for the first time, and then the fleshy lips and the moist teeth. Which meant that the same as the first time, the creature was smiling. Can you imagine, little Mikal? Abiel had no idea that that beard was now white, which might have confused him if he'd been able to see it. Sometimes, as a blind uncle in our family used to say, people who do not see, know.

Abiel sighed in obvious relief and joy.

'Jonah, I recognise you, it's you … it's you, but how can this be? how can this be? They told me you'd been swallowed by that fish and they all saw you in its mouth! Eli told me so, too, and he wouldn't have lied to me. Is it true?'

'They told? I don't know. I got out. It spat me out. Probably. I prayed.'

'But it's unbelievable! Uncle will be overjoyed! Your uncle, Jacob, that is,' Abiel added, not sure whether Jonah knew that the old man had permitted him to call him that. 'He was crippled with grief that you had been lost, you know, and I haven't met him since we reached port. I'm afraid he might be ill. I have no idea what has become of the other men from our ship. As for Elisha, he went to the inn just now, because that widow is killing those children, curse her! Tell me about yourself, how you escaped, what you have been doing all this time, where you went, how you got here.'

But Jonah's voice was incapable of storytelling, although for a time it had been capable of prayer.

'To the inn!' said the voice, and Abiel felt himself lifted up by a brawny arm.

With halting tongue

It was suppertime when the white-haired man and the blind man, striking the ground with his staff, reached the inn. Elisha was nowhere to be seen. In the ramshackle courtyard, the men who had stopped off on their way to Egypt were gathered in a circle around a fire, and the smell of baking fish wafted all the way to the street outside. Achim's widow was eating heartily a little way off, and a few mangy starving dogs and an old cat were circling the fire in the hope of snatching some leftover. The widow immediately noticed the two, but recognised only Abiel. What she noticed about the old man with the white beard was sooner the handsome bag slung over his shoulder, which showed that he had the wherewithal to pay for lodging. It never entered her head to interrupt her supper for anyone: she turned away from them and continued eating, heedless of them.

In a few bounds, like an enormous grasshopper, the man with the white beard was beside her and planted himself in front of her. The widow let him stand there, indifferently lowering her eyes to her dish as if she had not seen him. But above her thundered a voice:

'The children!'

Silence fell throughout the courtyard, and the men around the fire stopped eating and chattering and turned their faces to the other three all at once. The cat mewled and swiftly retreated into a corner. Only two words had been spoken, but they filled the whole courtyard. A shadow now burst forth.

It was Elisha, who, after standing rooted to the spot for an instant, approached, looked up at the old man, and let out a cry which, coming after the preceding thunderclap, sounded like a high-pitched squeak:

'Jonah! Jonah?'

First of all, he recognised him, and then he was struck with amazement. It was then that the widow too looked up, having shrunk beneath the power of the voice, as if it had struck her a blow. On her face could be read terror.

'The children! Now!' the thunder boomed once more.

The woman made to stand up, but she was gripped by terrible spasms and fell down foaming at the mouth. The two women from next door now arrived, as if sensing something was afoot. Abiel stood leaning on his staff and his ears followed everything that was happening. Elisha exchanged a glance with the white-haired man, who, although he did not look like Jonah at all, could only be Jonah, and, without a second thought, the two of them set about looking.

'Here!' came a voice, and this time the thunder was muffled, because it came from below the earth.

Jonah had found the children lying in chains, and their little bodies, huddled next to each other, undoubtedly to keep warm, made him recall the two skeletons in the cave. When Elisha went up to them, neither could get up, but the eldest murmured with halting tongue, 'Eli! We waited for you …' and tried to smile. His eyes were livid. The youngest gave no sign he knew what was happening and was unresponsive when Elisha called his name, leaned over him sobbing, and whispered in his ear that he would never leave him again. His little hands were as cold as ice, his cheeks burned with fever, and sweat beaded his brow.

'We have to get the old gaffer, he's the only one who knows the spells to make them better,' Elisha was scarcely able to say amid his sobs.

But Jonah had already picked up the children, holding one in each arm, carefully pressing them to his chest to warm them and impart the life in him.

'No,' he said. 'We go.'

'I know the house,' cried Elisha. 'I'll take you!'

At a run, they crossed the yard, where Achim's widow still lay on the ground, the two women from next door standing next to her: she was dead. She had died of terror.

They looked the same age

Jacob was on the way to recovery after his bout with the noonday demon, which, for about a week after he spoke his secret aloud had seemed to drain him of all his strength. He had therefore decided to go out every day, walking down into Joppa, quite a distance from his house on the hill, so that he could help as many people in need as he met on his way, since unfortunates were by no means scanty in the port. He would do so in memory of the man who was his nephew, if not more closely related than just a nephew, who had perished at sea in so unbelievable a fashion, an event largely Jacob's own fault, if not in fact wholly his fault. He took with him a bag of powders and ointments and a purse of silver, and he put on his new shirt, which the woman from Akko had brought him that morning. He was about to go down the hill to the seashore when at the end of the lane he saw a motley group on its way towards his house, moving with astonishing swiftness. His eyes were no longer what they were in his youth, it was almost dark, and this obliged him to wait. The shapes were unclear: a well-built man with a bushy beard carrying two young children in his arms, a young man, still not fully grown, and a third, holding a staff, yes, the third could only be Abiel. Jacob rejoiced that it was Abiel, he had long been intending to find him, to have him by his side, perhaps, but he had lacked the strength and the will.

The group had climbed the hill to Jacob before he knew what was happening. Although he was a man of great wisdom, what he now saw before his eyes surpassed his understanding. Think about it Mikal, enough of your tears! We men have to be strong, I want you to accustom yourself to what life holds in store, try to laugh at life, so that it won't laugh at you, think about it, my boy: standing in front of him was somebody who would have looked like a kind of Jonah, but the real Jonah had been swallowed up by the huge mouth of a fish, which was then swallowed up by the even huger mouth of the sea. And he was wondering what was with that white-haired 'kind of Jonah', who looked more like his cousin Amithai. Could it be that Amithai wasn't dead and was now bent on a reckoning with him? And what was with the emaciated, livid children he was holding in his arms? So, don't be surprised if Jacob thought it was all a dream, Mikal, or rather a nightmare. It was only then that he recognised Elisha and, in an instant, without anybody explaining it to him, he understood what was most readily perceived by a *medicus*—that's a word gaining greater and greater currency nowadays: the two pups in the arms of the supposed Jonah needed his help, right there and then. He set aside everything else for some other time and called the man holding the children into his chamber, which was dimly lit by two oil lamps. He stopped wondering who the man was or might be and told him to lay the children on the bed before ordering him to leave the chamber. He postponed understanding: life and the struggle for it came first, questions about it later.

The rest of them waited outside until dawn, now standing, now sitting by the wall, now pacing up and down. They felt no need to talk. At one point, Jacob's serving woman brought them food, presumably at the master's order. Elisha ate it all up without even knowing what he was eating, he didn't even realise he was eating, but swallowed the food the way a root drinks up the water after a drought, but Jonah and Abiel rejoiced in the warm soup and fresh bread. When milky dawn arrived, Jacob came out and said:

'They're going to live. It's highly strange, but both were dead drunk. How could such a thing be possible? They might even have died. They will sleep till evening, probably. In any illness, there is nothing more restorative than sleep, which is as the sun to the grapevine. Come in and tell me what happened. Speak already, but take care, for I am old and I don't want my heart to give out!'

He took the white-haired man by the arm and said:

'Is it you? Can it be?'

'It is I. It can be. By the will of God.'

*

Nobody now knows, my darling Isabella, what Jonah did after he left the family of Philistines that found him and before he met his uncle Jacob once more, or if Jacob really was his uncle and not his father. When my grandfather and then my father told me the story—you know that the story always has to be told by two mouths, so that it won't be forgotten—I was very little, I'd been ill, and I remember that my father Yeshua kept telling me: Don't cry, Mikal, you have to laugh at this life and its misfortunes, my boy, you mustn't cry, so that it won't laugh at you. But I see that you cried too, my little girl, you cried too at the part where Elisha met his brothers again, because it's not for nothing that you're my daughter. Let the others mock at it, but as for me, I'm glad that you don't have a cold heart. In seven days, you'll be wed, and so it's time that I passed on the silver ring to you, which now fits only my little finger and no further than this thick joint. It fits you perfectly, and I think you know already that this blue stone is a sapphire. When your first daughter gets married, put it on her finger. Or whenever you like, you can give it to her earlier, it doesn't have to be before her wedding, that's the tradition, but not all of us follow it. We live in hard and dangerous times, but don't forget that we're part of the line of Jonah, and though at first he was afraid and fled from God's commandment, in the end he became as brave as Don Quixote, so say I. And maybe he also became a bit of a dreamer and as eccentric as Don Quixote. My father Yeshua very much loved the author of *Don Quixote* and often he used to call me Miguel instead of Mikal. You're lucky that I put my foot down and refused to call you Dulcinea, which is what your grandfather wanted. Isabella is much more suitable.

I would have loved to have been there, in Jacob's room, when Jonah told him of his adventures. He must have helped a lot of people on his return journey and he must have been rewarded, because apart from his white hair, he looked well, he was handsome, and there was no shortage of silver in his pack. They say fear can make your hair turn white on the spot. I don't know whether it's true. Maybe it's not wholly true and Esther, the first storyteller exaggerated a little, adding a little colour, a splash of white. But let's not quibble, let's take a serene joy in this true fairy tale, which is still far from reaching the end. Anyway, I'll tell you what happened just as it was told to me, and where there's a gap or something unbelievable, I'll fill it in from my imagination, because otherwise, if everything has to be given a rational explanation, what's the good of telling stories? You know full well that life isn't rational, nor, alas, are people. Abiel had fallen asleep, my dear Isabella, and it was as if Elisha were deaf, he couldn't hear what they were saying, he had eyes only for the children, who were sleeping peacefully, and at intervals he would kneel by the bed and lightly touch their shoulders, as if to make sure they were really there and weren't going to disappear.

Whereas Jonah had aged, Jacob now grew younger, in the space of a single morning, when he understood that the man who was his nephew, if not more closely related than just a nephew, like I said, really was alive and that he would be able to look that man's mother in the eye once more, a woman still beautiful and forever good, albeit no longer young. That morning, uncle and nephew seemed both the same age. Jacob, who was telling jokes and talking in parables once more, even felt like boarding Don Amado's ship for a second time—actually, we don't know what the captain's name was, but that's what I'll call him from now on, so as to lend my own personal touch to the story—and returning to Spain, since it was here in our country that he had land and wealth, in Andalusia, near the mouth of the Guadalquivir, and he even felt like going to Gat-Hefer. But something had changed since their departure from the village. Now it was Jonah who made the decision, and he was adamant:

'Going to Nineveh. To prophesy doom. They're evil. Uncircumcised hearts.'

Jacob's fresh courage was dampened, since the worries he had only just left behind were now ahead of him again. His nephew had died young and been born again an old man, and Jacob now knew that his destiny was to accompany him and keep watch over him, to protect him, otherwise he would find no peace of his own.

But the departure for Nineveh, so Jonah announced, would be only after he had gone to see his mother. And daughter. He didn't mention Hannah, his nocturnal love, the woman with blue eyes, but her last words still consumed him: 'We will have a child.'

Deep roots

Like a storm wave rearing up and crashing down did the news of the Galilean's return spread the length and breadth of Joppa—the man with two lives, who had been swallowed by a monster of the deep and been spat back out. Dozens of times had the sailors told of how their passenger perished in the huge mouth that bristled with fangs of stone, and again and again their listeners had marvelled at his wretched fate. But now, from the inn of Achim's widow, where one of the dead woman's two neighbours had very quickly put two and two together, a new story made its way, a story such as had never been heard before in that little port. Jonah could no longer leave his uncle's house without people grabbing and tugging the hem of his garments or without them touching him at the very least. Given his tallness and the whiteness of his beard and hair he easily stood out, and when people realised it was him, many of them fell to their knees before him. Pregnant women begged him to place his hand on their bellies, so that when their babies came into the world they would be blessed with long lives free of peril. He took to going out only at night, furtively, and he pressed his uncle to hasten their departure from that port where he could not hide from people's love. In the end, that love, the same as any other love, was yet another huge mouth eager to swallow him and digest him at its leisure. In other words, a monster.

Jacob's house was spacious and he now played host to all of them: the three brothers, Abiel, and, of course, his nephew regained. Lately, despite the great differences between them, they had each experienced things that transcended all understanding, things so lofty that they were now bound together with cunning knots such as fate alone knows how to tie and, if it wills, to untie. The children, well fed and cared for by the two serving women, were restored to health with each passing day. In the morning, Jacob gave them powders to strengthen them and in the evening drops of an oil that tasted and smelled of fish, which he himself prepared and whose secret no one else knew. The elder of the two had regained his good cheer, his boisterousness, but the younger was still very silent, far too subdued, and even if he showed no more signs of illness, it was as if he hadn't decided between life and death. Nor had Eli fully recovered from the grief, the fear, and the guilt that had taken hold of him the day when he found them again, and not for a single moment did he take his eyes off the little boy, and he held his hand, as if thereby he might prevent illness from taking him away. But one day he told him to wait for him, as he would come back quickly, and rushed off like a whirlwind. When he returned, he asked one of the serving women for a bowl and filled it with water. This he took to his brothers. Listing, its broken mast bandaged with a rag, the ship fashioned by Sansón's eleven fingers bobbed on the rather cloudy water in the bowl.

'It's yours,' Elisha told his youngest brother. 'I went to the inn and found it.'

The little boy looked fixedly at the ship, but he didn't dare to reach out his hand and touch it. He didn't smile. The other brother had been given back his catapult, this time for good.

'How come she gave you it?' said the elder brother in amazement. 'Me and him'—here he pointed at the youngest—'we're afraid she might catch us again.'

It was only then that it occurred to Elisha that the boys didn't know what had happened at the inn that day, when Jonah had found them dead drunk in the cellar, because they'd drunk wine in their hunger and thirst. How could he have been so unmindful, so stupid? He quickly told them that the cursed old woman, Achim's widow, had croaked, she was dead and buried, and the inn was now kept by the two women from next door, who knew that God's justice caught up with you before you saw the back of your own neck, and they had given Elisha the toy ship straight away and smothered him with kind words, rejoicing that the little ones were safe and sound. The older of the two women had even given him a pile of pistachios to take the little ones. Neither of the two boys knew what pistachios were and Elisha was delighted to see how hungrily they ate them once he taught them to crack the shells with a stone. From that day forth, the younger boy started to eat other things hungrily too, and if he strove with all his might, Eli even managed to make him laugh. But the shadow of sadness never left his face, not even years later, when he had all but forgotten those terrible events. Let me tell you already, Daniela, my daughter, that later Elisha's brothers married and had children, lots of them, they had their own houses and flocks and vines, they had grandchildren, as if evil had accumulated only in the first days of their lives, after which it left them alone and never bothered them again for the rest of their days. Or at least that is what my mother and grandmother told me, although somebody else told me that they met their end just a few years after all that happened.

The sprightly Jacob went back and forth from dawn till dusk, he was busy now at home, now in the port, making ready for the new departure. He too had been reborn. After changing his mind back and forth over and over, he decided with Jonah, with whom he now took counsel a few times a day, to take all the others to Gat-Hefer with them: the three children and Abiel. After that, they would decide what to do next. He would leave the house in the care of the serving women, but till his return or till he sent a messenger with different instructions, the woman from Akko would live there and, with a few helpers, she would make and sell clothes.

On the eve of their departure, they received an unexpected visit. One of the guards—Jacob had hired men to drive away the people who came there determined to see the man from the belly of the fish—announced:

'There's a man at the gate, master. He says he's a ship's captain and that he knows you and won't leave till he talks to you. He talks like he's giving orders, like seafarers do. There are a few others with him. One has six fingers on one hand!'

Don Amado, the ship's captain, entered in a state of great agitation, and with him were Sansón, Hernando, and Siran. Jacob, who had got on well with him from the very start, greeted him like a relative and spoke to him in the language of the Tartisians.

'Peace be with you at sea, on land, and in my house. I missed you, captain, more than you can imagine! What news do you bring me?'

Jacob brought out a jug of wine, inviting them all to drink, and spoke as cheerfully as he had during their first days at sea. But the captain was there not for Jacob's sake but for Jonah's and to see with his own eyes that he was alive. If he was, then it meant that his little girl, who was now resting in port, was a *bruja*, a sorceress, and thenceforth he could be heedless of storms and monsters. As for the God of Jacob and Jonah, it meant that He was the greatest of all gods, and the captain had been praying to Him on board ship even before they reached Joppa.

Jacob's nephew was at home, busy with preparations for the journey, and Jacob called for him.

'Captain!' said Jonah in a quiet, serene, ordinary voice, by way of greeting, welcome, and everything else.

Don Amado, as our ancestor Mikal named the captain, was struck dumb. None of those who passed on the tale had told him what Jonah now looked like after being swallowed and spat out of the mouth that he still remembered all too well. He thought somebody must be playing a joke on him. No, this white-haired, white-skinned man could not be the proud man in the flower of youth, the man with the black hair and beard and sunburnt skin, the man who had done so many astonishing feats, a hero, no less: he had tended the sick Phoenician without a thought for the risk of death, thereby saving the blind man from the fury of the sailors, after which he had saved both them and the little girl, *begging* them that he alone be sacrificed. So, this was supposed to be the miracle everybody was talking about: a hoax. Some old man had come along, having heard the story, and now he was passing himself off as Jonah in order to get his hands on Jacob's fortune.

He looked at Jacob in dismay.

'It's not him at all! Well, then, wasn't I right to doubt what all those people said?' asked the captain, turning to his three companions. 'Nobody could have survived, let alone with his two arms and two legs intact, without even a scratch, nobody could have survived being swallowed by a huge fish like that. Come off it! I'm sorry, my friend, but I for one, unlike the other people you've led by the nose, I for one knew Jonah and I'd be able to recognise him. He was a strong young man, a marvellous man, with glittering eyes and a booming voice, and he had a good soul ... I'm sorry only that I didn't get a chance to thank him: if he hadn't sacrificed himself, we'd all have been dead, and my little girl would have been lying on the bottom of the sea.'

'Captain,' said Jacob in a harsh voice, 'didn't you know that he without sin has everlasting foundations and his life puts forth deep roots? All things are possible for Our God, or rather, for Him no thing is impossible—whichever way you want to say it, you will say well.'

Jonah gave all four a look of kindness and left without a word.

Hernando said, 'First I think it'sh him, then I think it'sh not him, because we shaw him in the monshter's mouth, after all. But moshtly I'd shay it'sh him, I'm telling you, it ish!'

Sansón was of the same opinion as his cousin, while Siran smiled as if he'd seen not Jonah but God Himself. Siran loved wonderful stories and even so, he still had not a trace of doubt that Jonah was Jonah. But none of them could convince the captain. They exchanged a few more words out of politeness, but the conversation foundered and a kind of embarrassment held them all in its grip. They left soon after, each with his own impression, not one of them the same, but it was from that time forth and from Don Amado that the rumour began to spread that the whole story was a fisherman's yarn.

The same evening, Jacob received news that froze him in shock: the woman from Akko had unexpectedly given up the ghost, nobody knew why. This after Jacob had rejoiced so greatly at being able to bring her some solace ... So, the house, as empty as it was large, would remain in the care of the serving women until his return, the same as his house in Tarshish: it was true that in this world all is dust and vanity. But despite this news, the joy of the last few days was still visible in his countenance and bathed him in light. He had grown young again.

One of his descendants

The motley convoy set off at the break of day. It moved slowly. Jacob led the way on a brown ass with a white belly and a white streak around its muzzle. Then came Abiel and the two children, rather cramped in a small cart, newly made by Jonah and drawn by a young ass, which kept stopping, thus giving the boys the chance to whoop and tug the reins. The elder of the two often climbed down to gambol alongside the others in the convoy. Elisha came behind his brothers, his long hair blowing in the wind, riding for the first time in his life and trying to hold his slender body as straight as he could. He looked at the world from above and was always saying something, although nobody heard him, apart from his long-eared steed. Last of all came Jonah, he too mounted on a sturdy ass, but with his feet almost touching the ground. All the men from Gat-Hefer they met in the port had seen them off, and when they left the city it was a procession fit for a king.

It was not the best season to be travelling: the days were short and rains came without warning. But when a man has no other choice, he trusts to God and carries on without looking back, lest he be turned into a pillar of salt, like Lot's wife, as Jacob said, in the best of moods. His health was increasingly fragile, the claws of the last month had left their scars, but little did he care. He was going to see Amithai's beautiful widow once more, to tell her the tale of the miracles he and her son had experienced together, and he thought no farther than that.

They reached the village without the slightest mischance, as if someone had guarded them for the whole length of the journey. When the hills bristling with vines loomed from the lava of sunset, Jonah reined in his ass and swept the heavens and the earth with his gaze, drinking in what he saw with the greed of a man athirst. The whole journey he had been stubbornly silent, my dear Jonathan, thinking about the events he had experienced since he left Gat-Hefer and about what awaited him and what he had to do next. He felt that his every step was guarded, and here, home once more, the light his eyes received seemed to be a heavenly sign. He remounted and drove his ass until, for the first time since they left the port, he reached the head of the convoy. He no longer had any patience.

He saw his mother running towards them, she who always walked with a slow sway, followed by a tallish girl whom he didn't recognise at first. He took them in his arms both at once as if they were small children. His mother was weeping, and the girl, after a moment's amazement, murmured, 'Father, Father!' As amazed as she, Jonah said:

'Esther! Is it you? My girl. You've grown!'

These were more words than he had spoken the whole journey. The others caught up and it took many words and stories on Jacob's part before everything that had happened became clear. But what I have to tell you, my dear Jonathan, who will soon become a father, what I have to tell you is about a meeting on the part of our ancestor whose fame is so great that the whole world knows his story, albeit minus the details that have been passed down to us from mouth to mouth, namely about how he met Hannah. For, in her belly an heir was developing. And even if they themselves had no idea yet, we know that it was going to be a boy and that he would have blue eyes and inherit all Jonah's fortune, except two things: this silver ring, Esther's ring, which, as you'll remember, was from Jacob in any case, and something far more precious than any ring, a fortune no money can buy: the story itself. So, we're Jonah's descendants on his daughter's side. Nobody knows his descendants on his son's side, and that's because unlike Esther they didn't care about memories, and their story was lost. But those descendants must exist somewhere in the world and they are our good relatives. I would so much have liked to meet them!

A woman came running to Hannah, who spent long periods lying down, because she didn't feel well:

'Your man has returned!'

It was the first time that anybody in the village had acknowledged Jonah as her man, and so he was to be from then on. When a woman carries a child in her belly, the man that made it is thenceforth hers, as is only just, my son, even if it turns out that once born the child won't live for even an hour. I'm telling you this as a woman and as a mother. It's time you knew that neither your father nor myself were joined together in marriage before the community, although I'm sure God doesn't take that into account. What He does take into account, however, is you, my child.

'He's here with his uncle and lots of other people, a blind man and some children, I don't know who they are, I'm going to go and find out right this instant. Come and see for yourself!' cried the woman in great agitation and left without waiting for Hannah, who didn't budge, as if the words hadn't reached her. Hope postponed makes the heart grow sick.

Actually, not only she heard the news, but also, it seems, the child in her belly heard it, because for the first time it made it known that it was part of what went on in her life and in the rest of the world. It kicked. Then came another two kicks. Tears of every kind flowed down her cheeks, tears of relief that the father of the child had returned unharmed, tears of annoyance at all the months he'd left her on her own, tears of joy that the lump inside her belly was alive and as annoyed at its father as she was. At which she laid her palms on her belly and stroked it in gratitude for the kicks. She didn't get up. She was certain that Jonah would come to them and she greeted him in her mind, picturing him as she'd seen him last, when she had *told* him.

It wasn't until midnight, the time he always visited her, that a man with white hair and a white beard appeared before her and the as yet unseen and unborn child. She recognised him straight away, in the glow of the rushlight, the way you would recognise a man you've only ever seen dressed in black, but whom you now see dressed in white. It might surprise you, but it wouldn't make you think it was a different man.

'You?' asked Hannah, and her blue, darkly ringed eyes looked straight into his, examining him. She wanted to see whether the man she knew before was still there, inside the body in front of her.

Jonah made no reply. She had changed too, and although he had suspected that he would find her like this, with a large belly rather than the slender waist he had once clasped, he was amazed: the same as she about him, he had constantly thought about her and seen her in his mind's eye the way she looked when he parted from her that final evening. He had been ready to embrace her, but he didn't feel like doing so now, he didn't want to hug the belly that carried his child, so he placed his hands on her shoulders and carefully sat her on the bed, which still showed a hollow from where she'd lain. And now her man took off her garment and, without reaching out his hand to touch it, he gazed for a long time at the huge pomegranate of her belly, and then, for the first time since his return, she heard his voice, and his voice filled the chamber with her name:

'Hannah!'

And only then did her tears well up. He went on:

'It's in your flesh. Prisoner. I was one too.'

Jonathan, you whose name contains the name of our ancestor, I don't know whether Hannah really understood what he was trying to say, but to me it's certain that he was thinking about how he had lain inside the fish, in a cage of flesh, the same as a sightless child lies in its mother's belly. Probably he understood that when he came to term, he'd been thrust forth from the flesh surrounding him, headfirst, the way a child comes into the world. Maybe what he was also unwittingly saying was that a part of him had been prisoner inside her, encircled by her boneless ring of flesh and hidden in the wellspring of life, when he made the child. By my reckoning, Hannah was in her fifth month when Jonah returned. It wasn't until the next day, after they slept side by side, that Jonah told her:

'I fled. From the Lord. He punished me.'

Hannah was to learn from others how it had all turned out. But from him she heard only:

'I'm leaving again. Going to Nineveh.'

She loved the voice, but sometimes she hated the words.

Like the moth

When they arrived in Gat-Hefer, there was a moment that only Jacob noticed. The moment when the beautiful smile of Amithai's widow met the so similar smile of her son, the way smiles fleetingly meet, and a third person is always required to see both those smiles at once. Back home in Tarshish, Jacob knew a man who could draw with unbelievable ease, nicknamed El Jorobado, or the Hunchback, since his back had an enormous hump. More often than not, crouching beneath his hump, he would draw only in the dust, and at the first breath of wind or under the first careless foot that passed, nothing would remain of his inventions. One day, after he helped rid him of his back pains, pressing the clump of flesh in a number of precise points, the Hunchback had drawn Jacob with a stick in every possible guise, he had filled the road with him. At the time, Jacob was still young, having arrived from Galilee just a few years earlier, and also seemingly taller. He liked to look at himself, but at the same time, it was then that he first thought about how all things are dust and vanity blown away by the wind, and a handful of dust is all that ultimately remains of our lofty pride. When he saw Jonah's smile meet his mother's, Jacob wished that El Jorobado had been there to draw the two of them on papyrus, on which, rolled together as one, he would have been able to preserve them, to keep them both as if time had stood still. I've heard, my son, that in our own day, in Toledo there is a man nicknamed El Greco, maybe because he's from Greece, who has the gift of painting people in a never-before-seen manner all his own, and I would have really liked to see his paintings and to ask him to capture the moment you hold your first child in your arms and make it stand still forever. But in Jacob's day, at Gat-Hefer, nothing like that was possible, and in any event, El Jorobado was very far away, beyond the Great Sea.

And time cannot be made to stand still, my son: like a moth feeding on wool and leaving holes everywhere, time eats the wool of life and destroys it. Only now that he had reached his goal did Jacob feel his illness and the accumulated weariness of long hours of travel gnawing away at him. As soon as he climbed down from his ass and embraced the woman who had been the wife of his cousin Amithai, and while all the people of the village flocked around Jonah, Jacob fell to the ground. His fingers were already blue with cold. They took him to a chamber and laid him on a low bed, waiting for the last heat to leave his body. Elisha and Abiel came to him, drawn by the people's cries. They had found him again only now to lose him once more. Abiel placed his hand on Jacob's face, the way he did when he wanted to see with his fingers, to greet a person or to bid him farewell, the way he had examined Zahra's face long ago and closed her eyes. This time, he felt eyelids that were already closed, he lightly pressed the hollow cheeks, then drew his hands back as if scalded:

'He's breathing,' he said in a strangled voice, 'he's not dead.'

Jonah's mother was stricken by too many emotions and had lost her head, but Esther, who, when her great-uncle last visited, had picked up a number of things useful in such circumstances, and who like him also seemed to possess the innate gift of healing, poured a tot of raki down his throat, at which Jacob spluttered and opened his eyes.

'I didn't drown at sea and now you want to drown me on dry land,' he quipped, in a good mood, but in quavering, panting voice. 'I fell down for joy ... maybe also from exhaustion ... After all, I'm old, as even I ought to admit, all things considered. Bravo, little girl, you remembered that I refuse to let water pass my lips. There is a time for all things, as the preacher says, a time to be silent and a time to close your eyes. Go now, all of you, I'm going to close my eyes, but don't worry, I'm of a mind to open them again ...'

They let him sleep until the next day. The fright of it had given them an appetite to talk and to laugh, the women looked after the guests, they washed their feet and dried them with clean cloths, they prepared a meal, and at midnight, when Jonah slipped away, the neighbours went back to their own houses, highly reluctant to part with all the unbelievable tales they had been listening to. The three children stayed where they were, and Abiel went to stay the night at the house of a widow who lived nearby.

Jonah's mother was unable to sleep for an instant, even though the spiritual trials she had undergone in the last few hours had drained her strength more than would a day's toil in the vineyard. She had been too fearful for her son's life, she had prayed, she had waited for him, but she couldn't understand why he now looked so old, when he was a young man, or why she felt him to be so strange and distant, when she wanted him to be closer than before, or how his terrifying tale could have been possible. She was resentful at the fact that no sooner had he arrived than he went off to stay with that blue-eyed woman, and her only comfort was that Jacob had come back to her, that he hadn't changed at all, but was keener than ever and gazed on her with the same boundless pleasure. She went to him as soon as dawn broke to tell him her complaints and ask him about all the things that had been accumulating in her during her sleepless hours.

She tiptoed inside. Jacob was awake and rummaging in his travelling bag. He didn't need to look up to know who had entered:

'How can the day not go well for me now if the first face to appear before my eyes is yours?' he said, although he was still looking for something inside the bag.

It was obvious that he spoke of other eyes, stronger than those made weak by old age. But it was those weak eyes that he now raised, and his face lit up with joy.

'You're still as beautiful as when I left you on my departure. The first one, I mean.'

'And you are still as dangerous.'

'Me? How so? I'm as gentle as the dove—and I don't mean Jonah.'

'That's why you are dangerous. You were always dangerously gentle.'

'Just as the face answers the face reflected in the water, so too your words answer my words. Were you able to sleep?'

Her eyes were ringed with shadow.

'Never mind that, it doesn't matter ... We're not talking about me now. I want to ask you about my son. I've gathered all by myself that he has been chosen by God, and it gives my heart a pang.'

'Why?' asked Jacob, raising his eyebrows and lowering his voice in reproach.

'You know very well why!' snapped Jonah's mother, but then lowered her voice too. 'I don't want him to be a chosen one, I don't want him to be swallowed by all kinds of sea monsters and spat out to die and be brought back to life, to turn white overnight, I don't want him to go to Nineveh to make horrifying prophecies, I want him here with me to dig the vines, to water them, to pick the grapes, to come home every evening, I want to see my grandchildren and for them to be many, and I want him, I want my son, to be just like everybody else! I want his to be the last face I see before I die!'

Jacob was silent, because he knew she was right. She now raised her voice:

'What about you? Why don't you say anything? What do you have to say? Tell me! Is he or isn't he a chosen one?'

'Probably.'

Jonah's mother began to weep softly, her eyes on the floor.

'But that means he is also very well-protected, as has already been demonstrated,' Jacob went on. 'Even if he undergoes trials more onerous than do ordinary men with ordinary mothers and ordinary children and grandchildren, the ordinary men you envy, he will still emerge triumphant, always triumphant, and his sufferings, since sufferings are an inseparable part of it, will always have a purpose, albeit a mysterious one for most people. And his name will live on with his story, passed down from mouth to mouth, and both name and story will weather the ages ...'

'Don't you leave too, the way you left once already, just when I needed you the most,' she begged him, making a reproach that had waited long years to be spoken.

Jacob's hands, which were still searching inside the bag, began to tremble.

'I always wanted to ask you,' he said in a voice now even graver than before, 'what I mean is ... anyway ... Jonah ... you know very well what I'm asking.'

'I don't know.'

Jacob understood her answer, Jonathan. It didn't mean that she didn't know what he was asking, but rather 'I don't know' was her answer to the question. But I think she was lying. A woman knows the answer as to who is the father.

When she left the chamber, Jonah's mother realised that for the second time in her life she had stood before him in her nightshirt. Her raw silk nightshirt.

BOOK THREE

The Green Shadow

Waiting for the sun to set

There are three things which go well, yea, four are comely in going, say the Proverbs: A lion, which is strongest among beasts, and turneth not away for any; a horse reined by an agile hand; a he-goat also; and a king, against whom there is no rising up. The King of Nineveh walks not on the ground but on air, borne aloft by others, higher than all other men, as stately as the lion, as taut as a horse about to break into a gallop, and piercing the heavens with the spike of his golden helmet, like the he-goat. When he passes with his archers, the people quickly bow their heads, lest they be blinded by lightning bolts from his diamond eyes, and if he opens his mouth, the crowd cast themselves to the ground, thunderstruck. The dogs turn tail before him, yelping in fear, and the birds descend from the upper air to behold his coming. Thus did every ruler of Assyria appear before his people since the reigns of Tudiya and Adamu long ago, magnificent was Assur-Uballit the First, so too Enlil-Nirari, may his name live forever, and Salmanasar the First, likewise Teglat-Phalasar the Second, and, as is storied, Tukulti-Ninurta the Second, whom many still remember, and likewise the king's brother, Assur-Dan, to mention only some of the greatest. Like unto them now is the exalted Assur-Nirari, the fifth king of that name, the sun of Assyria, may all the gods preserve him and may the goddess Ishtar bring safely into the world the heir whose bones are now being knitted in the darkness of the queen's womb.

Second only to the King, the great Belus shines like the full moon. He is his right hand and he it is who knows all the secrets of the empire. This courtier's cruelty is equalled in its magnitude only by his debauchery, and all of Nineveh knows both his cruelty and his debauchery and fears them. When he turns his head, beneath which hangs a long beard cut square, his earrings of gold and emerald jingle at the movement thereof, and the bracelets on his hand rattle when he makes the gesture of command. He is a man handsome of visage, proud of frame, albeit corpulent and, as a result of illness, he has no eyebrows or eyelashes. He likes to speak almost in a whisper, but the softer his voice, the more terrible the words he utters. His palace in the south of the city is only half the size of the king's, which is on the opposite side and the shadier, but the jewels that adorn his body when he is at home are twice as numerous. He doffs them not before mounting his slave girls should he be taken with lust or even when he is not so taken. If he is unable to penetrate them, it gives him pleasure to gash them with his sharp gemstones and to hear them groaning and howling in pain. Their cries and their blood arouse him, and his greatest delight is to terrify his onlookers, since he demands that there always be at least two watching, and sometimes he invites them to take part in the humiliation of the slave girl, who is permanently disfigured, while he himself watches. If he is not happy with the handiwork of his two assistants, he orders that they be gelded forthwith.

But that afternoon, an afternoon of a brief and unexpected rain shower, while the great Belus was idling morosely, playing with his wife the ancient game from Uruk and waiting for the sun to set, he was summoned before the king. This filled him with unease. Around his chamber wafted scents of aloe and vanilla, from the oils with which his wife had anointed her whole body. Her face was beautiful but marred by a slight asymmetry, which lent her an air of strangeness. She played with the black pieces, Belus, with the white, and his plump, ring-bedizened hand now held the four pyramidal dice. On the playing board, whose segments were chased with lapis lazuli, the red rosettes and mother-of-pearl eyes gleamed softly in the light of the torches that burned day and night. Belus shook the pyramids in his palm and cast them. They all fell with the unpainted, unlucky tip upward. Belus's face was impassive, for he had long since learned to conceal his thoughts, but his wife, who knew him well, could sense his turmoil. Sargina was the only person who was not afraid of him, for the simple reason that she was the king's niece. As they always played for slaves, one winning or losing them to the other, she asked:

'Are you so sorry that you will lose Mareil?'

Mareil was indeed Belus's most handsome slave, and Sargina was surprised that he had wagered him, whereas she had wagered only Kinara, whom she didn't particularly care about. However, she suspected that something else was wrong, because ever since her husband rose that morning all the signs had been bad, and Belus, who didn't believe in gods, did believe in signs. First of all, on waking, he discovered that he had broken one of his beautiful gold earrings, the ones with the palm leaves and emeralds. The earrings in question, which sometimes he was too lazy to take off when he went to bed, were a lucky gift from the king, who liked to see them swaying from Belus's earlobes and even insisted he wear them for that reason. Belus would therefore have liked to wear them that evening at the palace, but now it was impossible. After which came an intolerable piece of news.

One of the few living things Belus cared about was a parrot, in order to possess which he had commanded that its owner be beheaded: an aged traveller, who had arrived from who knows where and who had nobody in the world apart from his bird. The parrot had pined for the old man a long time, but in the end, it had grown accustomed to the large gold cage in which its new owner kept it, and, to be fair, Belus showed it a lot of love. The bird was grey, its head was yellow, and it had two orange spots to either side of its beak. It had a lovely crest of curved feathers, which, when it was alert, it lifted in a tuft, and grey tail feathers streaked with lemon yellow. Belus liked to watch while it cleaned its feathers, passing them through its beak one by one, an operation that lasted an endless time. Not even cats spend so much time washing themselves with their tongues. Sometimes Belus liked to give the bird a fright, just to see how it lowered its crest over its back, cowering beneath it. But then straight away he would make up for the fright by opening the cage and caressing the bird with his chubby, bejewelled hand. Every morning for eight years, the great Belus had visited the bird and he did not go to bed until he had spoken loving words to it, words such as he did not speak to anyone else, not even Sargina, whom, in any case, he had never loved, but whom from time to time he desired. As for his wife, she neither loved him nor desired him, but twisted him around her little finger.

No sooner had he awoken than he saw his young wife enter on soundless feet, her face in tears. With much coaxing, he managed to make her tell him that for some unknown reason the parrot was lying at the bottom of its cage with its little claws in the air, dead. If anyone else had brought him such news, Belus would have had her tongue cut out, but now his only reaction was to bellow, a cry that boomed throughout the palace, terrifying all those who dwelled therein. Little by little Sargina was able to calm him, telling him that the bird too had loved him the same as did all those around who loved him—she did not so much as blink as she said this—and that she would have the lifeless little body encased in gold and precious stones and mounted at the end of his bed, where it would keep watch over him forever from the world after death.

Even before he began playing the game with Sargina, Belus heard from the head of his spies that Rabona the ferryman had brought to the city two strange travellers, one a giant, the other very small, and that it was unknown what they were after or why they were there. The larger man did not speak at all, but the little one boasted that he was able to cure bodily ailments, which meant he might prove useful if the need arose. Everybody in the city went in constant fear of illness, and there were never enough healers. But here too came yet another sign. For the first time since they had played together, Belus was unlucky enough to be forced to move the last of his seven ivory pieces back to square one and start all over again. It wasn't only a game of chance, but also a game of strategy, which was why, as someone unsurpassed in machination, he always won.

'Roll again,' said Sargina quickly, 'one of the stones hit the box.'

Belus, who had been stroking his chest-long beard in agitation, took the dice in relief, shook them well, and made another cast. When yet again none of them fell with the white tip upward, both of them knew for certain that the will of the gods was to punish him, and that this would happen very soon.

They played on in silence and, with great effort and trickery, Sargina nonetheless managed to lose. Just as they were about to start another game, the trustiest man in the northern palace, Belus's brother, entered the chamber, making a very quick and not at all deep bow. He seemed preoccupied.

A break in the clouds

They heard the laughter of a child. It gurgled then broke off, only to tinkle forth again straight away, and two of the three men quickly turned their heads to see where the sound came from. They were on a raft gliding over an expanse of grey water so placid that it was as if it stood still. The youngest of them, who paid the laughter no heed, a well-built man with a scar that serrated his left arm from shoulder to elbow, guided the craft. He stood holding the pole, thrusting the raft shoreward, while the travellers, who though very different shared something in common, sat nervously watching him as he punted. One of them was strikingly tall and munched a flat cake, while the other was frail, seemingly very tired, and bore every sign of wisdom on his face, with its hazel eyes set deep below thick bushy eyebrows. The one was clenched within himself like a fist, the other, open to the world like an outstretched palm. The laughter came from the middle of the Ḥiddeqel River, which the Greeks call the Tigris. Some buffalos were bathing, their inward-spiralling horns, their backs, and the thick nostrils of their muzzles showing above the surface of the water, while a boy tried to ride the smallest of them, but kept slipping into the water, now on one side, now on the other, and he laughed every time he fell off.

Close to the shore the walls of the city could twice be seen: once lifting their crenellations to the heavens and a second time stretching slantwise into the river that mirrored them, as if its waters needed their crenellations to guard its depths. The boat glided towards the huge gate that towered to the sky and plunged into the water halfway across the river, and which bore the insignia of Adad, the god who holds bunched lightning bolts and wears the four-horned crown. The wall was forty bricks wide, as the ferryman proudly told them, and a hundred and fifty tall. The walled city approached them, and it was as if it glided across the water while they stood still, for rivers are enchanted roads that move and take you where you want as you sit motionless.

On the other side of the walls and battlements built of huge stone blocks could be seen two protuberances, the tips of stepped pyramids, which, given how high they soared, had to be intended as stairs for the gods to descend. The walls and pyramids swelled in size before the gaze of the astonished passengers in the boat and kept changing shape. The passengers had been silent the whole time. Neither of them had ever seen such grandeur fashioned by human hand and they were oppressed by the power they could sense behind it. Besides, at intervals the clouds cast an unsettling shadow over the city. But now the child's laughter finally shattered the solemn fear that had sealed their lips for so long.

'Nineveh,' said the older man. 'In the city of the strong the wise man enters and undermines their pride, it is said. How I would have liked to enjoy in peace all the knowledge that is gathered between these walls and the learned men who fathom the mysteries of the heavens and the earth. Once a man came to us in Tartessos, who brought with him a tablet written in Nineveh and I gave him a horse for it: a rare jewel! The tablet, I mean—my mare was just like any other mare, albeit young and mettlesome. I couldn't make out that writing at first, because the letters aren't like ours, but look like the spice they call the clove and are read from left to right ... But after I'd looked at them for days on end, I finally managed to decipher the name Inanna, written In-an-ak, the great Sumerian goddess of fertility, who is now called Ishtar: it appeared three times, always next to her eight-pointed star.'

The old man gave a slight smile at the memory before continuing:

'Even though I know you're more stubborn than a mule, forgive me for telling you so bluntly, the way only a close relative can talk, but I still harbour the hope that you will change your mind, my dove, and maybe, after we have visited the marvels of the most beautiful city in the world, we will go home, or at least you will go home, so that you can reassure your dear mother, because her tear-filled eyes have been watching me ever since I set out and at times my own eyes fill with tears at the thought of her. "Jacob, my dear—" it was the first time she called me that "—take care you bring him back to me, otherwise I never want to see you again and I'll hate you as nobody has ever hated you before!" Promise only this much: that you'll wait a few days until I prepare the highly placed people to receive you, so that you'll have some degree of protection. I have a plan, since I've done nothing but think of it the whole journey.'

But Jonah would not promise anything. Jacob said to the ferryman:

'Have we finally arrived, Rabona?'

Rabona did not have time to reply, since just then he poled the boat onto the sand and nimbly jumped onto the riverbank. He held out his hand to help his two passengers to disembark. Jonah did not take the hand, steadying himself with his staff instead, while Rabona had to lift Jacob out of the boat, since the old man had grown stiff after sitting for so long on the hard plank in the middle of the craft. Just then, it started to rain, a downpour that was brief but so heavy that it soaked them as thoroughly as if they had bathed with the buffalos in the river, and it shattered the crenellations in the water, as if prophesying their ruin or showing that not even they were eternal. Jacob was about to lose heart at this hostile welcome commanded by God, when Jonah stretched his arm towards a break in the clouds, through which slanting rays created a pyramid of light. Next to its magnificent beauty, the pyramids that had so frightened them were insignificant, nothing but timorous pullets of stone. Then, when they turned their heads once more, they saw how God's covenant with Noah, the last patriarch before the Flood, who had lived fifty years short of a thousand, was renewed even now, before them, the descendants of that patriarch: a perfect, vivid rainbow framed by a second that was higher and mistier. They didn't know that the men of that city also spoke of their own flood and had their own Noah, who had had a different name and saved his animals and the seed of the human race.

'It is good!' said Jonah, the first words he had spoken for seven days. In his fist he clasped the clenched fist of the staff Abiel had given him. 'So that you can protect yourself with it and bring it back to me! Please!' Abiel had told him when he set out, but Jonah had made no reply, except, perhaps, in his mind.

The young ferryman, who had not thereto heard his voice, turned in amazement, as if not the man he had conveyed but a god or some supernatural creature had spoken. He hastened to assist Jacob once more, as the old man had knelt down facing God's rainbow and couldn't get back up. He had shrivelled up during the journey, which started by sea, then stretched for week after week in the desert, and ended in the boat on that yellow water crenellated by the stones mirrored in it. Now only the high walls separated them from the dangerous goal of their journey. The sky had by now cleared and steam rose from the ground. The clothes on their backs dried almost as quickly as they had been soaked.

Rabona, who was a nondescript sort of man—apart from the scar—and who had a hesitant voice, offered to be their guide in the city and find them a place where they could stay the night. Jacob voiced a clear 'yes', while Jonah impatiently shook his head in token of dissent. The ferryman elected to listen to what he had heard and ignore what he had seen. They approached the gate, above whose arch stood Adad holding the light in his hand. It was guarded by another two gods of stone, with bull's hooves and men's heads with wavy beards, and two soldiers of flesh and blood, wearing helmets and holding spears. There were also bows slung over their shoulders, and each had a quiver of arrows at his hip. They stood talking, while one absently ran his forefinger over the stone knobs of one of the gods' beards. A little way off, other guards were sitting on the ground. When they saw the men approach, the two at the gate adopted a ferocious mien, and those seated on the ground leapt to their feet.

There was no need for Jacob or Jonah to speak, as the ferryman opened the way for them with gentle ease, giving each soldier a pouch on behalf of the two travellers, which vanished as if by miracle beneath their knee-length skirts. While this went on, Jacob looked fixedly at one of the soldiers, but spoke to Rabona:

'Tell him to seek me out whenever he wants, so that I can give him a healing balm, for war and anarchy rage in his body. I think he has an open wound, somewhere beneath his garments.

Only now did the others notice the beads of sweat covering the soldier's face and the unnatural redness of his cheeks.

Perhaps to conceal his infirmity, perhaps in gratitude, the soldier said not in Assyrian but in Aramaic, a language that both Jacob and Jonah spoke, the same as everybody else in the city:

'Keep your distance from the palace of Belus and stay out of his way. I think you value your lives, do you not? If he does appear in your path—you will be able to tell it's him from the way he glitters—you must throw yourselves to the ground without a word. Don't try to instigate popular rebellion, don't make a commotion or get drunk, don't raise your voices, unless you want to die in agony.'

'The laws are very harsh,' added the other. 'We can be sure that the great Belus, who has a hundred ears and a hundred eyes, has already learned of your arrival.'

A shudder passed through Jacob's body. It was not for himself that he shuddered.

While his member was erect

'The exalted Queen is very gravely ill and the time for her to give birth approaches. The heads of many courtiers and of the midwife rolled this morning,' Belus's brother announced.

Belus pushed the game board aside, scattering across the floor the pieces that had brought him bad luck. He clapped his hands together in surprise and his bracelets jingled. It was not very unusual for people to be executed, but nobody would ever have imagined that the king could sacrifice the midwife, who had been at the bedside of the queen mother when the king himself was born. Certainly, if Assur-Nirari's mother were still alive, such a thing could never have happened, but ever since they lowered her into her tomb, along with ranks of terracotta and cedar-wood servants, jewels and toys, combs and alabaster pots of ointment, needles and scissors, silver chalices and bronze strainers, antimony tubes, various dishes of food and amphoras of wine, writing tablets and styluses, ever since the day she had moved to the next world taking her mortal world with her, the king had done very many new and astonishing things. For a start, he loved his wife more than the queen-mother, he even loved her too much, and now that she was heavy with his child and he no longer bedded her, he was sick with both love and hatred for her. Unlike all the other men at court, he abstained from satisfying his lust with the slave girls. This caused him to find a vent for his lust in unpredictable, violent outbursts, at which times blood flowed in the palace, and these were followed by periods of humility, when he sought to suffer pain and sometimes made the queen lash him with a bull's neck ligament. This is what had happened now too: he had woken her up in the middle of the night and forced her to make an exertion while heavily pregnant as he stood naked before her, urging her to beat his back and buttocks, while his member was erect but bereft of anywhere to plant itself. His member did not remain in that condition for seven nights and seven days, as the wild Enkidu's did when he coupled with the sacred prostitute, nor did he make the beasts flee from his presence in shame, but for a good few hours at a time he showed himself like that to his wife, whom he constantly tortured with his strange desires. After that the queen fell ill, she took to her bed, she stopped eating, she didn't want to give birth, she didn't want to live, and Assur-Nirari seemed to have gone out of his mind with grief and guilt. The king was undecided as to whether to kill the woman he loved too much, so that he could forget the whole episode, or whether to let her give birth to his heir and to seek her love once more. He decided that only if his heir was male would he forgive her for the guilt of his being guilty.

All these things, spoken only in a whisper, reached the horrified ears of Belus. It was clear proof that the evil omens had not lied. Sargina, who heard only the announcement that had been spoken aloud, nonetheless knew quite well what to expect, because she had been told in great secret what was happening in the northern part of the city, and the king's strange outbursts of madness disturbed them all. She was not fearful by nature, but she could not help but see that things had gone awry, they had burst their banks like the waters of the river when the snow melted in the Taurus Mountains, and the people of Nineveh could dam neither the evil nor the madness. She too had a presentiment that something was going to happen, and very soon, but she did not know in what way the gods would strike.

I am old, my dear Abidan, and I have seen many things, I would even go so far as to say that my fellow man can no longer surprise me, but you, who will marry in a few days, would do well to beware of what a man is capable of and not place your full trust in anybody. How I regret that your mother is not alive, it was she who ought to have told you the story, and maybe she would have told it in a roundabout way, concealing certain things, but please don't doubt, even in this present century, when reason and scepticism are all the rage, that our ancestor really did find himself in a place where things were out of control. I can't say how Jonah knew this beforehand. We too live in the final decade of a debauched century: I've happened to see that scandalous book, *Justine*, an anonymous book full of perversion, but which turns out to have been written by a sick marquis, who perhaps even deserves compassion (I think his condition is similar to that of the King of Nineveh) and whom they locked up in the Bastille not long since, so I hear. His name is De Sade. They say that even in prison he continues to write things even more atrocious. It serves no purpose to lock up illness, and better we try to cure it. But anyway, such things— maybe we could call them sadistic, to coin a term—such things lurk in man. And you should also know, Abidan, that it is but a short step from lack of imagination to sadism. Some men torture you from a lack of imagination and then innocently ask why you are screaming, they torture you the way wanton boys torture small animals and are surprised when they die beneath their very eyes. It's of people like this that I'm most afraid, because nothing can stop them, but I also pity them. They lack any sense of the other person. As for the other plagues, the historical plagues of generalised cruelty, they don't go away by themselves or without claiming victims: mankind periodically feels the need to wreak slaughter. In Nineveh, the evil had begun to burst its banks, in waves as turbid as the waters of the Tigris.

That's why Jonah was so determined. There are some who even doubt that Nineveh existed! But now we have 'archaeologists'—I expect you know that this is what they have started calling those who rake among Time's innards, among what has been left behind in the ground, and who reconstruct the life of the distant past—and they won't rest until they unearth that city from the dust of ages that has buried it. It wasn't all that long ago that they discovered the bones of the unfortunates entombed by the lava in Vesuvius, Herculaneum, and Pompei. Likewise, I have no doubt that Troy really existed, it's not for nothing that it's described in the epic I read to you when you were little, and how wide-eyed and curious you were as you listened, my son. When they finally unearth the city of Nineveh, the story of Jonah, which we know because it's been passed down in our family, but which some of those who read the Bible deem to be pure fiction, will be believed by all. It's true that Jonah's story was written down, in highly abbreviated form, some four centuries after the events themselves took place, at the request of one of Esther's descendants, who was afraid she would remain without issue, and both she and the scribe adapted a number of things to fit their own times, to fit later history, but it's the essence that counts, not the stage scenery and the costumes.

In any event, Jacob was right: much book-learning, astronomy, mathematics, many myths collected on tablets illumined the life of the mind in the Assyrian city. The streets were thronged with folk of every colour and creed, speaking a mixture of languages, folk brought there in bondage from the margins of the empire and the conquered territories. Folk steeped in learning, the same as there are today, although in many respects, they wholly surpassed us. For the people of the time, Nineveh was the centre of the world, the same as Rome was to be later, and the same as Paris is today, in the closing years of this century. One of the largest and most valuable libraries in the world had been assembled there, that of Assurbanipal, alas subsequently lost. Who knows whether it will ever be found again, and if they succeed in deciphering cuneiform script, as our uncommonly intelligent ancestor Jacob was able to, if the story we pass down is true, and perhaps there were others like him, whose names are now forgotten, if they succeed, then the cornucopia of knowledge amassed over thousands of years will be poured out over mankind. My dear son, I am certain that Noah and the Flood existed, and that a far-seeing and resourceful man set out over the waters with his family and animals, just as I am certain that the experiment of the tower of Babel existed, and perhaps your descendants will discover its remains, likewise the remains of Atlantis. You or your children will maybe be lucky enough to discover the truth, and you can't imagine how happy I am for you! If my life lay before me rather than behind me, I would set out in search of the evidence for all these things, but it is to you that I leave this pleasant task, along with this ring of silver and sapphire, which you will pass on to your first-born daughter, if you have daughters, because the truth is that in the family of Jonah it is not the men but the women who have kept the story alive. But at a pinch, we men have fulfilled the task too, and no worse than they have, so I venture to think.

Belus realised that if he wanted to live, he would have to come up with something to mollify the king. His luck had not wholly abandoned him: he remembered the two foreigners brought there by Rabona. He knew the ferryman well: he had slashed his arm in a moment's fury, after which he had made him his spy. He knew that during the long hours they spent together on the boat, a kind of friendship sprang up between ferryman and passenger, and that willy-nilly all kinds of things would be spoken. Rabona was duty-bound to report everything he heard. One of the foreigners was a healer. And it was very good that they had arrived from far away.

'Bring me the healer who arrived in the city today, and bring him this instant!'

What is the fourth?

Spring had come to Gat-Hefer once more and the vines were in bloom. Bunches of tiny white fibres strained sunward. One day, Elisha remembered a saying that remained unclear to him, which Jacob had told him while they were at sea, on Don Amado's ship, just before the goat was sacrificed: There are three things in the world that leave no trace, or even four: the eagle in the sky, the snake on the rock, and ship on the sea. Jacob had said that it was too early for Elisha to know what the fourth was and that he would find out for himself. Elisha looked around him seeking things that left no trace: clouds that dissolved without shedding rain, the glance that settles on another's face, sand in the water, but he wasn't sure that all these left no mark, a mark ever so slight, on the sky, on a person, in the water.

'Abiel, remember what the old gaffer told me, that story about the traces you can't see, the eagle's, the snake's, and the ship's? What's the fourth? The one he said I'd find out later ... I hope it won't be too late before I realise what it is!'

'No, I don't remember. I for one haven't heard that proverb and it would be hard for me to picture it, because I can't see. But even so, I could list things that leave traces, and it seems to me that all things do. Take uncle Jacob's words and Jonah's goodness. Without them what would our lives have been? Can you imagine?'

At Gat-Hefer, the newcomers had been adopted as if part of one big family. Abiel was given bed and board by a widow whom he enlivened with his stories and helped with her basket-weaving and bread-making, for she was astonished that both his baskets and his dough came out as good as hers, even though he could see only with his ten fingers. All three brothers had remained in the care of Jonah's mother and her two serving women, one of them young, not even seventeen, a girl clever and pretty and bold, Ruth by name, the other old and fat and very skilled in household work. For the first time in their lives the children had enough to eat and as for Elisha, he could have capered for joy as never before had he not been so downcast at the prospect of Jacob's departure, as well as because of a disquiet he couldn't fathom and which was like an itch in his soul. And also in his body. He was afraid that he would never again see the old man, who had taught him so many things with a love he hadn't seen at the time, and his air of melancholy had become more evident even when he smiled. Despite the dimple in his cheek, he was one of those people who are unable to give a happy smile. With the result that women, particularly young women, wanted to erase the melancholy from his handsome face and many of them cast him winsome looks when they met. Lately, a soft beard had begun to cover his cheeks.

One evening, as behind closed eyelids he saw images of the past day jumbling together and about to dissolve into dream, the voice of the young serving woman sighed so close to his ear that he felt its warmth tickling him inside: 'Elisha, Eli, Eli ...' He was too torpid to reply, so the girl lay down beside him, wrapping him in her flesh, after which, not much differently than the hand of Zeuxidamos once had aboard the ship, she sought beneath his clothes. This time, Elisha turned over, he responded, and without knowing what was happening or why, although he had often heard men speak briefly and harshly about what a man does with a woman, he began to seek her with nervous fingers, clenching the warm flesh here and there, at random, awkwardly, and sensing, when he came to the wee horns of her large breasts, that something unknown, like a torrent from within, invaded him and made him weak, especially from the belly down. His ignorance did not prevent his body from doing what his unknown father and all the other unknown fathers of his race had done before him, and the girl's hand, having bared his sex, guided him. Elisha finally discovered one of the world's secrets. But only half that secret, since the girl did not scream.

'Elisha,' she said afterward, in a whisper, 'it was the mistress who ordered me to wake you.'

Obviously, the mistress had not ordered her to do so like that.

'You have to go with her to Jonah's woman. She's going to give birth. It's her time. Her neighbour sent word.'

Still dizzy, Elisha leapt to his feet:

'Why didn't you tell me?' he said, all of a sudden like an angry man.

'We have time. The mistress has gone to the midwife to ask her for this and that. The old woman is dying. She can't get up from her bed.'

'Ruth,' he said all of a sudden, with a smile, without listening to what she just said: it was the first time he had said her name. And he hugged her tightly, also like a man.

They both got up and they smoothed each other's hair. By the time Jonah's mother returned, with a few items she had taken from the midwife: a pair of scissors and some cloths, the pink flush had faded from the girl's cheeks, her head covering sat neatly, and she seemed as calm and as collected as ever. It was then that Eli glimpsed for himself the fourth thing that leaves no trace: a man's trace on a woman.

We'll go together

'Who are you?' asked Belus with a harshness and contempt that nonetheless belied a strange hope.

With a single glance Jacob took in the scene before his eyes and instantly drew what conclusions there were to be drawn. The man who had summoned him and who was feared by one and all, as Jacob had discovered at the city gates, half reclined on a kind of tall bed, while his wife, who was seated on a large, magnificently carved throne, but positioned lower down, was obliged to look up at him. Between husband and wife, on a small table, was a box that served as the board of a game unfamiliar to Jacob and whose pieces were scattered over the floor, betokening anger or perhaps surprise. But in the eyes of the large man, which lacked lashes, Jacob could sooner read fear. As for hope, this was certainly connected to him. Which was good, for the time being, as it remained to be seen what would be asked of him and how he might prove himself useful. His reply was deliberately cheerful, but the words were slipperier than olive oil:

'Who am I? How you hit the nail on the head with your question: I have been trying to find out all my life. But I think you actually want to know something more specific, and in all humble obedience I shall hasten to tell you, lest I prompt you to anger. Exalted Belus, I am a Jew, my name is Jacob, and, drawn by the fame of this peerless city, I have come all the way from Galilee, together with my sick nephew, whose wits are slightly, ever so slightly addled, the poor man, but he is as gentle as a lamb—he was not allowed to enter and your men pushed him around a little, as they did me too, as a matter of fact, I'll have you know—I came here in the belief that the customs and knowledge of the most glorified city on earth, some of which have been collected on tablets—I don't wish to boast, but I have learned how to read them all by myself!—will help me cure him. For my nephew, whose name is Jonah, is as sinless as the dove that is his namesake, and the wise men of old teach us that the light of the sinless burns brightly, but the lamp of the evil is quenched, and likewise that sinlessness preserves the innocent, but evil—'

'Are you a healer or not?' interrupted Belus, impatient at the proverb. The hope in his voice and tigrine eyes was now more visible than ever.

'But evil brings destruction to the sinner, as the proverb says. Forgive me, but I never leave my sentences hanging unfinished and tattered in the wind, and yes, I hasten once more to inform you, with a guest's humility before his host. The second question is as penetrating as the first: I cure ailments of every kind, both bodily and spiritual, and therefore I am a healer. A good one, so they say, but this only if it also be the will of the almighty healer,' and here Jacob jabbed his finger up at the very high ceiling.

Jacob had quickly realised what was to be his weapon in this unequal battle, a battle in which he would have to fight to save his nephew, if nephew he was.

'Are you skilled in midwifery?'

'I have some experience, you might say that, yes. In my life I have helped seventy-six women to give birth, of which only sixteen have died, but of those sixteen, I saved the lives of nine babies. I know this because I have kept meticulous records. Of those who died, I would nonetheless have been able to save a number of them, if their husbands had allowed me to touch them. A healer's battle is also against people's fears and bad customs, and these things are plagues like any other. Allow me to tell you that no midwife has a better tally than I do. Forgive me for speaking so highly of myself, although it is the mouths of others that ought to praise you, as the proverb rightly says, rather than your own mouth, a stranger ought to praise you, rather than your own lips and tongue, but there is nothing I can do about that, because there is nobody here who knows me better than I know myself, not even the nephew I told you about. I keep mentioning him because I wish to place him under your exalted protection,' Jacob concluded, abruptly shifting to a ceremonial turn of phrase.

'Don't bore me with all this, Jew, and beware: nobody tells me what to do. You are garrulous by nature and far too loose of tongue. People here are fearful of me when they speak.'

Sargina, who had not spoken a word, thereby confirming what Belus said, bestowed upon the guest an encouraging smile, which gave Jacob to understand that the threat was not serious for the time being and that so far things stood well for him. She wore a wreath of golden leaves, which came down over her forehead as far as her eyebrows. Her face was mysterious, evincing a strange power, and Jacob noticed a slight asymmetry in it. As her body was slender and she did not seem to be with child, Jacob wondered who it was that Belus was so concerned about. He immediately spoke up.

'This is to do with the queen, is it not? She feels ill, nauseous, she's virtually stopped eating, she spends all her time lying down, she is sick of living, is she not?'

Belus's face remained expressionless, in which it was helped by the fact that he had no eyebrows, but the feline eyes, three-quarters concealed by his eyelids, registered amazement. He knew that the old man had only just arrived and nobody could have told him such a thing, since the secret was well guarded, unless he was one of those who could read minds, and he knew for a fact that such people existed. He stroked his long beard.

'Yes,' he replied, seemingly indifferent. 'You will now be taken to the other side of the city, to the palace of the king, then ... in fact, no, wait, I wish us to go together!' and at this, with a nimbleness unexpected for all his great bulk, he leapt down from the bed. 'Wait for me here!'

As soon as her husband went out, Sargina, in a whisper, lest the slaves overhear, and looking into the very lively hazel eyes, filled Jacob in on everything he needed to know about the royal couple in order to be of assistance to them. Otherwise, she warned him, the lives of strangers could be quite short there in Nineveh. She had taken a liking to Jacob from the very first moment, and since her days seemed long and quite lacking in novelty, she wanted to have him around her, to hear him speak, because she had never heard anybody speak in that fluent way, as if he were reading from a tablet. Jacob, too, liked the woman's intelligent face, and her dark eyes struck him as joyful without cause.

'I would like to ask you a favour, my dear, exquisite creature,' said Jacob, deciding to put his full faith in her. 'Without there is a man as tall as your glorious husband, but slenderer and with a white beard, although he is young. He is my nephew, Jonah. Let him be locked up in a room, but not cruelly, until my return, and have these dried flowers put in boiling water for him to drink, it will help him sleep. The whole pouch, please!'

Sargina had no time to reply, for Belus, dressed with great care, but wearing fewer jewels than when he kept to his own palace, now reappeared and nodded for Jacob to follow him. Jacob noticed to his puzzlement that Belus was wearing a single earring with gold palm leaves and an emerald, whose pair was missing from his right ear.

But he was a prisoner too

'As thou knowest not what is the way of the wind, even so thou knowest not how the bones do grow in the womb of her that is with child,' so Jacob explained to Belus on their way to the palace in a chariot adorned with the carved heads of animals painted vivid colours. Jacob was sitting very comfortably among large soft tasselled pillows, but he was dizzied by the passing buildings and walls that he saw as the horses hurtled along and he had the impression that above the city the sky didn't even exist. It was as if he found himself in some monstrous otherworld governed by other laws. The setting sun lengthened the shadows of the houses to the utmost hugeness. It was not for nothing that Rabona had told him in a whisper that the people of Nineveh feared shadows and words most of all. He was so astonished at what he saw—the broad streets, the tall, wondrously beautiful buildings, the countless statues, the fountains in the squares, and things to which he could not even put a name—that he preferred not to look up. Likewise, he also tried not to look at the people who threw themselves to the ground as they passed. At one point, an old man leaning on a staff didn't get out of the horses' way fast enough and was left prone on the cobbles behind them. Jacob, who had read the terror in the old man's eyes, thought that he resembled himself and that it was he himself who had been left lying on the ground behind them, probably dead. He sensed something evil in the air, something that told him he would never return to Gat-Hefer or see the widow of his late cousin Amithai again.

In fact, the saying about the woman with the child in her womb, a saying attributed to him known as the Preacher, was somewhat different, but Jacob didn't think it was the moment to tell his all-powerful and all-terrified listener the whole thing. Maybe it was because of such an insufferable combination, one of power and terror, of mistrust and, above all, pride, that Belus was silent the whole way. A long time passed before they reached the king's palace. Jacob fell asleep on the way, even though the horses raced at a dangerous gallop, and when they arrived, night had fallen. The entrance was lit by dozens of torches, some of them in bunches, some of them in rows. The two men walked down passageways with enamelled walls illumined by torchlight on either side, in which, at intervals, were half-embedded stone animals, as if their sculptors had not wished fully to release them from the stone, to emphasise that they too were prisoners, like everybody else in that place except the king. But ultimately the king too was a prisoner, pent inside the walls of his illness.

They came to a room, at whose highly polished door, studded with glossy knobs, stood two slaves. Without a word, in a single smooth movement they crossed their spears. They evinced self-importance and curled their lips in scorn. The next moment, the door was opened from within, and the slaves withdrew their spears in the same single smooth movement, half turning as if to assist the entry of Jacob and Belus, although the look of scorn remained on their lips. The two now entered a room as blue as the water of the Great Sea. The walls shone with lapis lazuli and, here and there, red carnelian and mother-of-pearl. The burning torches made the air hard to breathe, particularly for Jacob. A bare-breasted slave girl, so beautiful that she looked like a sculpture, was playing a harp whose wood was painted bright red and which was adorned with the gilded head of a gazelle that seemed to regard them with solemn attention. The notes produced by the plucked strings tinkled soothingly on the ear. Another slave girl, dressed in yellow, was singing a love song in a low, slightly hoarse voice. A few young women sat cross-legged around the harpist, but their eyes were on the king, such was their readiness to fulfil his every wish even before they heard it spoken.

Little by little, Jacob caught the words of the song: *My beloved husband, I tremble before thee, my beloved husband, I tremble before thee, O Lion, let me caress thy mane, let me caress thy mane.* The harp then played on its own before the woman's voice continued: *Sweet as honey is my caress, Take me to thy chamber, Take me to thy chamber, That you might give me caresses sweeter than honey ...* The voice grew hoarser: *My lion, my dragon, my god, My lord, I tremble before thee, I tremble before thee. Caress the soft place*—here, Jacob wasn't completely sure he had understood rightly, nor was he sure which particular soft place the woman meant—*Grasp it in your hand, Grasp it in your hand.*

Jacob, who walked a step behind Belus, remained standing as Belus kneeled. It was only then that he saw the king: he wore a plain dark blue garment, which bared one shoulder, and he was almost invisible against the blue wall behind him. It was as if he were another sculpture half embedded in the wall. On his face—the eyes resembled those of the gazelle adorning the harp—Jacob glimpsed a cold, sickly sadness. He knew that a disordered soul was harder to cure than a disordered body. It would be very easy for him to go wrong here, and probably he now found himself at the most perilous moment of his life. He made a deep bow, but it seemed the king did not notice him. Belus was still kneeling and did not dare look up or open his mouth. Jacob saw that his copious, overflowing flesh was trembling like the woman's in the song. As for Jacob, because of the smoke given off by the torches, he was convulsed by an unstoppable cough, which sounded like an impertinent shout, clashing as it did with the gentle atmosphere created by the tinkling notes of the harp and the whispered words of the song. The king gave a start and turned his head towards him, his eyes flashing with fury. All those in the chamber knew that this was enough for the old man to cease to be. It remained to be seen in what way he would cease to be, since the imagination of Assur-Nirari knew no bounds.

While Jacob struggled to suppress his cough, a cry rang out from quite far away, the same cry that he had heard exactly seventy-six times in his life, and he knew very well what it meant: a woman in the throes of labour, feeling as if her belly was splitting asunder, was about to give birth. It could be none other than the queen. Belus, who now heard this cry for the very first time, trembled even harder, but since his instinct for survival was infallible, he too realised quite swiftly what was going on. He addressed the king without being given permission to speak:

'The best healer in the world, your radiance! I summoned him from distant Galilee, as a precaution and knowing that the moment approached when the royal infant would enter the world. Hitherto he has assisted at a hundred births, absolutely all of them successful. Not one of those infants died. Order that he be taken this instant to the mother. We both came here in the utmost haste lest it be too late.'

As many lies as words. And once more Belus lowered his face to the floor, having raised it like a beaten dog, but from beneath his eyelids he subtly studied the king's face. The king had collected himself and looked at the two men before him as if having abruptly woken from sleep. Jacob did not see the sign in his eyes, but Belus saw it: Belus had won, if not the whole game, meaning his life, then at least another night. For that longstanding game with the king was for further days and nights won or lost. At the same time, Belus knew that it meant the death of the stranger: no man who saw the queen as Jacob was about to see her could be allowed to live afterwards. But this was none of Belus's concern. As for Jacob, his face remained calm and trusting.

Two burly servants lifted him by the armpits and more or less carried him down another enamelled passageway, and then another, along a labyrinthine route. A few moments later, the same cry was heard again, this time at close hand, and Jacob was admitted, alone, into the queen's bedchamber. He immediately saw her frightened gaze, which darted back and forth begging for help, and the same as in all the other seventy-six cases, he collected his strength to do battle with the invisible but always lurking rival of life.

'Make sure it's a boy!' the king had shouted at him.

The same as every other father he had encountered thitherto. Except that this father had added:

'If you want the mother to live.'

Tell me about yourself ...

Since it made her uncomfortable, Sargina took off the heavy head covering with the golden leaves that came down to her eyes—her husband forced her to wear it in his presence—revealing her arched eyebrows. She put on a plain, woven band she had been given by a guest from Egypt, which was adorned with translucent pieces of amber. Catching the rays of the setting sun, the amber matched her skin. She had a face like copper. The tiny ringlets of her black hair tumbled in a glossy cloak over her shoulders. If she hadn't been alone, she wouldn't have been able to let her hair down, either. The roof of the palace, where she awaited her guest, or rather prisoner, was luxuriant with vegetation: star-shaped russet blossoms, shrubs and small trees in which hung like earrings other flowers with red buttons framed by jagged bright yellow petals. Conveyed from the Tigris by a many-storeyed system of aqueducts, there was water aplenty, the same as in the whole city of Nineveh. Sargina had ignored her husband's request, as she was too curious to see this Jonah, a man still young, but with a white beard and 'slightly addled wits', and to discover the reason for his and his companion's strange visit. She had chosen the rooftop to meet him: it was the safest place in the palace, which is to say, it was inaccessible to spies, and besides, the air was pleasant, the birds sang there, and sometimes, in that season on the threshold between spring and summer, the dragonflies alighted on you, fluttering the rainbow fabric of their wings and showing their bulging eyes. She was somewhat afraid of this traveller who had to be placated with soporific herbs, like a wild animal, but she also liked it, because otherwise she cared about nobody else, not even the king or the dreaded Belus, and atop her long throat, her mysteriously asymmetrical face was more often than not covered with a veil of boredom. She therefore demanded that she be left alone on the verdant rooftop and that the man from Galilee be sent to her.

Jonah appeared in front of her abruptly, like the gods appear, causing her to start. He struck her as exceptionally handsome and gentle, despite his frowning countenance, although the beard, it was true, was out of keeping with the rest. Unlike all other men, he was blind to her beauty and that of the palace's rooftop garden. His eyes looked wholly inward and he did not even greet her. Maybe he really was ill.

'The old healer with whom you came says he's your uncle— is it true?'

She had spoken to him in Aramaic. Not a word of reply. It was as if he had not heard her or had not understood what she said.

'He left you in my care. He told me that we should give you herbs to make you sleep until his return. But I should warn you that he might not come back, you should be prepared for ... but now tell me about yourself!' she tenderly urged him, as if she were speaking to a child.

Jonah, who gazed straight through her, began to open his lips, but abruptly stopped before uttering a single word.

'Why did he tell me that your wits are addled?'

The man looked at her and heard her for the first time, and the astonishment in his eyes might have been at either what he saw or what he heard, if not both at once. In satisfaction, Sargina gave him a smile that was haughty but also encouraging. Nevertheless, Jonah did not seem to have an answer to her question and made a sign with his hand to this effect. A bird was chirping intermittently, as if speaking in his stead, the way people in a hurry do, when they put the words in your mouth if you're too slow in answering.

'Is it true that he is a healer and that he brought you here to cure you?'

The man moved his head in time with the words she spoke: first a nod, then a shake, and then, as if changing his mind, he changed the shake to a motion that signified 'probably'. He spoke meaningfully, albeit without words.

'Are you mute by any chance? Are you one of those who lack a tongue? Here in the palace there are three slaves and four slave women whose tongues have been cut out.'

'No, woman,' came the deep voice of Jonah all of a sudden, and Sargina started for the second time.

Nobody had ever spoken to her like that, nobody would have dared. It was lucky that nobody else had heard. A brutal reply, but in a gentle voice. How can you be brutal while speaking so gently? A smile the likes of which Sargina had never seen before accompanied those words, a smile like a moonbeam, capable of lighting up the night. 'Gentle as a lamb' the old man had said, but he had not told her of the power of the words his nephew uttered. He went on, with wholly unexpected sadness:

'Forty days left. From today. City will perish. Destroyed by the will of God.'

Sargina felt a pleasant excitement all over her skin and deep inside her. The voice utterly astonished her, as if it issued from outside him. Her face was grave. Her large painted eyes first paused on his, and then she looked him up and down, in a way nobody else had done before, as if she were casting a black velvety net over his body:

'Why?'

The question had been spoken in a voice in which a slave-owner's command mingled with consolation, revolt with sub-mission, boldness with fear. But Jonah's words were at an end. He was the first to lower his eyes. Too late, because the woman had already caught him in her closely woven net, like a fish, and he knew: he would struggle in that net for a long time to come, even until his dying day, for he had seen so many times how the fish leap in the fisherman's net, first swiftly, then more and more slowly, more and more wearily, until finally they leap no more. Nevertheless, he opened his mouth once more, and by now he wanted to tell her everything:

'Not my uncle. My father.'

It was a delayed reply. He ought not to have said it.

Let's wash him

Elisha had witnessed a birth before. Two women from Joppa once helped his mother give birth. They chased him out, but his curiosity got the better of his terror at her screams, which were intermittent at first, then more and more frequent, louder and louder, and he had pretended to leave but then turned around and came back, by which time they were all too busy to notice him, they didn't even realise he was there. And he couldn't comprehend what he was seeing, until the same two women took her away from there, her mouth still open after her final scream, her face unrecognisable, terrified, along with the baby that had not lived to see this world, a crumpled little girl, covered in blood and suety fat, with greenish-brown streaks on her little legs, the colour of withered salad leaf. The mother and little baby girl were wrapped in the same shroud, but Elisha didn't go to the burial. He had been left alone with only his younger brothers, to whom he was now mother, father, and brother, too. At first, the two women looked after the orphaned children, coming once a day, then once every few days, then once every few weeks, until finally they left them to fend for themselves—they had troubles of their own, troubles aplenty, and they had no room for yet more small children at home.

Now Elisha wanted nothing more than to be left in peace, to be by himself, bathed in the light of the full moon and to think of Ruth and what had so unexpectedly happened to him with her and because of her, to relive it over and over again in his mind, her whispers, her caresses, and the invisible trace a man leaves on a woman like a snake on a rock and an eagle in the sky—he had absolutely no desire to be present at another birth, an event that could only be atrocious. He hated births. When they arrived, they found Hannah lying in a strange puddle, and she, who had given birth five times previously, and had had two babies who died before they could open their eyes, knew what it meant and seemed very downcast. Eli tried to turn around and leave the room, but Jonah's mother, along with the neighbour who had summoned them and the mother of the girl from the well, who had also come in haste, spoke hurried words to make him stay close at hand so he could assist them. They told him to fetch firewood, to lay a fire right there in the room. Unlike his mother so long ago, Hannah did not scream, but her silence struck Eli as all the more terrifying for that. With tears in her blue eyes, the woman opened her mouth at long intervals, showing her teeth as if she were laughing. Eli kept his eyes fixed on the floor as much as he could, but he could still glimpse her sitting splay-legged on a low stone, and it seemed that things were not going the way they should, they were not progressing at all, in fact. Jonah's mother and Milkah's mother took counsel among themselves, in agitated voices, then the woman from next door fumigated her, she gave her boiled herbs to chew, in order to hasten and induce labour and keep her awake, but Hannah seemed wearier and wearier, she was dozing off, she soundlessly opened her mouth again, she threw her head back, baring her teeth.

Nothing stirred, not even time. It was as if the birth would never end. The women woke her and forced her to strain every fibre, and Jonah's mother pressed her belly in a special way. Elisha managed to slip outside and leaning against the wall, on the threshold, in the moonlight, he cleansed his mind of the images of Hannah, pushing them far away, and summoning up images of Ruth, he fell asleep caressing them.

The mother of the girl from the well woke him just as day was dawning:

'Quickly fetch a pail of water for us to wash him.'

It took him a long moment to understand that he ought to be overjoyed at that 'to wash him'. When he went in with the bucket, Jonah's mother was cradling a child in her arms. Like the little girl that would have been his sister, the baby was covered in blood and a thick fat that glistened in the candlelight, but its little mouth was moving and from it issued a bird-like little shriek, and the two little red hands, each minuscule finger precisely moulded, were stretched hesitantly in front of it. The three women were all smiling the same smile, each of their smiles an extension of the other, as if all three had given birth at once.

'My grandson,' said Jonah's mother. 'He looks like my son.'

'And like you, Hannah,' said Milkah's mother.

'And like you,' the neighbour told Jonah's mother.

'Jonah,' said Hannah.

'Do you want us to call him Jonah?' Jonah's mother quickly asked and then blushed.

Hannah replied with a look from her shining, bright blue eyes. In the meantime, the neighbour was rubbing the little creature with a wet rag, and to Elisha it looked as if she were pressing too hard, hurting him. From the navel hung a comical stalk. Then the women placed the infant at its mother's breast and finally they covered it and let it sleep. Its first sleep. The wider world had received a new creature, and nobody knew what awaited it. But it was a full moon, and it was known that this meant not only luck in being born but later luck in living.

Right then, of course, my dear Amos, since the mind doesn't need horses or mules to travel, since it speeds faster than the steam locomotive, they write about so often in the newspapers nowadays, right then in Nineveh, just before he fell asleep after finally being given an infusion of the herbs left by Jacob, Jonah remembered Hannah's eyes, and it seemed to him that they were the colour of lapis lazuli. He had seen the same full moon, but he had no way of knowing that its light kept a protective watch over the birth of his son in the village far away. The blue gleam of Hannah's eyes was then eclipsed by the hazel eyes of Sargina, the strangest woman he had ever seen and within whose power he now found himself, and this made him very unhappy. At which he fell asleep, laid low by exhaustion and excitement. I've experienced it myself, this double love, and I know what it's like, my son. Now that you have fallen in love for the first time, I would do well to warn you that just as you don't know the way of the storm wind, you don't know the way love will take in life. When Elisha saw the little Jonah, he grew fearful about what he had done with Ruth at the beginning of the night. It was as if somebody were to compress time and see the fruit of his action not nine months later but the very same night. He understood that the proverb about the trace a man leaves on a woman was not true at all. And for the first time he thought that when the little Jonah grew up and became as big as the elder Jonah, he too would leave his trace on women, of which only a few traces would live, and after a time he too would die, the same as everybody else, the same as every other trace man leaves on a woman. Likewise, for the first time ever, he thought that he himself would eventually die. Theretofore he had thought himself immortal.

We shall give a banquet

In the northern palace, Assur-Nirari ordered Belus to rise to his feet and stop trembling. And Belus instantly obeyed the order in each respect. You might say, my son, that fear only makes you start trembling, it doesn't make you stop if you're ordered to, but the king had trained his subjects in such a way that they could control their bodies according to his will and his word. They both proceeded, the king went before, his spine straight and his head slightly tilted back, Belus went behind, half bent so as not to exceed him in height, down halls of enamelled brick they went until they came to the 'yellow room', as the place where the king issued his commandments was known. Assur-Nirari asked for two scribes to come with fresh, soft clay tablets and styluses.

'On the occasion of my son's birth, we shall give a banquet such as the world has never seen. Let me hear you!'

Belus did not dare contemplate, let alone ask, what would happen if the king's son proved to be a daughter or if, gods forbid, the birth did not go as it ought to and the child died. He knew that in such an event, he would have every chance of immediately joining the child taken by the gods. He therefore answered in a thin voice, which grew the deeper the more he saw the king was satisfied:

'The most splendid banquet recorded on the tablets, if my memory does not deceive me, was held a hundred years ago, in the time of the marvellous Shalmaneser III: thirty thousand guests were invited. One thousand two hundred oxen and cows and eight thousand sheep were slaughtered, five thousand kegs of wine and four thousand barrels of beer were drunk. It is fitting that what we should do now is to double the amount, and the fame of the banquet, which we shall pass down in writing, shall never perish! Let all the earth know that a son has been born to Assur-Nirari ... erm, yes, a son of divine origin. All the city, all the inhabitants must learn the news and take part in the joy, we shall place tables of food and drink everywhere, in every square and all along the walls. We shall send messengers to all the neighbouring lands forthwith, who will bear invitations that cannot be refused. Even the gods, may they be magnified, will look on our celebration with joy, wishing to take part in it, and we shall feed them with sacrifices and offerings.'

The scribes, two youths, looked at their tablets in wide-eyed wonder, believing that the birth had already taken place, and unsure whether the birth should also be recorded, they lifted their eyes, but Assur-Nirari made a sign for them to wait.

Belus was about to continue, well pleased with himself, but the king grimaced and grabbed Belus by the earlobe, tweaking it as if he were a small boy.

'What have you done with the earring we gave you as a gift? If you have no earring, you have no need of an ear, and we can cut it off for you.'

His voice was calm, the most dangerous voice of all. The scribes sat smoothing the soft clay as if they were deaf. Belus gathered all his wits to make an appropriate reply.

'I left it with your exalted niece, Sargina, to take care of it. I am in this habit whenever I leave her side. In this way we remain bound to the glorious king and also to one another, when we are far away.'

'Hmm, yes, not bad.'

'To the southern palace—' Belus avoided saying 'my palace' '—a traveller has come, he arrived with the healer, and we don't yet know what he is about.'

'You place my niece in danger?' the king now yelled, while the scribes busied themselves sharpening their already sharp styluses, as if they were not in the same room.

'Not at all. I would not do so even under torture. The traveller is as gentle as a lamb, but he seems to be addled in his wits, and the healer hopes to cure him here in our city. I mentioned him because the exalted king ought to know everything that goes on in the city, and it is certain that this Jonah, for such is his name, also has unknown powers that might be harnessed.'

Assur-Nirari seemed satisfied with this response too, and he ordered the scribes to record all that Belus told them about the banquet, so that preparations for the event might commence forthwith. From where they were could be heard the queen's screams, and the king stopped his ears in irritation.

The Great Priest of the Great Temple of Nineveh and the Egyptian priest who had come especially for the birth were now announced. They entered with solemnity and the appropriate demeanour. The Great Priest had a thick beard which rivalled that of Belus in length, while the Egyptian priest was shaven from head to foot, which made them a pair whose contrast was endlessly fascinating. The king was informed that in all the temples of Nineveh and Alexandria, the priests were praying for the king's son or daughter.

'My son! It's a boy! Teglat-Phalasar will be his name. After my younger brother.'

'If the gods wish it, it will be a boy,' said the Great Priest, 'and if it is a girl, then you may be assured that this time next year she will be followed by a boy.'

The Great Priest was the only one who was allowed and even obliged to contradict the king from time to time—albeit seldom. His power was bound up with that of the temples, even if some of them had walls of reeds through whose holes the wind whistled. Assur-Nirari did not see fit to grow wroth. Looking at the Egyptian, he asked:

'Why do you not have a single hair on you? Even women have more hair! Are you ill by any chance?'

The Egyptian gave a thin smile He wore papyrus sandals, and his white linen garments, which looked as if they had just been washed, contrasted pleasingly with the hue of his skin. Around his throat was coiled a five-layered string of differently coloured beads, which he stroked at intervals.

'The custom is that we shave our whole bodies every two days, so that no impurity, no louse, no flea or other insect might nest in our hair and disturb us as we serve the gods or, deep in meditation, as we gain wisdom and approach the great mysteries. Some of us nonetheless leave a tuft on the chin or conceal their hair beneath a white head covering, but the true servants of our temples' immortals do as I do. There is no nation more religious than the Egyptians, who surpass all others in their fear of the gods,' said the priest and made a bow that wasn't deep enough.

'Mind what you say, I beg you!' interposed the Great Priest in annoyance.

But the king, who sometimes became enraged at what you least expected, did not seem put out, and was perhaps even pleased to see the Great Priest humbled by a foreigner. He made a sign that the audience was at an end. The queen's cries had not been heard for a while, and as nobody arrived to announce what was happening, the king hastened to his wife's bedchamber, followed by Belus and the priests. Looking at each other, the two scribes, now all alone—they were nothing but boys, almost children—began to laugh and whisper about the things they had heard. For they had seen nothing, having kept their eyes lowered and fixed on their tablets. They both fell to chewing the ends of their styluses.

An ordinary woman

As thou knowest not what is the way of the wind, nor how the bones do grow in the womb of her that is with child, even so thou knowest not the works of God who maketh all—so said he who called himself Ecclesiastes, or the Preacher, a saying which Jacob had not dared to tell Belus in full. He hadn't wanted to mix God up in it. Now, however, he needed God's help, not for the birth, which, as far as he could see, would go quite well, but so that the new-born would be of the male sex, a matter in which not even all his skill could have any influence, as the works of God might go either way.

The reason why the king wanted to kill the mother if the infant was a girl presumably had to do with his illness. Jacob was certain the king would do it without hesitation, since, as the proverb says: As dead flies cause the ointment of the apothecary to send forth a stinking savour, so doth a little folly to him that is in reputation for wisdom and honour. A traveller from the Orient had once told him a story he would never forget: A tyrant goes among his subjects and none is allowed to lift his eyes from the ground. Nevertheless, a woman who was about to give birth, having waited a long time in the road, in throes of labour, lifted her sweating face towards the tyrant. The next instant, the edge of his sword or maybe one of his soldiers' chopped off her head. Like headless chickens that carry on hopping for a time, the woman gave birth to a boy, who was raised by a charitable man, the boy lived like any other child, but not knowing the circumstances of his birth, and grew to be a man in his prime. Life cannot be stopped, if life there must be. Jacob now knew that his duty was to save both the mother and the child, whatever its sex.

The reason why the king wanted to kill Jacob, regardless of whether the new-born baby was a boy or a girl, was clear to the old man, however. He knew it as well as did Belus: a strange man who would have no choice but to touch the queen in labour could not be permitted to live afterward. But if his God, and the God of Jonah and Jonah's mother, came to his aid, then all would be well, as it had so many other times before, whether at sea or on dry land, he had been in the presence of life's unseen rival. And besides, he was elderly enough and had lived through things aplenty, so that all he wished for now was to see Jonah return safe and sound to his beautiful mother, who would ever after hold Jacob in gratitude and perhaps even a little love. Sin, the God of the Moon, was auspicious, said the women of Nineveh, since he revealed the full roundness of his face and his heavenly house was filled with light, which meant the birth would be an easy one.

In the chamber where the queen lay there were twenty-one midwives, who had been picked from among the populace of the whole city. There were six-score thousand people living between the walls of Nineveh and in the last year, according to the latest count, four thousand four hundred and ninety-one children had been born, of which two thousand six hundred and ninety were boys. Of these boys, in one thousand nine hundred and twenty-nine cases both the infant and the mother had survived. And it was only from among the midwives who had assisted at the births of live, healthy boys that the three times seven had been chosen: those that were the strongest, the gentlest, and the most pleasing to look at. When Jacob entered, small groups of the women were arguing together in heated whispers, their faces all showing differing degrees of alarm. From the queen's screams, Jacob knew that the moment was coming when the pain would become uninterrupted. He would have to lay the groundwork swiftly. Taking advantage of the midwives' amazement at his entrance, he told them that the king had chosen him and him alone to assist the queen, but only verbally, without touching her, since he was a healer whose fame stretched from Galilee to Tarshish, and he gave them the sacred task of praying on their knees to the goddess of fertility, Ishtar, for the birth to be easy and the infant to be a boy. Only they, as women, could do this in such a way that the goddess would hear.

Jacob then whispered in the ear of the midwife next to him, a plump woman dressed in green, with lively eyes, a round face, and a kind smile. He learned that her name was Emmita. He secretly told her that if the infant were to be a girl, they would all die: the queen, he himself, and likewise, there could be no doubt, all the midwives. He enjoined her to silence and obedience. He then spoke aloud, asking for a screen behind which to conceal the queen and himself. A screen was immediately brought, carved with fierce-eyed lions. Behind it he spoke once more in a whisper and at greater length to the midwife in green. She answered him with nods of her head, after which she tiptoed out of the room, before tiptoeing back inside, a round, green shadow. In her arms she brought something covered with a cloth and slipped behind the screen. It was a baby. The women were too busy with their prayers to the goddess to notice her, but the queen stared wide-eyed and screamed once more before her final, loudest scream. She understood.

Jacob was afraid of two things: lest the child's head be too large, in which case there would be nothing he could do, both child and mother would die, and along with them he himself and the twenty-one midwives. Secondly, he was afraid lest the placenta be left inside, in which case only the mother would die. But after this befell him a few times, he had quite simply thrust his hand inside the uterus of one brave little woman and taken out not only the placenta, red and as spongy as a mushroom, but also its tattered membrane, thereby saving her life. He was prepared to do the same thing now. Jacob felt drained of strength, but he didn't have time to be tired, as a famous inventor lately said.

What else can I tell you, my son: we, who have never given birth and never will, cannot even imagine the terrible pains a mother endures, the same pains when the very first woman, Eve, suffered the throes of labour as they are today, in this age of progress. The truth is that we have electricity and running water and I for one cannot imagine life without them, although there are plenty of people who fear such novelties like the plague, we have railways and steam ships, a different miracle happens every day—for example, they're building a tower of iron in the middle of Paris that will be taller than every building in the world—but when it comes to giving birth, women do it the same as they did in Nineveh and Galilee, and I speak as a physician whose very business it is to help women give birth. Let me add only that in Nineveh the problem of running water had been solved in an ingenious fashion: it was conveyed to the palace from the Tigris via splendid aqueducts, as I already said, built by the engineers of the time, who were as good as Monsieur Eiffel. In many respects, I think the people of Nineveh were our equals, my dear Amos, and the education one had there was more thorough than in the schools you attend, at which most of the time the pupils learn next to nothing, I'm afraid. In any event, our equality with them is most obvious in the pains of labour, which Assur-Nirari's wife suffered the same as any other mother, since when she gives birth or dies, even a queen is an ordinary woman.

So, she too urinated on the doctor's hands, like any other woman in such pains, she too bled, quite a lot, but Jacob, our ancestor was right that her hips were generous, and the birth went well. He grasped the hair on the top of the child's head, which was longer and thicker than other babies', and he pressed the mother's belly: the head slid out without any great impediment. Tears, blood, other discharges: this is how life begins, my son, I tell you as a doctor, but after she gives birth, every woman becomes not only a queen, but a goddess, she floats as light as air, relieved of the weight and the pain, and after she eliminates the placenta, once the infant is at her breast, invisible threads must form that envelop them both in love. I have no doubt that in future science will discover this, even if now it strikes you as fantasy.

With great trepidation Jacob waited for the lower half of the body and, alas, he saw not the nubbin of a boy, but the smoothness of a girl. He did not lose his head or succumb to despair! You should know that this ancestor of yours, this Jacob, was full of character, he was strong, brave, intelligent, and above all charming: how happy I would be if you took after him and became a physician too, my son! He immediately smeared the other infant, brought by the midwife, with some of the fat and blood from the little girl and cut the umbilical cord in three rather than two pieces, as is usual, placing one on the wailing boy. The midwives were still praying softly and had begun to cast frightened glances at the cruel-eyed lions on the screen, which guarded the secret of those behind it. Jacob cleared his weary throat and stepped into view. He spoke to them in Aramaic:

'Listen to me with great attention and repeat after me all together: This night a miracle has taken place!'

'This night a miracle has taken place!' repeated the women in unison.

'Pass on the word, in the palace, let everybody know, let them praise the birth, young and old: the gods were with the exalted queen. Repeat after me, the gods ...'

'The gods were with the exalted queen,' murmured the twenty-one women obediently, without knowing where what they were saying would end up.

Some of them nudged each other, whispering, 'a boy, a boy, a boy, a god ...'

But no: 'The exalted king has sired two children at once, twins, a boy, who was first to come into the world, and a girl, who immediately followed him.'

A murmur went around the room, but Jacob sternly spoke:

'Repeat after me: The exalted king ... let me hear you!'

'The exalted king has two children, a boy, who was first to come into the world ...'

'And a girl, who immediately followed him.'

'And a girl, who immediately followed him.'

'In such cases, bear in mind, so that the boy might be healthy, his sister must always be at his side, as she was before they both were born, in the unknown darkness of the womb. And both of them under the protection of the mother. Repeat after me: So that the boy might live ...'

'So that the boy might be healthy, his sister must always be at his side, as she was before they both were born ...'

'Go forth and make sacrifices to the goddess Ishtar, who helped us in her benevolence, in her great kindness ...'

But before they could leave the chamber, the king entered, his face discomposed, panting as if it were he who had given birth. Jacob knew that his fate would now be decided and that it depended on how heavy was the heart of Assur-Nirari. For it is said that heavy are salt and boulders, but heavier is the soul burdened by a hidden sin.

She is like Gilgamesh?

Jonah, who didn't know a son had been born to him, just as his son didn't yet know he had a father somewhere in the world, was as deeply asleep as his son, who was sleeping his first sleep since entering the world. True, the father's sleep had been helped along by some herbs. My dear Amos, if somebody had been able to shrink the earth so small that he could see both of them asleep at once, he would have delighted to see the swaddled little Jonah in Gat-Hefer, submerged in the waters of a dreamless sleep beside his mother, weary and joyful after giving birth, and at the same time the big Jonah, in Nineveh, in the palace of Belus and Sargina, worn down by excitement, worries, and the burden of his task. Sleep had also come to the northern palace, overtaking both the royal daughter and the three-month-old son of one of the serving women, who was thenceforth to pass as the king's own son. Also asleep were most of the inhabitants of Nineveh, six-score thousand people of various races in all, as I have already said, and all the villagers of Gat-Hefer, probably some four hundred and fifty souls, including Hannah, and the woman from next door, and Jonah's mother, and Abiel, and the widow with whom he lodged. Jacob was also asleep, the poor chap. I say 'poor chap' because the old man's body could barely cope with the strain any longer and was withering in plain sight, like a weeping candle. Asleep were the archers, and the merchants, and the high officials, and Emmita the midwife, and, after his first encounter with a woman, Elisha too. Asleep were the animals in the forest, and the fish in the rivers, and the sea, but without closing their eyes. Perhaps, God too was asleep, also without closing His eyes? But that's not a question I'm able to answer, my son.

Apart from Jacob, the queen, the midwife, and the real mother—the father was dead—nobody in the world ever found out that the royal son was not the king's. But in the end, wasn't every child in Nineveh symbolically the king's? You must have a ready understanding of symbols, because you read all those new-fangled poets that I don't like. It's also what Jacob told the midwife, to help her keep up the lie: all the children in Nineveh were the king's. True, the baby boy struck Assur-Nirari as exceptionally large—he was three months old, after all!—but Jacob, Belus, and the two priests were unending in their astonished admiration of that choice specimen, so different from any other new-born, which served as proof of his divine blood. Maybe he wasn't quite two-thirds a god, like Gilgamesh, but like the hero he certainly had the strength of a wild bull, given how chubby he was, and he would match the fame of the famous vanquisher of Humbaba, the monster with the tail of a serpent and the talons of an eagle.

*

Sargina's prediction was borne out: Jacob did not come back. Not because he was killed, as her words had hinted, but because Assur-Nirari kept him at the bedside of the queen, who was recovering her strength only very slowly. As for Sargina, she kept Jonah at her side, and Belus made no objection, up to his neck as he was in organising the banquet in honour of the new-born heir to the throne. He had to draw up the guest list: from the king's entourage to captains at arms and high officials and high priests, and even lower officials, craftsmen of every variety, farmers and shepherds and ship's captains—you can imagine how hard it was not to leave anybody out. So, those two ancestors of ours were each being held prisoner, each by a different woman in a different palace. They may as well have been separated by the Great Sea, or the Mediterranean as we call it nowadays, because they had no way of communicating with each other. But Belus's wife had to keep her guest under guard, since he had announced, in words sparing but unequivocal, that he intended to quit the palace in order to carry out his mission. Sargina found various pretexts to go to his chamber. With the greatest nonchalance she told her slave women:

'I dreamed of a falling star above me. I'd very much like to find out how the Jews would interpret such a dream. I know, I'll go and ask *him*.'

She didn't specify who this *him* was, everybody knew, and everybody also knew why she was going where she went. Women sense instantly when someone is in love, but nothing of the kind had ever happened to Sargina before. This Jonah resembled no man she had ever met before. He was a foreigner, and therefore attractive thanks to the allure of faraway places. Unlike everybody else, he was not afraid of Belus or even the king. He had some mission that was the most important thing in the world to him and, it seemed, he spoke with God, the only god he recognised, as far as Sargina could tell. She couldn't understand how the Galileans managed with only one god, or more significantly, how only one god managed all the affairs of a whole nation.

Since it was inappropriate that she enter another man's chamber alone, she took with her a woman, who knew that she would have to be both blind and deaf during the visit, and above all, mute afterwards. Jonah sensed Sargina's approach, lowered his eyes, raised them when the door opened, and when, treading lightly, she came to within a footstep of him, he gulped: he had never desired a woman so much, not even when he was very young, but this was something he dared not think about, didn't want to think about, and above all must not think

247

about. It wasn't for the sake of that woman that he was there. Sargina noticed his excitement, which surprised her and very much excited her in her turn, so much so that it made her feel weak, and it gave her pleasure to see her effect on him over and over, to feel his effect on her over and over:

'I dreamed of a falling star above me. I would very much like to know how the Jews interpret such a dream. How they would interpret it, how you would interpret it ... I came to ask you!'

Jonah said nothing, but looked at her asymmetrical face, at her eyes, which as always cast dark nets over him, so that he could see them again in his mind in the long hours of solitude and in the nights when it was hard for him to sleep. Sargina had known from their first meeting, on the rooftop, that she would have to be the one who spoke, so she settled herself comfortably on a chair while Jonah and the slave woman remained standing.

'Gilgamesh had the same dream of a falling star before he met Enkidu, his lifelong friend. I think you resemble him somewhat. You are Enkidu,' she whispered.

Jonah listened tensely and made an effort to speak, talking about her as if she were not present:

'And she resembles Gilgamesh?'

The voice was loud, far too loud for the chamber in which they found themselves, but the words spoken astonished the two women. The slave woman quickly lowered her eyes, and her lips trembled. In Nineveh, there was not a man or woman, not a slave or merchant, not one person young or old that did not know the story of Gilgamesh. The man from a faraway land seemed to think that the powerful, magnificent, all-knowing hero, the man who was two thirds god and one third human, was a woman!

'Sargina does not resemble Gilgamesh,' said Sargina rather curtly. 'I will tell you the story,' she then added, with a gentle, joyous laugh.

248

Jonah liked to hear her laughter—nobody had ever laughed liked that around him, and like a snuffling stag, without wishing to he sniffed the scent of fruit, aloe, vanilla, musk from the perfumed oils with which she anointed her body.

'Enkidu, a wild man, lived with the wild beasts and his herds of gazelles, he grazed the grass and drank at the water-holes with them. His hair grew long, down to his waist, like a woman's, he went naked and was so hairy that it was as if his whole body were covered in a pelt. The gods commanded that a hunter send a child of Innana—' Sargina did not mention that this was the term for a prostitute '—to teach this noble savage what a knowledgeable woman is able to teach an unknowledgeable man. The hunter told the young woman to disrobe in front of him, to bare her breasts and make him her prisoner, to hold him like a fish in the fisherman's net.'

Jonah gave a start at the mention of the fisherman's net.

'Which came to pass. For six days and seven nights in a row they made love, because he was never sated and constantly wanted to be a prisoner of her body.'

The storyteller now looked deeply into his eyes to see the effect of what she said, now demurely looked away, but Jonah did not pick up on the full meaning of her words, which were spoken swiftly and rather unclearly—Sargina had a speech impediment—but even what he did understand embarrassed him greatly. He then said something that was not wholly inapposite, although to her it seemed that way.

'Forty days. Counting from my arrival. Nineveh will be destroyed.'

Sargina pretended not to hear, even though Jonah's voice resounded all the way to the end of the passageway outside. It could have endangered them both.

'Afterwards, Enkidu went back to his wild beasts and herds, but the animals did not want to look at him any more, the herds of gazelles were ashamed of him. His knees were weak and his whole body was limp. The young woman tore her garment in two and covered herself with one half and him with the other. Then she told him the dream of Gilgamesh, the magnificent, the strong, the all-knowing Gilgamesh of Uruk, who had the strength of a bull and flawless beauty—unlike Enkidu, who was merely a savage—and who was as invincible as the gods. The dream of the falling star, which Gilgamesh himself had told, presaged their lifelong love and friendship. But before they could become friends, first they had to do battle, Enkidu had to show Gilgamesh, who had overstepped every bound and become evil—a real tyrant!—that he was not above everybody else, that he was not a god, and during their long battle it turned out that neither was stronger than the other. Such a thing seldom happens in love ... More than friendship, although that was what they called it, what they felt for each other was love.'

Sargina stood up and abruptly left the room, with the slave woman behind her, tripping over the hem of her gown in her haste, and Jonah as limp as Enkidu, was left behind to ponder the woman who could speak of such things without blushing.

When evening came, Sargina returned with a different slave woman and further told him:

'And after the death of his beloved friend Enkidu, whom alone the gods chose to punish for the wrong both had done, for the gods are more often than not unjust, as you already know, don't you? After the death of his friend, Gilgamesh understood that he was not immortal. He had always thought he was before that, for that is what we young people think. And he went to his ancestor, who had escaped the flood after building himself an ark—'

'Noah,' said Jonah to himself, but aloud, much to Sargina's amazement.

'Utnapishtim was his name,' Sargina continued, without comprehending. 'Gilgamesh wanted to learn from him the secret of immortality. He was unable to, but his ancestor, on seeing him disconsolate, said that somewhere, at the ends of the earth or the bottom of the sea, or as they now say, at the bottom of our river, the Ḥiddeqel, there was a flower that restored your youth if you ate it.'

Sargina looked at Jonah's face as if picturing how he would have looked with a black beard. Jonah looked back at her in silence, and Sargina understood: he was saying that she had no need of such a flower. Her youth was plain to see: she looked like a young girl.

'He found it, but he wanted to try it on somebody else, since Gilgamesh was mistrustful by nature, the same as all those who hold too much power. And one day, when he was bathing, he left the flower on the riverbank and a serpent swallowed it. Ever since, it is serpents whose youth is restored, every spring when they shed their old skin. Human beings' youth is not restored, even when spring comes, as it has now. Human beings remain in the same skin. But as for me, I think that every spring even human beings feel as if their youth might be restored. When I first heard the story about the snake, I was a child, and I didn't understand it. But right now, it strikes me as terribly unfair! Why should snakes have their youth restored but not us? Why shouldn't we be able to shed our old skin to reveal a new, glossy, youthful skin beneath?'

Sargina didn't say all this for her own sake. She then whispered something to her slave woman and left. But the slave woman remained.

Stupidity

In the royal palace, Emmita, the midwife who had played such a decisive part in the royal birth and in saving the lives of all, told Jacob, 'To their good fortune, snakes never grow old. They who soundlessly crawl swallowed the flower of youth. They are the same as certain people who keep low, go unnoticed, but steal from everyone everything that is good. The women here often grind up snake skin and sprinkle it in their food to restore their youth, and the queen has ordered me to do the same for her. She thinks that after she gave birth she lost her charm and her youth.'

She showed Jacob the skin of a snake, which looked like tree bark, and which she was about to grind up. She was dressed in green, as always, and her round face was all smiles.

'Stupidity, and dangerous stupidity at that,' replied Jacob. 'Look, I'll give you some cassia powder, tell her it's snake skin, and it will remain our little secret, since I've seen you know how to keep a secret,' he added with emphasis. 'It will help her feel lighter and invigorate her.'

'She wants to see the prophet, she believes in him, and she wants to make the king at least touch the hem of his garment, to cure his sickness.'

Jacob didn't understand straight away. It was the first time the word 'prophet' had been spoken in his presence. It meant that news of Jonah must have reached the northern palace too, and for the second time he realised that the people around him drew no connection between himself and Jonah. The first time had been on the ship, at a time of great danger, when, in the end, he had been unable to save Jonah, his son or nephew, whichever he might be. He was fearful lest it turn out the same this second time, he had dark premonitions, but also a faith that transcended premonition. For Jonah to be saved the first time, God had had to intervene. Yes, it was God who had saved him.

He looked at Emmita in gratitude. She was abreast of everything significant that happened in the palace and in the city. As soon as the queen had given birth to a little girl and been given the little boy, Jacob had, out of caution, requested that the midwife also remain at the palace, to take care of her—he wanted to make sure that she did not speak of the events to which she had been privy. And indeed, she did not. With her plump body and affectionate, open face, dressed in robes as green as a palm tree and always ready to help anyone in need, it was easy to like her. The queen too had liked her from the very first, and so now the midwife was at her side day and night. And she was Jacob's best friend: he took counsel with Emmita, it was her that he asked about the rules of the palace and about everything he was unable to work out for himself. Jacob had never thought of Jonah as a *nabi* until then: it is hard to disrobe those closest to you of their old skin, the skin you have seen them wear day after day, since they are not snakes, and it is just as hard to see them all of a sudden clothed in solemn splendour. He immediately told the midwife that the prophet's name was Jonah and that he was his relative.

'My nephew,' he added, somewhat doubtfully. 'For in thee, O Lord, do I hope. For I said, Hear me, lest otherwise mine enemies should rejoice over me, when my foot slippeth, they magnify themselves against me. For I am ready to halt, and my sorrow is continually before me. For I will declare mine iniquity, Emmita, as the great David said so simply.'

'Don't worry, they say that our city will soon be destroyed, in less than forty days,' the midwife went on, without realising what she was saying and making Jacob smile. 'People think the end of the world has come, and they grow more and more afraid with each passing day. When I heard it for the first time, it made me laugh, but now everybody is talking about it, albeit in a whisper, and even I am starting to get worried.'

Emmita looked at Jacob, hoping that somehow he would cure her soul of the illness of fear.

'All I think about is those two children, especially the little girl, the one I saw coming out of her mother's womb a week ago and who is so pretty ... and about all the children at whose births I've assisted. Whenever I heard a child laughing, the way only a child can laugh, endlessly and without the slightest trace of worry, I was as happy as that child. At least for their sake I'd like the world not to end ...'

Assur-Nirari too had heard of the prophecy, from none other than the queen, as nobody else would have dared repeat something so monstrous to him. He even set the day of the banquet for Jonah to be brought to the palace and be allowed to speak. He regarded it as a kind of performance, like that of the dancers and singers, as a surprise that he was to lay on for the guests at the banquet, who would marvel at the prophet and the prophecy alike. Only then would he decide the prophet's fate, on the whim of the moment: he might shower him with gifts and seat him at the banquet table next to him, he might give him to the women, for them to delight him and drain him of all his strength, he might have him tortured and killed in front of the banqueters, he might have him chased away with stones. Such moments stimulated the king's imagination, and in his eyes could be read the sickness of cruelty as plainly as in the eyes of the lions on the ceiling.

Jacob was among the first to find out what the culmination of the banquet would be, and his velvety eyes, shaded by his unruly grey eyebrows, now showed an almost continual alarm. He did not need to learn every single detail, as he was sharp enough to know what was going to happen. He told Emmita everything that weighed on his soul and together they made a plan to send somebody to Belus's palace and warn Jonah of what was afoot, to tell him to feign illness, a swoon, even to pretend to be dead when the day of the banquet arrived. Jacob had some drops that would make him genuinely sick for a day or two. In the end, Emmita took upon herself the dangerous mission. She did so with the help of the queen, knowing that nothing was easier to employ than curiosity if it came to it: it was curiosity that made the world go around.

'I might venture to go to the southern palace myself, if it be pleasing to my queen, to see the prophet and ask him about his prophecy. The queen needs to know in detail what that man is about, what he looks like, what he has to say, and so on, rather than knowing only what the commoners have heard ...'

The little girl was whimpering in the cradle, the little boy was gurgling in Emmita's arms and opening his crooked mouth, and the mother, bored of her weakness and protracted lying-in, rejoiced.

'Yes, you will be my envoy! Let him tell you everything, whom he worships, why us and not some other city, and how he knows ... And let him know that I alone can save him, which means he would do well not to conceal anything. Tell him that he is going to be summoned here, to the banquet ...'

There were another thirteen days until the banquet.

Thirty-three days until the end of the world foretold by the prophet.

So amazed she had fallen in love

When the midwife arrived at the palace with the drops from Jacob and the message from the queen, the southern palace was in a ferment. Sargina's slave woman had returned the night before, her eyes downcast. With doleful sighs, her head lowered, she told how Jonah had driven her out, how he had first pushed her away with his eyes and then, when that didn't work, raised his hand against her to push her out of the room. Sargina herself would have liked to be the one who had been pushed, just to feel the touch of his hand. He had not touched her yet. Other than that, said the slave woman, he spoke not a word, as if he had forgotten how to talk or simply had not wished to waste words on her. But the greatest shock came the next day, when Sargina, burning with impatience to see him again and to rest her gaze on his hands or maybe even to touch them, went to the chamber in which Jonah had been locked up only to find him gone. He had vanished like smoke and everybody was looking for him. Sargina didn't know what to do with herself, and the asymmetry of her face was now more pronounced, disfiguring her. The slave woman swore that Talya, the slender guard at the door, had done his duty: after she left the guest or prisoner, she didn't know which to call him lest she err, she heard the heavy lock being turned twice. But the mistress knew her slave woman was enamoured of the guard and would not have betrayed him. Maybe they had both lost their heads and Talya had left the door unlocked without realising it, maybe they had taken advantage of the fact that they were alone to hold each other tightly, insatiably, fleetingly, lest they be caught, and forgot about everything else. Or maybe Jonah really did have unnatural powers? Otherwise, how could he have passed so many doors, all of them guarded and locked, in a place unfamiliar to him and in which he could not help but get lost, and still not be captured?

The midwife returned to Jacob and the queen, telling them that Sargina had naturally sent a large number of men to look for Jonah both inside and outside the palace. It was lucky that Belus was constantly away, busy as he was with the royal banquet to honour the birth of the great Teglat-Phalasar, who was still so little and helpless (as for his sister, the rightful heir to the throne, her name was never mentioned, as if she didn't exist), which meant that Sargina had complete freedom of movement. Nothing more than this was known for the time being, and there was nothing else anybody could do.

That evening, by which time Sargina had lost her patience, her appetite for life, for food, and the colour from her cheeks, one of the men sent out to search for Jonah asked to speak to her. He was the only one who had any news.

'Let him come! Let him come, right now!'

The man entered and bowed as low as his age allowed, since he was elderly and rather stiff.

'He was in a market a day's journey from the gate of Adad, and he was speaking of ... forgiveness ...'

'He was speaking of forgiveness?'

'No, I mean I beg your forgiveness that I dare repeat his words ... he was speaking of the destruction of the city of Nineveh and the death of all the people who live there, begging your forgiveness, from the richest and even the Great ... but I dare not utter the name of the Great Belus. There are still thirty-three days left. This is what the ferryman told me the prophet was saying, begging your forgiveness, your highness.'

And he attempted another, deeper bow, but his stiff back was having none of it, so he groaned instead.

'In other words, you didn't hear him with your own ears? Why then are you wasting my time and trying my patience? Bring me that man, the ferryman, and bring him this instant! Bring the one who saw him!' yelled Sargina, clenching her little fist in chagrin.

Nonetheless, Sargina had to endure a long, excruciating hour before they brought Rabona, the ferryman with the jagged scar, an hour in which all she could do was pace up and down the hallways, from her room to Jonah's room, where she tried to sniff the traces of his scent and hoped to see him reappear as if by miracle. Rabona was a quick-witted young man who seemed to be very devoted to Belus, although Sargina was not convinced of his loyalty—how could you love and obey somebody who had scarred you for life like that? But now she was happy that she knew him. The ferryman recounted in words plain and clear that he had just brought some guests who were to attend the royal banquet when, in the small star-shaped plaza he saw a crowd gathered around a man talking to the crowd, a man tall, slim, still young, but white of beard. He immediately recognised him since he had never yet forgotten a face, so he boasted, and people's features left an imprint on his mind like the characters the scribes make on soft clay tablets. He joined the throng of bodies pressing in a circle around the speaker, and managed to elbow his way to the front through the agitated men and the women standing frozen, with their hands to their mouths. By now, Sargina could barely breathe.

'And his voice boomed out as if from the bowels of the earth, all the way to the heavens. When I brought him on my raft, he was as silent as a fish, and for a while I thought him weak-minded or mute, but now he was speaking or rather thundering like I've never heard anybody thunder before, in a voice that was unearthly.'

You could sense the admiration in the ferryman's words. The tiniest of smiles fluttered on Sargina's lips. It was a smile of pride.

'What was he saying? Be so good as to try to remember everything he said, word for word!'

'I don't need to try to remember. It's not something you'd forget. He was looking all around him, fearlessly, like a lion tamer, and he said: "The Lord God said unto me: Yet forty days and Nineveh shall be overthrown! Seven days have passed. Thirty-three remain! Cleanse and purify yourselves! Put on sackcloth, cover your heads and lower your eyes. Learn to do good, to be just, to succour the poor, to protect women without husbands and children without parents. Let both you and your oxen and your sheep and your goats keep a fast. The Lord of justice keeps watch! Woe unto the evil man, for he will reap what he has sown, for him there will be no mercy, there will be pain, darkness, weeping and wailing, and the gnashing of teeth. There is not a man here in your land who has not sinned, beginning with Gilgamesh and Enkidu, the chiefs of sinners ..." And then he started all over again: "The Lord said unto me: Yet forty days ... seven have elapsed. Thirty-three remain ...'

Rabona's voice was sweet, almost a whisper, it was hesitant, and his words did not make a very great impression on Sargina. All the more so since she knew that it was from her that Jonah knew about Gilgamesh and Enkidu, and that seemed to lessen the impact of the prophecy. She did notice, however, that Rabona had said nothing about Belus, which meant he wasn't being completely honest. She wasn't interested in that part, however. All she wanted was to save the man with whom she was so amazed to have fallen desperately in love.

She thought about how ironical the gods were. It was the first time in her life that she had fallen in love and now the end of the world was nigh. When love actually ought to herald the beginning of a world. But the whole city could perish for all she cared, as long as he escaped. Preferably taking him with her. Also as far as she was concerned, everybody could carry on living in the city with its walls intact, as long as the two of them managed to run away together, maybe to Alexandria, to the land of the wig-wearing Egyptians, or to one of the Greek cities, where the men oil their muscular bodies and wrestle each other, or to his home, to Galilee, where the men obey ten commandments and just one God. There were so many places in the wide world that could welcome the two lovers, so many places whose inhabitants would let them live among them, since they would hardly do anybody any harm, each caught up in the other's eyes, each entwined in the other's thoughts as in an embrace. All of a sudden, she couldn't stand Belus any more, or his big black beard, or those eyes of his, bare of lashes, that forehead of his, bare of eyebrows, his limitless brutality, his body barren of love but bursting with jewellery. She wanted to feel she was loved, and the silent Jonah, Jonah with the commanding voice, loved her, of that she was sure. And in any event, that was the only thing that counted.

'Take with you the guards and bring him to me. If need be, you can tie him up, but don't do him any harm, make sure of that. We don't wish to bother your great master or let such matters distract him from his preparations for the royal banquet. I myself will take charge of everything. Don't be afraid. But if my husband and your master finds out, you will be sorry!'

When Rabona turned around to leave with the other, having made the customary bows, Sargina repeated breathlessly:

'Don't do him any harm, I have to speak with him, because ... erm ... because he knows certain secrets ...'

Was she imagining it or did the messenger smile? After the men left, Sargina suddenly burst into tears. She didn't know why. Nor did she know that she was not the only one who wanted to protect Jonah and save him. What is for sure is that the gentle Rabona was wholly on Jonah's side. And presumably God was too, just a little.

His heavy voice, for minutes on end

In the huge hall of the northern palace, the royal banquet surpassed all imagining. Nobody had ever seen the like before,
so much plenty and so much splendour all at once, and nobody would have believed it possible. Belus had proved a true
magician, and people were no longer surprised that the king
valued him so highly and placed so much trust in him. When
he put his mind to it, he could do anything, for he was a born
constructor. The table was in the shape of a hexagon, but with
a large circle cut out of the middle, where a living tree had been
placed, with its roots planted in the ground, since the floor had
been dug up to make room for it, and its boughs, laden with
yellow flowers, reached almost to the ceiling. In the tree were
hung cages of songbirds.

At each of the table's six corners, an artist-craftsman from
Babylon had combined seasonal fruits, vegetables and flowers, using an art known to him alone, to fashion six heads of
gods and goddesses, which looked as if they had descended
straight from heaven. You couldn't take your eyes off them.
The gods had real bull, gazelle, and stag horns and antlers,
but everything else was fashioned by the artist's hand and
displayed a lifelikeness that was consummate in its mastery.
Among the gods, the most striking was Marduk, fashioned
from brightly coloured petals large and small, and among the
goddesses the most beautiful was Ishtar, as was only fitting.
On the table were rows of star-shaped oil lamps, as yet unlit,
since it was still daytime, but arranged in a snaking pattern
which, once they were lit, would draw the eye like the stars in
the heavens.

For the king, the queen and the priests there were gold goblets encrusted with rubies whose handles were shaped like lions' heads, for the high officials there were silver goblets encrusted with sapphires, and for all the other guests, bronze goblets with tigers' eyes, and all the goblets gleamed as one. Flatbread, pita, and fresh loaves were arranged in seven-stepped pyramids and had their walls not been soft, you would have thought that the most beautiful structures in the world had been reduced in size and brought inside to be set on the table. Barrels of blood-red wine and bitter beer had been rolled up from the cellars and crammed into an adjoining room where they would be handy. In the courtyard dozens of rams were roasting on spits, along with hundreds of nicely browned birds. The hall smelled of roast meat, freshly baked bread and, from the very entrance, the sweet waft of the flowers in tall vases.

Servants swarmed, while the harpists and singers, gossiping about the guests, had been waiting for hours on end for the moment when they would finally play. Around the city, in squares and parks, copious but far simpler tables had been prepared for the common people, so that everybody would be able to rejoice and to glorify the heir to the throne. Guests filled the streets, and the palace was packed to the seams. All were caught in the choppy waves of joy.

That the royal heir for whom so many preparations had been made was in fact the son of a servant was a joke to be enjoyed by the gods alone. No one could have had even an inkling of something so strange. The queen did not love Teglat-Phalasar. She tried to suckle him as if he were her own son, but the boy, in great agitation, would grab her nipple too greedily and hurt her. She thought he drank too much, that he didn't leave enough milk for his poor little sister—or rather, his sister in a manner of speaking—who was frail and quiet. It was a good job Emmita was there, who had forgotten that the boy had been

263

made rather than born the royal heir, and every day she brought a wet nurse full of milk, a cheerful, garrulous woman, whose stories made the queen now laugh, now take fright. That very morning, the wet nurse had told her about the prophet again. They kept trying to catch him, apparently, there were countless soldiers and spies on his trail, but whenever they were about to grab him, he vanished like a ghost. He had been to eight public squares already, each time thronged with an even larger crowd of the curious, and always he told the petrified listeners the same thing, except that the number of days remaining kept diminishing, doom kept getting closer, and the people were more and more ashamed. The prophet was worried about them and downcast. It was obvious he cared about the people of Nineveh, that he wanted them to wake from their slumber and become better people, but he was also unrelenting and left them no other escape. And so it was that the people started to count down the days they had left to live: and that day was one of exactly twenty that were left. Each thought about what to do first before the city was destroyed, some gave themselves over to debauchery, others made love and neglected their daily duties, and others still, in large numbers, got ready to flee. If the gates had not been so well guarded and the punishments for those who tried to leave the city without permission so dreadful, Nineveh would be deserted, said the wet nurse as she laid in his cradle the chubby little boy, who had fallen asleep while he suckled—he had no idea the end of the world was nigh!

Jacob, the most significant keeper of the secret of the birth that took place on the night of the full moon, was feeling ill. As for him, he didn't know whether he would see the prophesied end of the world or whether the end would come sooner for him. He missed Jonah very much, he also missed Jonah's mother, but there were days when above all he missed Elisha and Abiel, to whom he was bound by the voyage, and he even missed Don Amado and his little girl, and Sansón and Hernando. He realised now that more than certainly the most beautiful period of his life had not been his youth, when nothing gave him peace and he could find no place for himself in the world, but his old age, aboard the ship, with all the others, when he gave lessons to Eli, when he tended the sick Phoenician, when he saved the blind man, when he saw the great fish, *dag gadol*, when the storm abated, a sign which at the time he had not interpreted correctly. He then thought about Gat-Hefer, and in his mind he relived the scene with Jonah's mother over and over and over again: 'I've always wanted to ask you, then ... finally ... Jonah ... you know very well what I'm asking.' 'I don't know.' And he kept changing his mind about how he ought to interpret the answer. He hadn't asked her at the time and now he no longer had any way of asking her. He hoped only that it was how he felt it to be. But he would die without knowing, the way all people die: without finding out anything of what was important and hoping it would be better than he imagined. And without having tried to restore Abiel's sight. Others would come later and they would certainly do that, but with different Abiels.

Emmita's news, which she gave him along with the unused drops, overwhelmed him. Henceforth it would be nothing but the will of God, since Jacob's business in Nineveh was done. He knew that when a man gave himself up to the will of God, it meant he was in genuine despair. A place of honour had been set aside for him at the banquet table, on the side where the most important guests were seated, but even though he liked people and merriment, now he would have preferred to languish alone in his bitterness. He tried to encourage himself, saying that he had to be there, in case they caught Jonah and brought him to the palace, or in case his reckless nephew got it into his head to enter the lion's mouth all by himself and prophesy doom.

Do you hear that? A *nabi*, a prophet! Jacob gave a snort. He went to put on the sumptuous garments the queen had sent him.

*

The banquet was in full swing and everything was as it should be, the people were in good spirits, many had already grown tipsy on the red and the white wine that gurgled into the goblets no sooner than they were emptied, and on the beer that was slightly tart on the tongue and left a bitter taste in the mouth. Let it be noted in passing that drink was poured into the bronze goblets more often than the gold, and therefore thirst was greatest where wealth was least. The small lamps had been lit at last, and each flame-scaled snake caused the vessels on the table to glint. Bunches of torches clamped in iron rings on the walls brightly illumined the rest of the hall.

Then something happened. Nobody knew how. With the utmost swiftness, one after the other, like ears of wheat bending in the wind, the heads of the guests all turned toward the door. There on the threshold, beneath the beautifully painted archway, stood a tall creature, as if having sprung from the ground, with the glaring eyes of a beast-tamer. His legs slightly apart, he leaned on a pommelled staff. He stood as motionless as a statue and, strangely, the people at the table, the servants, the musicians all froze like statues, too. Sargina let out a brief cry. After her cry, all other sounds ceased. It was like in a fairy tale, in which the world has frozen, in which everything is still. Only the birds in the cages continued their heedless chirping in the tree with the yellow flowers.

Emptied of sounds, the whole room was filled with the voice: 'The Lord God said unto me: go and tell them of their doom. Forty days. I have been here for twenty. Twenty yet remain! I have told you! Do what the Lord demands! Pray! You must!' Then his words flowed in a torrent: 'Behold, their ear is uncircumcised, and they cannot hearken. The wife will perish with her husband and the child with the youth and with the old man, a wasteland shall stretch where now you shamelessly build and pierce and wound the heavens and your bones shall be ploughed into the earth. Desolation gushes from you like a spring and nobody knows how to blush with shame any longer. Greed throttles you, all steal and deceive without surcease. You glisten with evil and with grease. You care for none and you know not God. How is such cruelty possible? How is such heedlessness possible? You have eyes, but you do not see, you have ears, but you do not hear, you have thoughts, but they are vile, you have mouths and tongues, but not one good word are you capable of uttering therewith. Woe and bitterness and shame! Woe to the new-born babes. Let the animals cease their lowing and bellowing and roaring, let the birds restrain their chirping, and let them hear me, and let the earth and the air and the water hear me: all things shall be one, mingled with the dust and ashes, for all that now is and all that now lives shall be reduced to dust and ashes. From your minds has issued nothing but evil and your minds shall wither like the mown grass, and your bones and your hearts and your tongues shall be ground to dust, leaving only your eyes to weep unending tears. I am full of the wrath of the Lord who will cause you to perish without trace! The hour is nigh!'

And all of a sudden, the entrance was empty once more, the man had vanished without trace, but the heaviness of his voice still filled the large hall, and did so for a number of minutes. He had spoken with the voice of the voice. Gradually, the voice began to fade, like a scent dissolving, but in the banquet hall the people's murmurs and whispers now spoke only of the words of the prophet and all were in thrall to them. Nobody ate, drank, sang. Belus was the first to rise to his feet, bursting into tears. Having seemed as hard as stone, he now crumbled. His eyelids, which lacked lashes, had turned red and for the first time in his life, his face was tortured, full of repentance. Likewise for the first time, his face lacked its wonted self-pride. The queen followed suit, she too wept, perhaps thinking of her little daughter, her only child, wronged by king, courtiers, and prophecy alike. Within minutes, weeping gripped them all, passing from man to man as laughter had during the feast, and around the six sides of the table, tears flowed as the wine had flowed not long before, and the strength of the tears surpassed that of the wine, it dizzied them. Even Jacob wept, he wept like never before, he wept like a young man, sensing that he would never return to Gat-Hefer. And so it was that the repentance began. In the heavens, the moon was a half disk.

There were yet twenty days till the appointed hour.

Maybe just like that, without reason

The full moon that kept watch over the birth of her grandson had now waned to a half moon. Jonah's mother looked at the moon with a sigh, thinking of those who were not with her to rejoice that everything was as it should be. She had prepared a modest meal, which, in the absence of the father, she herself was giving in honour of the boy's birth. Only the green olive sprigs picked by Ruth and placed on the table showed that it was a celebration. With her light footstep, Ruth seemed to be everywhere at once and she was the trustiest help. There were only twelve guests, including Hannah, of course, whom Jonah's mother now regarded as her daughter-in-law, there was the mother of the girl from the well, hand in hand with her Milkah, and there were Elisha and Abiel, Jacob's protégés, whom she had invited because they made her feel closer to the two who had gone to Nineveh: they were always reminiscing and talking about the weeks they spent on the ship. And even if they did repeat some things over and over again, she was still glad to hear them. Naturally, she had invited the widow with whom Abiel lodged, lending her comfort in her loneliness, and then also a few friends from the village, and Esther, who softly hummed a hymn of rejoicing. For nine days (she had counted them!), Esther had known she was in love for the first time—ever since Eli had said her name, also for the first time, and helped her carry a bucket, taking her by the hand. My dear Eidele, I don't know what Esther's song would have sounded like in those days, but let me sing you a song that you'll hear in a few weeks, when you get married. I don't know why, but the song, which is quite recent, always captivates me like a magic spell. I imagine Esther too hummed something like this, not exactly the same, but close:

> *Hava nagila,*
> *Hava nagila,*
> *Hava nagila,*
> *Venis mecha.*
>
> *Hava nagila,*
> *Hava nagila,*
> *Hava nagila,*
> *Venis mecha.*
>
> *Hava neranena,*
> *Hava neranena,*
> *Hava neranena,*
> *Venis mecha.*
>
> *Hava neranena,*
> *Hava neranena,*
> *Hava neranena,*
> *Venis mecha.*
>
> *Uru, Uru achim*
> *Uru achim belev sameach,*
> *Uru achim belev sameach,*
> *Uru achim belev sameah*
> *Uru achim,*
> *Uru achim*
> *Belev sameach.*

Everybody was gay and melancholy at the same time, maybe because the father wasn't there, maybe because the moon was waning, maybe for no reason at all. Jonah's mother had begun to look like a grandmother, lately her face had become furrowed and her hands trembled slightly. Above all else, her eyesight had grown poor, and when she sewed she had to hold her work right up to her eyes. But her smile was as beautiful as ever and when she looked at the little one in his swaddling clothes, it was as if she were his mother rather than his grandmother.

At intervals, Eli would get up from the table and go out, whereupon Esther would follow him with her eyes, and when he came back, he would be frowning and sullen. He was trying to get Ruth alone, but the other serving woman, the plump old woman, noticed something and without knowing that the thing had already occurred, she planted herself in the young man's way, much to his exasperation, and pointlessly guarded the tender young woman.

'I dreamed of Jonah!' said Hannah all of a sudden, causing the other women to start and to freeze.

They all remembered the dream of foreboding once told while they were picking grapes and the nasty episode that had followed it.

'Oh, why didn't I realise it before? How could I have forgotten? Your dream back then turned out to be true, my dear Hannah, maybe it was the very same moment when Father was swallowed by the sea and saved by the fish. Yes, I'm sure of it!' said Esther, hoping to catch Elisha's eye, but he was oblivious to her, even though right then she was as pretty as could be, speaking with childlike joy.

Unlike the last time, when Jonah's daughter had been spiteful and unyielding when it came to her father's lover, now she fully took her side and kept asking her permission to hold her little brother in her arms. Maybe it was because she understood many more things now than she had then. Hannah's blue eyes lit up whenever Esther asked her for the child, and she would hand her him, albeit always with a certain trepidation.

'*Dag gadol*,' said Abiel with a smile, and to the surprise of all, he started to whoop, crying 'yooooooooooooooo, ffffyoooooooooo, yyyoooooooooooo.' Elisha placed a piece of goat's cheese in his hand. Elisha alone knew why Abiel had whooped. As he ate the cheese, Abiel added: 'My staff will protect the *nabi*. It was from Zahra, my sister. She had special powers. I'm not worried. He'll win through and bring my staff back to me.'

In the village they had started calling him *nabi*, or prophet. The word had hovered around Jonah, but it had never been spoken until recently. Previously, Eli would have been quick to repeat the story of the monster, but now his mind wasn't on such matters. It was as if Ruth had swallowed up his world, along with the great fish and the sea and the storm and Jonah and the ship. The only thing he saw was Ruth: she was his beautiful monster, whether one that would save him or kill him, he didn't yet know. Esther, who was truly beautiful the night of the celebration, her hair neatly combed, her eyes radiant, her cheeks rosy and her face full of life, was at a loss as to why she couldn't make Eli notice her. She couldn't understand that he was inside and she outside. At Hannah's words, which were somehow reinforced by Abiel's, Jonah's mother froze.

'We were all sitting at this table, this is exactly as I dreamed it, and he arrived too. He didn't know I had given birth to his son. His beard was as black as it was before. When he saw me with the baby boy, he frowned at first, but then he embraced us both, and I can't describe how warm and safe I felt in his embrace, as if I were in heaven. Behind him was a beautiful slender woman holding a net with a big fish in it, I didn't know her, she was standing still, but at the same time she was beside him as he walked, I don't know how that could be ... And all of a sudden, the table, which looked like this one, as I said, was transformed into a table of unimaginable opulence, laden with all good things, all I can remember is that it glittered like gold and there were many unfamiliar people around it, and Jonah started shouting at them, and then he vanished, along with the woman holding the fish, and straight away I woke up, because Jonah was crying, as if frightened by his father's yelling in the dream, and I gave him my breast.'

Jonah's mother sighed in relief.

'It's a good sign,' Esther was quick to say, speaking up before anyone else, as usual. 'The opulence of the table shows that my little brother is going to be an important person. And the woman behind Father was his hidden guardian, that's why she moved beside him without taking any steps, the way the messengers of the Lord do. The fish in her net is a sign that he lacks for nothing in the place where he is and it shows that the monster has been tamed this time too, because it was in a net.'

'Let it be so,' said Milkah's mother, 'even though there's something I don't like about that slender woman in the dream. It's as if he's thinking about her, not about us. Did you see her eyes? What colour were they?'

'I can't remember. I don't know.'

The neighbour's words hit Esther full on, even though they weren't to do with her. Ruth slipped past, a slender shadow, on her way to fetch some wine and, as if struck by lightning, Jonah's daughter understood why Eli didn't see her and whom it was he sought with his gaze. Ruth was behind him all the time, moving alongside him like the woman in the dream. The evening lost all its lustre. They raised their wooden beakers of sweet wine and drank in silence to both little Jonah and big Jonah. In telling her dream, the mother of Little Jonah had unburdened herself of her disquiet. The mother of big Jonah had not dared tell her own dream. For she had dreamed of Jacob. But not a good dream. She had dreamed of his kind, velvety eyes, framed by unruly eyebrows, and there were tears in those eyes, which seemed to convey to her a huge regret. She felt the need to make some unexpected gesture to banish the badness of the dream. She looked at her hands, which Jacob had praised so many times and on whose fingers there was no other ring than the one he had given her, the gold ring with the ruby. As her fingers were swollen from how much she had toiled that day, she couldn't take it off straight away, but after she wetted her hand with a drop of wine, the ring gradually slid off her middle finger. She placed it on Hannah's finger without difficulty. She then clasped all her fingers in her hand as tightly as she could, and covering that hand with the other, which was just as large but warmer, she said:

'It is my gift to the two of you. It will protect you and the little one.'

The blood rose to the cheeks of Jonah's woman. She felt as good as could be that evening, accepted by all, reconciled with all.

The meal was over quickly. Abiel left with the widow with whom he lodged, weighed down with sadness. He had sensed, as only he was able, the sadness of Jonah's mother and in some indistinct way he had divined the reason. Jacob! Ever since his first talk with 'uncle' he had clung to the hope that he would by some miracle heal his eyes. 'If you don't call them miracles, you can safely believe in them.' He now knew that it was not to be. He was overwhelmed by the thought that he would never see the way all other people did, that he would not be given what is so readily available to all, that he was destined to suffer. He knew that he was not guilty of anything and that it was unjust. Eli was helping Ruth to clear up, although Esther had tried to object, saying that he wasn't needed, that he was in the way, but then she realised it was in vain and fled home. Giving love orders is like commanding the wind not to blow or the sun not to come out from the clouds. She couldn't even give her own love orders, to command that it be victorious or, if not, then not to exist, and she certainly couldn't command Eli and Ruth's love not to exist. She didn't know enough about life yet to understand that nothing lasts in love and that, without wanting to and without caring about it, she would see Eli and Ruth's love dissolve and vanish like smoke. But for the first time in her as yet tender years, she understood that the realm of the love between man and woman was separate from the realm of what is just and that nobody could ever be happy in that realm for more than a few weeks, months, or measly years. To her had been granted nine days.

Outside, Ruth suddenly and boldly looked Eli straight in the eye, and he told her gravely and fearfully:

'What will I do if you have a child by me?'

But the girl laughed in his face:

'How stupid you are!'

Their bodies lay useless

Two weeks had passed since the day of the banquet and Sin, the God of the Moon, was now hidden. Six days remained until doom arrived. The city had fallen silent. It was now as silent and solemn as it had once been noisy and boisterous, when the streets had teemed with crowds, when they had resounded to voices speaking words in all the languages of the empire and those from beyond its bourne, voices that called out and quarrelled in Assyrian, divined the future in Babylonian, haggled in Aramaic, whispered in Hebrew, bid farewell in Phoenician, plotted in Persian, told tales of journeys by land and sea in Greek, cast spells in Egyptian. Before, the people were never content with anything or anyone, the poor cursed, the rich grumbled, the evil fought and killed, the weak got drunk, the multitude prattled idly and, even when they made sacrifice to the gods, they did so only with a mind to immediate gain, be it wealth, love, or power. It was true that Nineveh was a seat of great learning, and of the more than one hundred thousand permanent inhabitants, there were many who had knowledge of the stars in the heavens and all kinds of wonderful things on earth and in the sea, things which they spoke of in a whisper or aloud, and almost a fifth of the population knew how to read, write, and use a dictionary.

Eidele, my dear, don't pull faces—they really did have dictionaries! As one of the people of the Book, you ought to be able to appreciate that. Don't just read fashion magazines, my darling, because there are other wonderful things in the world too! In fact, go ahead and read them, because you look good when you dress in daring, modern fashions, with your star-like little eyes with eyelashes for rays, and with your gazelle-like ankles. Nineveh was to the ancients what Rome would later become, and you know the proverb about all the roads leading there, or what Paris is today, in the Jewish year 5690, or if you prefer, Anno Domini 1929. Obviously, Nineveh had its own Moulin Rouge or more than one, it had its public baths, and I've already told you that they'd built a system to deliver the running water they used to sprinkle their gardens and crops, but I know, what you care about at your age is not how all that technical equipment worked, but how the apparatus of love works, and that's why I've been telling you all these things about it. You can be sure that it functioned the same as it does today, and back then only the stage props were different. But now we are in the fast of Esther, before the celebration of destiny, and in our family it's a celebration holier than all the rest, because it reminds us of Jonah's daughter, Esther, the first storyteller. The biblical Esther, the famous and beautiful Esther whose fast we began today, the young woman from Persia who, as I hope you know, defeated the Babylonian Haman, the one who hated the Jews and wanted to exterminate them. I always picture that Haman as a Humbaba, rearing up on its legs like a huge frog, with its pug face and too many teeth in its mouth, which Gilgamesh and Enkidu fortunately slew.

Please don't forget to give alms to two people in need, you have so many beautiful clothes in your wardrobe that you don't even wear, there isn't any more room in there, and also to take food to two friends, as tradition demands! Traditions are a good thing, Eidele, even if you sniff at them now and can't be bothered to keep them, because they connect you to the world when no other connection holds you to it. And our people don't have any bad traditions, Eidele, remember that!

So, as I said, two weeks had passed since the banquet, and Jacob had spent them in his chamber lying alone with his thoughts. None went in to him except the green-garbed

Emmita, who had covered her head with a white shawl. Although she tried to put on a sad face, she didn't succeed. The goodness of her nature was too obvious on her trusting, radiant face. She brought him food, but he didn't touch a thing, and when she returned in the evening, she would spoon-feed him like a child. Even now, Jacob was looking at the door through which he expected the woman to enter, although it was not yet sunset, when his heart leapt: Jonah was there, large, worried, filling the doorway from top to bottom like a column. It might have been a hallucination, because lately the faces of those dear to him had kept appearing, each lingering a little before dissolving into the next. But this apparition had a definite outline, it stood out against the air around it, and it now approached him, sat down on the floor, and took his hand. To his surprise, Jacob felt his hand being kissed.

'Father! Get well!'

Jacob thought he smiled in reply to these words, but probably the smile was unable to make the too long journey from heart to lips. Jonah had spoken in a whisper, but it thrummed like a thick string beneath the bow, producing a solemn note.

'Why do you say that?'

Jacob had whispered, too, because he could no longer speak more loudly. His whisper was barely audible, but Jonah answered it. It was not the answer expected.

'I say it to make you well. I can talk just like everybody else when I want to. I'm silent for most of the time because I'm afraid of what happens when I speak words aloud. I was about twelve years old when I first noticed that my words weren't like other people's. My words bore fruit, like seeds bear fruit, putting forth green shoots that you can grasp in your hand, or like the vines do in our vineyard on the hill, when they bring forth grapes you can eat. My words *made things*. At the age of about fourteen, I felt sorry for a girl, because she was ugly and they all made fun of her, and I whispered in her ear, without knowing why, I whispered, "You're beautiful!" and she started to cry, thinking that I was making fun of her too, but then, two months later, when she suddenly turned into a beauty, she came to me, kissed me, and said that I had cast a spell on her with what I told her. It was the first time my words bore fruit, and it brought me my first kiss. I told Itzak, a lad who lived nearby, "You're a pauper!" because he didn't want to give me some of his bread when I was hungry, and in two months, his family, which was rich, lost everything and he really did become a pauper. And he reproached me for it with his eyes whenever our paths crossed, and only the two of us knew my guilt. And so the words I blurted without thinking became reality, whether or not people realised it, whether I spoke the words to them or said them in passing and they picked up on them without me being able to prevent it. It was then that I started to be silent. I did it out of a kind of fear. My words oppressed me. Somebody once told me that my words were possessed of grace. Who am I to have the right to change the world with words, when the world seems so crooked to me? And what if I do harm with words thinking I do good? What if I myself make the world crooked thinking I straighten it? What if I destroy it, thinking I repair it?'

This time, the smile from Jacob's heart showed faintly on his face.

'But the soft ... tongue ... breaks the hardest ... bones,' he quoted, with long pauses between words.

'God gave me this gift, but He didn't tell me how to use it or if I was allowed to use it when I saw fit, not just when He commanded. Now He has sent me to destroy the people of Nineveh with my words. I didn't want to, I didn't think that I would be able to, that I would be good enough to, and I fled. Not in fear of them, but in fear of myself. When I was in the belly of the monster, I said the word "stars" and straight away the stars rose above: I had emerged. Now I have said those dreadful words and doom will come. Father, I want to take you with me, out of the city, to save you.'

Jacob shivered as if with cold, although the word 'father' had suddenly warmed his frozen body.

'And there's also that woman ... I'm going to take the woman too. I want to show her that I can do good with my words, not evil ... Nineveh will be overthrown. In six days. I came to make you *well* with my words and you will get well through me, thanks to God.'

Jacob nodded:

'I'll come, I'll come with you in two or three days. Let me regain my strength. See, already I'm talking more easily,' he said, panting at every word. 'I'm not going to die with them!'

Although Jacob said nothing more, Jonah thought to hear: 'I'm not going to die with them, I'll die before them.'

Then, scarcely audible, Jacob said:

'Why do you say that? Why do you say "Father"?'

'I know from Mother. She told me. Before we left. She told me to tell you only if you're ...'

Jacob understood. Jonah didn't want to say the word 'dying', so that he wouldn't make it come to pass.

'Do you like Belus's wife? She's not really a beauty. Hannah is as beautiful as can be, with those blue eyes of hers, and you should know that the woman waiting for you is more precious than pearls.'

'I'll be back in three days to take you with me. Live, Father!'

To Jonah's surprise, Jacob started talking very fast:

'The woman waiting for you is more precious than pearls. Death is stronger than grace, my little Dove, and be sure that I loved you even when I was far away, I loved you from Tartessos, and if God wanted to destroy the city, he wouldn't have sent you. He sent you to save it, my boy, not to destroy it, and those who have sowed in tears will reap in joy, for you will eat the toil of your hands, blessed are you and it will be well for you, your woman will be like a fruitful vine within your house and she has given birth to a boy for you, a strong and healthy boy, sons like the branches of the olive tree there will be around your table, behold, so blessed are you, like the turtle dove, my little dove ...'

It was impossible to make out the rest. Jacob was delirious.

A good few minutes passed and Jacob's face was slick with sweat and very pale. He opened his eyes again and smiled at the face that studied him with visible alarm, but also, behind the alarm, with love. He said, more softly:

'Yes ... come in three days, my turtle dove, come without fail. I have many things to tell you. I long for us to sit and talk more than we have up to now, how bad it was all that time when we didn't talk. We'll talk at last. Don't take things to heart so much ...'

Jacob's eyes, hidden beneath his unruly eyebrows, had grown moist, like a spring abruptly welling from the earth, then the waters receded just as abruptly. He didn't want to sadden Jonah with his sadness. His face was bathed in light, shining like the face of a loving mother. Jonah grasped his hand. It felt thin, moist, warm in his. He didn't have the courage to clench it too tightly. It was the first time that father and son had held hands.

*

From the day of the banquet and the prophecy, nobody had made love in Nineveh. It was strange, in a city of six-score thousand inhabitants, more than half of whom were capable of love-making, for there not to be a moment or a day, but days on end when that self-forgetting occurred, which is named in so many ways, but which no name fully captures, that suspension within a reality higher than reality, the moment when two bodies become one and speak their own language. The most ordinary and the most unusual of things, the most predictable and the most uncontrollable, which you can rightly mock and just as rightly glorify, and however you might name it, nicely or nastily, you won't be wrong, since like God, every name can fit it. It was as if in the city-fortress, the Ninevites had suddenly all forgotten how to speak the language that all understand equally, the language of bodies. It was as if their bodies no longer served any purpose, as if they were like a snake's skin, detachable from the soul and painlessly shed. They no longer touched each other with their lips or hands or even their eyes, words, minds, they had forgotten that caresses exist in this world. Nobody now felt any lust. Marriages were no longer celebrated. They ate with bitter mouths after sunset, when they fed their sheep and cattle, but even then, sparingly, without hunger and without consuming flesh. They drank water sufficient only for them not to fall ill, they sprinkled their wine in the road to settle the dust, and the earth drank it with its vast insatiable mouth. By the decree of the king, who sat in ashes for days at a time, the Ninevites had put on sackcloth, from the greatest of them even to the least of them, they even covered with sackcloth beast, herd and flock that they fed and watered after sunset. Many mothers even wrapped their infants in coarse sack and their wailing was ceaseless. From king and queen to the humblest courtier, in the northern palace they comported themselves as if they were bodiless shades. As if the catastrophe had already struck, depriving them of the flesh of which they were made and of all their lusts and appetites. They were trying to love the one god of Jonah.

In the palace of Belus, the change was even more visible. All the jewels had been put in wooden crates and buried. Sargina now wore next to her delicate skin a sack whose neck she herself had cut out using a pair of golden scissors. The fibres of the sack made her itch, her hair hung down over her shoulders, uncombed, and no oil or dye now enhanced its glossy sheen. But she was still attractive, and her hazel eyes gleamed from within the dark rings that now framed them. Belus had lost weight, his face had become melancholy, and having lost its cruelty and vainglory, it was now even pleasing to look at. His voice, too, now grown sad, had become more pleasing. His wife could not believe that the same man as a few days before now stood before her, and it was as if she were seeing him for the first time. This miracle had fulfilled the words of the foreigner, perhaps in order that she continue to be protected. But she had not changed on the inside, even if on the outside she wore sackcloth. She was tender and desperately preoccupied not with Jonah's god, but only with Jonah himself. Her mind was set on him. She missed her guest every second of the day, she felt like crying out for him, going after him, finding him, clinging to him, but she knew that he would have driven her away, that she would have annoyed him, preoccupied as he was only with the prophecy. His god did only what he wanted and made you do what you didn't want. But sometimes woman is stronger than a god.

The destiny

Gat-Hefer and its scattered houses would have fit inside Belus's palace in Nineveh with room to spare for the hills of the vineyards. And the whole of the cottage where Jonah's son was born would have fit five times in one of the chambers of the palace. But for Hannah and the baby there was room enough. The little one was now a month old, but looking at him, his mother saw in her mind only the goat breeder she met at the well. His mouth had reeked of poor-quality wine, he wanted to touch her, and when she recoiled in fright, he shouted words of mockery at her. First he railed against the prophet: 'that madman who thinks he's the mouth of God,' then at her, 'you slattern, the only men you haven't had are the ones who didn't want you,' and finally at their son, 'he'll turn out crazier than his father, and mark my words, you'll never see him again as long as you live, he's found some other woman, a younger and a richer one.' The ugliness in the souls of some people is like the worms in the bellies of others: it tickles them and gnaws them and is eliminated through the mouth, whereas worms, which are more innocent than words, are ejected through an orifice different but just as dark. As for the mouth of little Jonah, it was sweet, he had soft toothless gums with which he grasped her finger and gnawed it, tickling her. When he cried, he revealed the pink little roof of his mouth, where teeth as handsome as his father's were to grow. Big Jonah tore the flesh he ate with teeth as sharp as a knife's blade.

Hannah gave a start. She hadn't heard Esther enter. The girl was in tears. Nobody had ever seen Esther in tears before then, not even when she was little and hurt herself when she fell, or when Amithai taught her to play rough boys' games, or later.

'What's wrong?' asked Hannah in a strangled voice. 'News?'

Esther shook her head, and the relief was plain to see on Hannah's face. The baby had started to whine and Esther took him in her arms, carefully holding him to her small, almost flat breast, whispering to him something inaudible. Her eyes turned red again, as if she had only just remembered something.

'I miss Father.'

'So do I,' smiled Hannah, taking from her the child that connected her to the man so far away.

But then Hannah looked at Esther more closely:

'But it's not that, it's something else, isn't it, Esther? Has something bad happened? You can tell me …'

All of a sudden, Esther, who had never opened up to anybody since her grandfather Amithai died, felt the need to tell her everything, to tell this good and simple woman, who knew, or rather had known, what unhappiness was and would not judge her. And her complaint was that of an orphaned child:

'Why did God have to make such a botched job of *that*? What would it have cost God to make people happy at least in love? Does He or doesn't He want us to multiply? Why then doesn't He help us all? Why does He want us to love only Him? Why is there so much pain and suffering in the world?'

Hannah took fright, she put the baby down and hugged the trembling girl to her chest like a mother would.

'Oh, Esther, you don't even know how to suffer like everybody else, like all we other women … Instead of hating and ridding yourself of the bad, you forgive, so that you can rid the other of it. Instead of forgetting and moving on, you bottle it up inside. I haven't had any peace since I dreamed of that woman, either. Men need to sow their seed in as many furrows as they can, to make sure that their line won't die out: it's the law of their nature. After they do it in one place, they go looking for different soil.'

'But Elisha won't come looking for me. He'll never look at me. Now I know it.'

And she began to sob soundlessly again. Hannah was not surprised.

'He'll see you, he'll come looking for you when he gets bored of whoever serves as his furrow right now, and if he doesn't see you, another will, and you'll fulfil your purpose in this world.'

Esther didn't want to know about that purpose, Dvorel, my little bumblebee! We're on the threshold of the twenty-first century, of which I'm very afraid, lest it bring something worse than this century, which has been the most terrifying our people has ever known! Today you can understand such a thing, because women also find their fulfilment in purposes other than the one Hannah was obviously thinking about, but in Jonah's day it was impossible. Only today I read on the Internet that women have stopped making marriage an ideal, rather they make a game of it. Apparently, if you're a man, you have to get married, but if you're a woman, you don't bother. Parents don't understand their children any more, mothers don't understand their daughters. To our misfortune, mine and your father's, you keep putting off your wedding, even if you and Bastian have been together such a long time, and I think you'd have got on well with Esther in that respect. And just then, Esther meekly bowed her head: how can you tell a mother with a darling little Jonah, who suckles the milk of life and who swallows up her world every time he opens his mouth, like a good and unbearably darling monster, that other purposes in life exist? It wasn't only that Hannah's blue eyes would have filled with amazement and incomprehension, but also not even Esther understood what was going on with herself. She missed Elisha, the Elisha with the melancholy smile and the dimple, the Elisha with the long curly eyelashes who had started to grow a soft beard perfect for stroking, the Elisha with whom she could have read and filled the world with children, and at the time she didn't know that her purpose in the world was to keep the story alive. Or that her monster was to tell the story and it would swallow up her life. Today, Esther would have been a famous writer, there would be lots of photographs of her, maybe she would have two lovers, and who knows? Maybe she would have met Amos Oz and dined out with him. As for children, Esther was nonetheless to have one, a girl, in order to fulfil the purpose of telling the story. But not Elisha. He was to have twelve children who survived childbirth—back then they didn't count the still-born—with Ruth and two other women, and he had about a hundred grandchildren. Esther had only one man, one daughter, one granddaughter, and one story.

But it was from her daughter and her story that the legend of the father was born, and even Elisha has survived thanks to her and, perhaps, precisely because she loved him, he appears here in a better light than what he was actually like. That's what stories do: they do people justice or injustice. As for the story of Jonah, it was to be read by all those eyes that have ever read the Book of Books, and it looks like it has every chance of entering the twenty-first century with us, the people of 1999, Dvorel. Our numbering of the years is more difficult, and you know I prefer the simpler one, even if your father always pedantically corrects me, as if I were training to be a rabbi. Dvorel, don't let me catch you having surgery on your nose! It's more than certain that you get the small bump on your nose from our ancestor Esther, and you ought to know it suits you very well. Or have a nose job, if that's what you want, after all, it's taken more than three thousand years for such things to be possible. But even so, you're pretty with your nose the way it is, you know!

Before the disaster

It was the eve of the day of destruction foretold by the prophet, as all the inhabitants of Nineveh now called him, unbeknownst to the inhabitants of Gat-Hefer, who called him the same. Jonah returned to the northern palace to collect his father, convinced that he was cured, that he had cured him, that they would go home together, but Jacob was hidden from his sight beneath a newly dug mound of soil. Beneath that soil already dried out by the scorching heat now lay the velvety eyes whose lids Emmita had closed, the bushy eyebrows and the always unruly beard, the delicate feet shod in calfskin sandals, the fine-fingered hands, the ear with the golden earring and, more precious still, the gift of listening. Buried beneath the ground forevermore were his unexpected sayings, such as that people ought to wish each other a 'good death' rather than a 'good night'. There beneath the freshly dug mound were the proverbs fitted to every circumstance: 'As thou knowest not what is the way of the wind, even so thou knowest not whither love might wend' and 'A word fitly spoken is like apples of gold in pictures of silver', there his memories of the beautiful wife of Amithai, the True, on the night of the sin that was to bear the fruit of a prophet, there too his term of endearment, 'my dove!' which nobody would ever call that prophet again. That name had died along with Jacob, now that God, who only lends us our names, as the old man used to say, had hastened to take it back again with all the other things. Jonah lay face down and threw his arms around the mound of soil, as if he wanted to bite it. From his throat came a soft, hoarse, cracked lowing sound:

'Why, Lord, why did You do this to me? I'd found myself a father and You took him away again! Wasn't it enough that you made me suffer the death of a father once, only to make me suffer it all over again? Why do You kill the fathers? Were you jealous? Did You want to be my only father? You are a jealous God! What harm did he do You, this creature who saved so many lives, so many children and so many mothers, who saved the queen and the girl in the well and me, who was to blame for her falling into it? Why did You, who are capable of all things, not let him return home, to rejoice in life and in us for at least another twenty years, or at least another ten, or at least just one, so that he could feel I was his son, at least now, in his old age? You know that I lied to him, because my mother didn't say anything to me, and you know why I did, so that he would have a reason to go on living! As soon as anyone takes pleasure in anything other than You, You punish him along with everybody else, indiscriminately. You are not just, O God! Why did you create us if it was only to torture us like this? Why? Answer me, enlighten me, I beg you on my knees! You know that I love You.'

In fact, he knelt only in his mind. But the voice that in his childhood had scolded him, castigated him, encouraged him did not answer his cry, as if it had gone unheard. But somebody did hear it. Emmita came up to him on quick feet, swaying as she went, and as always, her round face was full of goodness and concern. Her white shawl had slipped off her head. She had given up wearing her green robe and put on sackcloth like everybody else. She gently took the giant by the armpits and moved him aside from the grave, murmuring how it was unseemly. Then, with the corner of her shawl, she carefully wiped the sweat, the dust, and the tears from his face. No sooner did she dry his cheek than it received another wetting, but every time she wiped it dry anew, never tiring, and spoke to him without pause.

'He didn't suffer one bit, my dove. He told me to call you that from now on, "my dove". He passed away; he was like a lamp that goes out when its oil is spent. The queen gave the order for him to be buried in a *quburum*, she herself chose the gold leaf that they placed over his eyes and mouth, and all the other things needful. His spirit is now like that of a high official, wherever it might be. He will be honoured and loved. There were no women to wail him and there was no funeral repast, because we are in a time of fasting and prayer. He left you nothing, but he told me to tell you that what he used to say instead of 'good night' is a wish that has now been fulfilled. Do you understand what he meant by that? I couldn't really understand it, and I didn't even hear it very well, because by then he was barely breathing, the poor thing ...'

'He has left me all alone.'

'Don't talk like that, you're not allowed to, Galilean!' said Emmita sternly. 'The healer told me you still have a mother, you have a woman at home, and that she was to give birth to your heir. I'm positive she's given birth to your son—a midwife comes to divine such things—and that's what the healer thought too. Do you have other children?'

Jonah's voice grew gentler, but it was still hoarse. He looked at Emmita, but it was Esther he saw:

'I have a daughter. She's clever and ... but not even her will I ever ...'

With a shudder, he swallowed the words at the very last moment.

'Oh, but you will, I'm certain of it! You'll *see* her and embrace her and you'll forget all the evil in the world, which is what happens when you embrace your future. For that's what our children are. I don't have children, but I know, because I've attended so many women in labour. Don't be angry with me, but I don't believe in your prophecy ...'

Jonah's tears no longer flowed in streams, but his mouth remained a little crooked from weeping.

'The people aren't as bad as you say, as bad as you said at the banquet. Not all of them steal, not all of them think nasty thoughts. Some of them are even as good as a mother's milk, and you ought to know that I've seen many of them blushing for shame and shyness,' Emmita said, herself blushing as she did so.

For a moment the prophet regarded her pensively, weighing her words. If she had embodied them in her softness, her purity, her benevolence, it would have been sufficient. But Jonah was now assailed by the accidie of which the Psalmist sang, his soul was consumed by the destruction that wasteth at noonday, and which often spreads in close proximity to the grave. The death of his second father, his real father, if such he was, and the scorching heat made him blind to beauty, oblivious to goodness, uncomprehending of modesty, impervious to gratitude. He stood up and, without realising what he was doing, pushed Emmita aside, almost knocking her over, as if she were in his way.

He left, full of hatred and fury. Rabona followed him, having stood there at a distance all the while, but Jonah didn't even notice the man who had guided him, who had been at his side and protected him, for all he could see was the man who was gone. He felt only the empty, not the full. Henceforth and forevermore he would be without Jacob. He left the city by the gate through which he had entered thirty-nine days before, and the guards bowed down before him, still holding their bows and spears. Jacob's remedies had cured the guard who was sick.

'Did you pass on my thanks, master?'

'I passed on nothing. He is dead and buried,' replied Jonah savagely, as if he rejoiced at the words.

'Oh, *lā libbi ilimma*, woe and sorrow, may Anu protect him. I for one will always be grateful to him. This evening I will make sacrifice for his departed spirit!'

The ferryman took Jonah across the river. He then bid him farewell and returned to his family in the city:

'Pray for us, prophet, pray that we live,' he said in a soft, comforting voice. 'I have children, sons, and I still have my mother and father. If it is you who prays for us, we can be saved. And we too will pray for you.'

The words didn't find Jonah, but flew wide, like arrows shot by a poor bowman. Beneath the sun that beat down on his head, Jonah climbed a nearby hill, for, yes, there was a hill there. He glimpsed something flashing. A motionless snake was basking in the heat. With a stone, he smashed its head, continuing to pound it savagely even after he killed it. He saw how a few tiny scales were scattered over the ground with the splattered blood and he saw the eyes covered with a film, like when the fishermen's wives gut fish in the yard. But all he wanted was to see the disaster, to watch as the city was reduced to dust, with all its houses and temples and flower- and star-shaped plazas, and hanging gardens and ziggurats. All he wanted was for the hinges of the world to be burst asunder and for endless weeping and wailing to fill his ears. The combined din of destruction and lamentation was the only thing that could now appease him and respond to the pain inside him. He didn't want to hear anything else in the place left empty by the voice of the God who had forgotten him and no longer spoke to him, in the place left empty by the voice of Jacob, who had forgotten him and no longer spoke to him and was deep below the ground, with gold leaf covering his eyes and mouth, in the place left empty by the voice of his mother and of his daughter and his secret wife, who had forgotten him, or whom he had forgotten, it was the same thing, and who were far away and no longer spoke to him. In the place left empty by the words of Sargina, which sometimes he didn't even understand—Sargina, who probably didn't care about him any more either. In the place left empty by the whine of the child who was probably his son and which he thought he would never hear. In despairing love, he clutched the fist of Abiel's staff, as if he were clenching in his own fist all the people he missed. It was strange that the staff that Zahra had given her blind brother was the only thing that still anchored Jonah to the world. That and the hazel eyes of that woman. He missed Sargina, that strange woman married to the worst man in Nineveh, he missed her more than he had anybody else before. He was unhappy.

Reaching the top of the hill, Jonah saw the huge, silent city below, the city that he wanted to be destroyed so that his prophecy would be fulfilled. The prophecy had to come true so that he himself would have some meaning in the world. The voice that had hidden from him spoke to him once more: 'I am weary, O God. I have had enough. You have tested me till you broke me inside. You knew from the start that you are the strongest! What kind of a game is this, which you always know how to win? Take me already, have mercy, stop my torment. I want to die, O Lord!' The sun that baked the top of his head gave him the merciless reply.

The green shadow

Jonah had an extensive vineyard in Gat-Hefer, where he had used to hide away from people sometimes, savouring the coolness of the green leaves. He missed his vineyard. He now set about making himself a booth to sit under it in the shadow. He was sweating, dying of thirst, but he didn't want to drink the water he had with him, he wanted to suffer, he wanted finally to see his prophecy fulfilled, and then to die. He knew that every living thing, be it a man, be it a beetle, had to drink water to live. If you want to die, you stop drinking. It takes two days, and in heat like that, maybe with a little luck, he would die too, on the very day of doom. He poured out his water skin on the ground and then began building his booth from dry stalks. He stretched the mat of stalks above him, propping it up on four poles. He now had a ceiling like a dry net, through which rays of sunlight pierced unhindered, and he thought of the good, moist net of the woman's eyes, the one from which he couldn't untangle himself. The fisherman's net. He looked out over Nineveh, the huge city, fenced in by its yellow walls, half of it clasped in the lazy embrace of the river, the city whose houses stood in neat rows, unlike in Joppa or Gat-Hefer, each stood straight, one next to the other, and now all seemed so small that a child or a God could have played with them. Rabona was there now, somewhere, perhaps telling his boys about Jonah. There, beneath a mound, was Jacob, his mouth covered with gold leaf. There in the southern palace was the gentle Emmita, keeping the queen's spirits up and chattering away with the wet nurse— Emmita, who thought the world was good and that people were still able to blush the way she did, even for things they hadn't done and for what they were not. There was the sick king, who for ten days had sat in ashes. There, among the houses and the temples, were all those who had listened in fear to his prophecy and who had then changed from one day to the next, beneath his very eyes. There were the two lively youths who had chewed the ends of their styluses. There, too, was the unloved Belus. He quickly turned his gaze to the southern palace, which towered over all the houses around it. The rooftop where he had first seen her who caught him in her fishing net was a little green rectangle. And she too was there, somewhere, in one of the many chambers or perhaps even among the trees and flowers of the rooftop. His eyesight was sharp, but not sharp enough to see anything more than the bluish-yellow walls, and the straight lines of the streets, and the flower- and star-shaped plazas.

He turned his aching eyes back to her palace. For a few moments he imagined her crushed by toppled masonry, immediately after which he imagined her crushed by the heavy body of Belus, crying out beneath him, and this second image was more painful to bear than the first, that of her dead beneath the masonry. From under his useless booth he too cried out. And then, because the senses of those in love are excruciatingly keen, he almost heard Sargina's answering cry. It didn't come from beneath fallen masonry or from beneath Belus—she never even saw him any more—but rather it came on her learning the news that her emissaries had not found the man she was looking for, that Jonah had vanished yet again. They both cried out at the same time, at a great distance from each other, my dear Dvorel, like the cry two lovers make when coupling, which is the word they used back then, and which reduces a man and a woman to the level of beasts, a word which I don't know whether is appropriate or not.

The next day, Jonah was to watch the city's destruction. Like in the cinema, Dvorel, my darling. It was going to be like one of those Hollywood big-screen spectaculars, with smoke, fire, screams, buildings collapsing in on themselves. Explosions and implosions, although Jonah wouldn't have known words like that. He was like a director waiting to watch his film at the premiere. He was an artist, that's what he was—the first in our family, which has known no shortage of artists!

But he hoped that God would spare one person in Nineveh. A woman. It was with her that the world could then begin after it ended. The same as always when you're in love, it wasn't a question of him not caring about others, but rather he cared so much about Sargina that she had engulfed without trace all the other people he knew. She was now his monster, from whose belly he didn't want to emerge, or rather he wasn't even trying to emerge. He didn't want to be spat out, because more often than not, my darling girl, we love our monsters. Everything else was just small change to him, everybody else was invisible, even God, whose voice didn't show itself to him any more. But it was late in the day for him to fall in love, just as the world was about to be destroyed.

And even so, every fibre of his being was waiting for her, drawing her to his body, once strong, now weak, sorely tested and so eager for love. He spoke her name aloud a few times, to make her come to him, using the gift he knew he possessed, or which at least he had once possessed. He spoke her name to make her exist. After which, thinking that that wasn't clear enough, he said: 'Sargina coming. Now. To find me. We escape. I save you. We go away. Our tribe will be numberless and it will be good.' When I married your father, my darling girl, we wanted to be Adam and Eve, we wanted to give birth to a new mankind, in a better world, and I think that that's what any-body with a brain wants when bringing a child into the world. But children always slip through their parents' fingers, they belong to all, they're not just ours, as we like to imagine, heed-less as we are.

His words no longer possessed any power. God had taken away his gift, his only gift. Now he was just like everybody else, a man like any other. The sun turned red, the sky straight away turned black, and Jonah, exhausted by thirst, was plunged into a dreamless sleep, after which the sky was filled with light once more: the day of doom had arrived, the fortieth since he entered the city by the Adad gate. When he woke up, there was a green shadow above him. Some large leaves from one of the stalks of the sunshade had sprouted while he slept. All metamorphoses occur by night, you know.

Probably the large leaves of the gourd had sprouted like the buds on Aaron's rod. Let's not forget that Aaron had experienced something similar not long before Jonah, or rather something even more spectacular, because what sprouted from his rod was good to eat, namely almonds. I think maybe the stalk had been wetted by Jonah's water skin, when he poured it out wanting to die? But he didn't think about that. The leaves gently shaded him, and for Jonah, ill with pain and withered by thirst and lovesick, it was as if he had heard the voice anew. The joy overwhelmed him and eased his suffering. It meant God hadn't abandoned him after all: even if He didn't talk to him any more, He protected him against the searing heat. He comforted him with His green shadow. Sargina would come to him too. His whole being was waiting for her to come up the hill to him before the end of the day, before the end of the world. Like a child, but now one that was obedient, he prayed that God would allow her to come. Exhausted, but full of hope, he fell asleep again, under the shade that had come to life overnight.

But instead of the one creature he loved most of all in the world, God sent him a creature that nobody had ever loved at all. A worm. While the weakened Jonah slept in the shade that he thought was for him alone, while he slept wrapped in the miracle made for him alone and from God's love for him, the worm, probably as hungry and thirsty as Jonah was, and as glad as he was at God's miracle, to which it too had a right, the same as any other creature on this earth, large or small, loved or unloved, busily began to nibble the tender leaves, until the only thing left was tatters through which the sun once more shone. Its belly full and its hunger sated, the worm then crawled back inside the hole in the ground whence it came.

It was afternoon when Jonah woke up and he felt the dry heat hitting him with a vengeance. Sargina hadn't come, the city hadn't been destroyed, Jacob hadn't returned to life. His words possessed no power. The leaves that he thought had been created for him to comfort him with their shade were no more. Instead, a hot wind was blowing from the east and from God. Jonah felt as if he were swimming in the sun, which engulfed him in its pitiless light as the monster once had in its darkness, as if his ankles were shackled in chains of light as they had once been shackled in chains of darkness. An unbearable thirst had dried out the walls of his mortal frame, leaving nothing but hardened silt: he was like a dried-up well. He felt humiliated, ashamed, made a mockery of, alone.

His eyes filled with darkness. In his swoon he argued with God, praising Him with all his heart and in the utmost annoyance: 'You are good and merciful and long-suffering and rich in endless goodness. You repent of evil. Why did you send me here, far from my own country, to foretell something you didn't want to do? Why did you let me waste my words and why did you humiliate me? Words were all I had. I loved them because they came from you. That's why I fled, because I was sure you would take them back from me. You give and You take away as You please. You didn't care about me, You care only about the evil. Why then do you create good people, if you're just going to humiliate them in this world full of all things bad? You worry your head over the bad man a thousand times more than you do over the good man. You let the good suffer because of the bad. Why didn't you just make me bad from the outset, Lord

God, so that I could feel your love and your care and your endless joy in setting me right, and so that you would answer me straight away? So that you could hold me in your arms? Why didn't you make me a worm? At least I'd have felt better about myself if I'd been in my own skin. Why did you pull me out of one monster only to thrust me into another?'

But even as he said all this in his dream, he also found a good answer, one of many: 'So that I could meet her!' And all of a sudden, he heard the voice he missed so badly. But it no longer comforted and encouraged him, but scolded him: 'Doest thou well to be angry for the gourd?' In the dream, Jonah saw his rage seething and he felt it to be justified. And he snapped back in his own justification: 'I do well to be angry, even unto death.' The voice descended on him like the setting sun and as never before or after it calmly explained: 'You felt sorry for yourself and for some leaves that shaded you and which not you but I caused to turn green, as I once did to Aaron's staff. They appeared while you were asleep and they disappeared while you were asleep. You didn't worry your head over them and you didn't even have time to get used to them, you barely had time to see them. And you want me not to take mercy on the largest city in the world, with six-score and three thousand people like you in it, plus the five that were born today—God knows their exact number, the same as He knows the number of stars in the heavens—poor, helpless people that don't even know left from right, let alone good from evil? And quite apart from the people, there are all the cattle, birds, and flowers, and thousands and thousands of green leaves that give shade, the same as these that were eaten by the worm!' 'Worms ate my green shade. I want to die, and I want to die right now!' Jonah said to the voice, without understanding what was being said to him or what he was saying. He was aggrieved to the death. But it was God who had the last word, as usual.

The fish's tail

Instead of dying as he wished, he woke up with a wet face. He thought he was on the seashore once again, washed by the waves, the same as the night when he emerged from the darkness of the creature, if creature it was. Now he emerged from unendurable light. But it was still night. Next to him were Sargina and two slave women, who were pouring water over his face and through his crusted, welted lips. The sky was sprinkled with myriad stars, as it had been then, too. And he felt as weak as he had then, and there was a lowing sound in his ears. Sargina was stroking his bare chest, whose whiteness almost shone in the night, she thrilled him with her light, wet hand, with her small, soft, cool fingers. All the women in Jonah's life, even his mother, had had hard fingers, callused by hard work, and it was for the first time that he felt the softness of a woman's hand. His eyes adjusted to the darkness and in it he was able to glimpse the gleaming black of her eyes, the eyes he had yearned for so much. He could barely hear what the slave women were talking about among themselves. If it had not been for him, the prophet, the voices were gaily saying, people would not have changed and God would have destroyed them all. The whole city was grateful to him. So, they knelt and they thanked him for saving them as if he were one of their gods. Then the sun rose. It was the forty-first sunrise since his arrival.

The women looked out over the city that lay at their feet, great, just and powerful, in the half-embrace of the waters of the Tigris, which glinted softly in the first rays of the sun. Beyond it stretched the annihilating desert, and within its walls lived people who could not tell right from left or good from evil, but who nonetheless felt guilty without knowing why and desperately wanted to escape with their lives along with all their loved ones, and quite simply, along with everybody else. In that city lived children, cattle and goats, birds and flowers, thousands of leaves that shed their green shadow over the world between the walls and innocent hungry worms hidden in the ground. And snakes whose youth was restored every spring because they had stolen the flower of youth. Most of the inhabitants had stayed awake all night. And now, at dawn, when everything was the same as before, a great sigh of relief rose up between the walls. Joy gripped them all, it overwhelmed them, dizzied them, and like a whirlpool it caught up and mixed together slaves and masters, children and parents, the moribund and the strong, and they embraced each other, they wept and they laughed, they cared about nothing other than that they were human beings and they were alive.

Life had won, God had won, Jonah had lost, he had wasted his words, but the women kept saying that on the contrary, thanks to his unfulfilled words, he had saved them all. And because you are twins, my dear Hannah and my dear Natan, I want to tell you that sometimes, in fact almost always, good and evil go together, like twins, and one doesn't occur without the other. Jonah, as is clear today, and as I think I've told you, was an artist by nature, or better still, a poet, and that's why the whole world is so fond of him and why everybody smiles when they hear his name. Hence too his fame, which is, how can I put it? Ambiguous. As over the top and as touchy as any other poet, and always giving all the people around him a headache. He wanted his words to be fulfilled to the letter, but what he didn't understand, and what the slave women, ignorant as they were, did understand straight away, was that the power of his words was something entirely different than what he thought it was, and that this was made manifest only when they weren't fulfilled. Because their power derived from the power of God, who surpasses human understanding. His words had built lives rather than torn down walls. Which is to say, the work outgrew its creator, as they say nowadays, and in this particular case, it did so in spectacular fashion.

And the same as with so many poets and prophets, since the one is often mistaken for the other, the place where his bones are laid to rest is unknown, which means you can't go somewhere and say: here lies the man who was swallowed by the fish, the leviathan, the sperm whale, the *dag gadol*, and was spat back out three days later. Some say that his resting place is in Gat-Hefer, where he's supposed to have returned, others that it's in Nineveh, where he's supposed to have remained. Not that it's important given that his story is visited all the time—it's his highly beloved final resting place. Don't keep pestering me to tell you what became of his love, because I haven't got a clue.

How do we know he was inside the fish for three days if he didn't have a mobile phone with him, like you two do, or even so much as a watch with a luminous face? It's not nice to ask questions like that, Natan. A whale isn't a fish and there weren't any hills outside Nineveh, you say? Don't take after your brother, Hannah, we all know you're an inveterate nit-picker. There are lots of details in this story that are as slippery as eels, but how could it be otherwise, when it all took place so many centuries ago, whereas we don't understand and don't even remember what happened yesterday?

Back in those days, my dears, time relived itself year after year. It didn't make a din, it didn't tick, it didn't chime, it didn't have bells to ring or gongs to clang, it didn't have intermeshing cogwheels and mechanisms to hold it prisoner. It glided like a shadow rotating around a stick planted in the ground, it trickled, it spread like a puddle, and what people are beginning to lose an understanding of is that it moved in a circle, it kept coming back and starting over again, as if it had never passed and would never pass, as if ahead and behind were completely the same to it. Like your names, which are the same whether you read them left to right or right to left, Hannah, my little monkey, and Natan, my little quibbler. Like the date today, which is the same back to front and front to back: 02.02.2020. Like this story, which is recreated from time to time, depending on the century when it's told, and whose time blends so well with our own.

They say that our family is directly descended from Jonah, my dears. My mother told me this story, which her mother told her in words differently arranged, which her father told her in words polished according to the time he lived in, and so on, ninety-two times, the story has been repeated and each time altered a little, passed down now from a man's mouth to a woman's, now from a woman's to a woman's, now from a woman's to a man's, all the way back to the boulder-like words of the first father who knew the story, Jonah himself. For Jonah rolled his words like boulders. His words were few and heavy. I'm the ninety-second to reconstruct the events. Probably in this way not much is left of the true story, or maybe nothing is left at all. You are the first twins from this line of seeds nurtured in a woman's belly like in the soft, good earth, and maybe you'll be the first in our family on which fate will look kindly, because many terrible experiences have been inflicted on us by God and we've suffered plenty of mistrust on the part of our fellow man, starting with the things our ancestor of rather dubious fame endured and down to the present day. May God preserve us!

The story has an ambiguous conclusion, ending like the tail of a fish, as the saying goes, which, my dears, I think is a highly appropriate way to end in this particular case.

EPILOGUE
IN THE 21ST CENTURY

Dear Jonathan,

My mother died last night, at twenty past eleven, in our little house next to the photographic studio on Parížká street. Both Viki and Moni and I myself were at her side, and although she was very weak and I don't think she was aware of very much, it was as if she smiled at us whenever she opened her eyes. She celebrated her ninety-seventh birthday this April. She had a long and eventful life, with more bad events than good. She taught us not to fall prey to sadness, to confront our misfortunes without taking them too seriously, likewise not to take ourselves too seriously, and above all to laugh. With that adorable humour of hers, which you know very well, lately when we wished her good night, she would say, 'You ought to wish me a good death, not a good night!' And Jonathan, I think this wish of hers was fulfilled.

Yours, in great sadness,

Astrid

MUNICH

The end of July was horribly hot, a parched wind was blowing, the tourists were swarming back and forth, licking their ice-cream cornets, and they looked dizzy and exhausted. Absolutely all of them were wearing sunglasses and hats or caps, as if they were in disguise. They'd disguised their children, too. They were looking for shade. We walked from the Marienplatz to the old town hall to see the zodiac clock. The large hand was on Scorpio, and the small hand on Pisces, right between the two fish: ten to two.

'Ah, look at that, the clock is laughing,' I told him. 'That's why in all the clock shops the hands are set to ten past ten or ten to two.'

'Like an emoticon. With a mouth of gold.'

'Which writes the gospel of time.'

'Oh, come on ...'

His tone was harsh. I quickly made to erase what I'd said—it really did sound ridiculous—by changing the subject.'

'Let's go back to the Marienplatz, to the Glockenspiel, to catch two o'clock. Let's watch the jousting knights slide past each other without ever crossing their lances, the cowards.'

'And you think they'll suddenly pluck up the courage? The glockenspiel only plays at twelve! And I can't understand you: wasn't it you who said that the figurines were too high up for you to see them properly? Anyway, we don't have time. I want to catch the museum before it closes.'

We want to catch it, I softly said to myself. We have time, in fact. I remembered the inscription on a different clock that I'd taken a picture of the day before: *Nur gute Stunden möcht ich zeigen / Die bösen aber wohl verschweigen.* If I were a clock, that would be my motto. Anachronistic and completely against the current. All men find it hard to tolerate the heat. Some find it hard to tolerate life. Others find it hard to tolerate love. Others still, travelling.

So we went to the Alte Pinakothek without going to see and listen to time. There were lots of people there, but they were all silent. It's strange, but museums are like a sieve, they strain tourists and keep only the quiet ones. The entry fee was seven euros a head. After a while, I found the painting from which I chose a detail for the cover of *The Book of Questions*: Jan van Kessel, *Europe.* It was one of only four continents at the time.

In a narrow room on the ground floor, I remained transfixed, all alone, in front of a not very large painting, perfect for seeing all the details in it, which represented a whale familiar to me. A compact group of visitors quickly went past it, luckily for me. It was by Jan Brueghel the Elder, not by Pieter, his father, who was also 'the Elder', who could be found a little farther on, where there was a crush. Back then, all fathers were elders.

I stood quietly, looking the whale in the eye. And before me the painting metamorphosed. The monster had the radiant upraised eyes of the penitent St Mary Magdalene, or the eyes of Mary praying for her son. But this time I noticed, for the first time and with a joy that verged on fright, a detail unfamiliar to me and which you have no way of seeing in reproductions. Within the left eye of the whale, tiny in His grandeur, was God. From the whale emerged a man with white hair, in a red, completely dry robe, he emerged blind, like children when they are born, his hands joined together, helpless, and his eyes too were raised to heaven, but blinded by the light, unseeing. Terrified and terribly alone. I read the inscription: *Jonas entsteigt dem Rachen des Walfisches—Jonah emerges from the throat of the whale*. In the painting, only the mother-whale was holy, and it was Jonah who was the sinner. To me, the real title of the painting ought to be *The Holy Mother*, but obviously that would have been deemed a heresy.

He walked up to me, joining me in silence, and he looked at the painting. I pointed out to him the eyes of the whale, particularly the one on our right and what was visible within it, small but huge.

'*Gott sei Dank!*' he said, completely unexpectedly, and put his arm around my shoulders. We laughed, while other visitors, having come to a stop behind us, tried to see what had escaped them and amused us so greatly.

Outside, sparse snowflakes were falling, enough to wet the streets. In Piccadilly Circus, Sabra-Yerusha greeted the graceful Anteros, god of requited love. 'Please remember that I allow you to hit me with your arrow, since I'm sick to the back teeth of your insolent brother's. You'll find me in Ljubljana most of the time, if you're looking for me.' She couldn't have said such things aloud. The boys, one of them twelve, the other sixteen, would have laughed at her or looked at her with vague scorn, and in any event, they wouldn't have picked up on the allusion to Eros. They couldn't wait to finish with the museum and go off about their own business. They were to meet back at the hotel in the evening. The same as always when they left her to her own devices in a foreign city, her feelings were contradictory: on the one hand, she felt free, happy, determined to reclaim herself as quickly as she could, on the other, from the first steps she took she would be disconcerted and not know what to do with herself.

She headed down the left side of Piccadilly Street, walking along the wet pavement, feasting her eyes on the shop windows festooned with Christmas decorations. She walked for a long time, not knowing where she was going or why. Finally, she entered a café, more to get warm than anything else. She hadn't been inside a café for ten years. She hadn't smiled for twenty. She drank a cappuccino, which she thought a drink fit for the gods, and she munched the crunchy biscuit on the saucer with enthusiasm. She set off again and saw the mullioned window of a bookshop. It was Hatchards. At the entrance, there was an advertising board on a stand and tied to it a Beagle wearing a green coat clipped around his belly. The dog looked desperate and gave a short bark. She squatted down to talk to it, speaking soothing words to it in English, but all she managed to do was make it give a heart-rending yowl and to tug on its leash. Probably her English was to blame.

Inside it was warm and there were a lot of people, surprisingly many. She walked up and down the shelves, flicking through now one book, now another. She picked *A History of the World in 10½ Chapters*, beneath whose title it said, 'Stunning ... a flawless diamond.' Usually, Sabra-Yerusha didn't have any faith in such one-fits-all puffs, but in this particular instance she knew it would be justified: Julian Barnes was one of her favourites. Back at the hotel she was restless. She dipped into the chapters of the book, but when she came to the story of Jonah, she remained engrossed. After she finished it, she sat smiling for a long time. 'A fisherman's yarn,' Barnes called it, and she was amazed at how simple it could be. Strangely enough, her family had an especial liking for Jonah, it was even a kind of obsession, although nobody knew why.

When the boys returned late that evening, they found her in an unexpectedly good mood. The youngest was really downcast, however. He'd lost the tooth talisman which, like his brother, he wore around his neck, a large, perforated canine from some unknown animal, meant to guard him against evil. It really was a serious loss: it had been a family heirloom and was very old. The oldest brother took off his talisman, a tooth the size of a finger, and tied it around the youngest's neck. Then he looked at his mother, awaiting her approval. Yerusha stroked his sweet, feminine face, with the curly hair that was overrunning his cheeks: she had good children, of that there was no doubt.

'A 9.5-metre sperm whale was found dead in the waters off an island that forms part of the Wakatobi National Park, south-west of Sulawesi. The park is famous among scuba-divers for its reefs and marine life. The cause of the sperm whale's death is not known, but in its stomach were found almost seven kilos of waste, plastic bottles, 115 plastic cups, plastic bags, countless flip-flops, and more than 1,000 pieces of fishing line of various lengths and thicknesses, declared park officials, according to the BBC.'

THE DEAD SEA

From between the three tall palm trees by the shore there appeared a youth of about seventeen arm in arm with another, a few years older, who was wearing black sunglasses and held an aluminium cane.

'It smells of brine and I hear people paddling. How many metres to the water's edge?'

'Three or four. Look, Michael, I promise that once you've had the operation, in a month's time, I'll bring you back, right to this very spot. Now you can only imagine what I told you, the sea, the sky, the lumps of salt, that tattooed bloke sat in the water reading, and all the rest, but in a month, you'll see them.'

A pleasant breeze was blowing from the sea. It was the end of February, but not at all cold, so there were plenty of people paddling in the sea, while others, wearing sweaters, walked up and down the beach. The salt created a thick crust of crystallised lumps up and down the shore, like a hardened line of surf. A man with tattooed arms was indeed reading a magazine a few metres from the shore, seated as if in an armchair afloat in water so salty that it held it at the surface.

The young man with the cane sighed.

'If only!'

'Not if only, Michael, but for sure! They've made incredible progress. The doc says that ninety-five per cent of operations are a perfect success. Stop harping on about having all the bad luck.'

Michael laughed, unconvinced.

'Can you imagine?' added his guide. 'You'll be able to see us all and you'll be able to see yourself, to know what you look like! And you look really good! I told you before about mirrors in which you can see yourself ... If you ask me, you're better off feeling my mug with your fingers, the way you do now, because it's really ordinary. But I'll take the risk, for your sake. I've got narrow eyes, I'm warning you!'

Michael smiled and then said, almost in a whisper:

'Last night I dreamed I was on a ship, a yacht or something like that, and there was a storm, and one of the people on board had the same voice as the doctor ...'

NAPLES

'Il tempo di prendere un caffè e andiamo!'

The two sisters didn't even sit down to drink it. Gina, wearing a short skirt and fishnet stockings, was the more beautiful of the two, although her face was slightly asymmetrical. Dark hair, as thick as a wig, tumbled in small curls over her shoulders. Her sister's hair was dyed green and she was heavily made up. They were at a café in Dante Square, dominated by the ascetic statue of the poet, which no local so much as noticed, but which the tourists photographed ceaselessly with their phones. As if knocking back shots, in one burning gulp they drank the thimble-sized cups of coffee they had already paid for, then they went to their scooter, parked next to a booth selling all kinds of tat. Gina drove. They took the Via Toledo to the port. They were meeting a bird vendor there. Gina's son was about to celebrate his tenth birthday and she wanted to buy him a nymph parrot, a species from Australia. The lad was crazy about ornithology, he studied bird species and their songs on the internet, and some of them he could even imitate.

The vendor, a cigarette hanging from his mouth, was waiting for them with the cage under a portico whose columns were scrawled with graffiti. The ground was strewn with litter and reeked of fish. Gina stopped the scooter right next to the man, prodded a dustbin out of the way with the tip of her Nike trainer, and dismounted while simultaneously taking off her helmet, a kind of reflex gesture. Her sister remained seated on the scooter, resting one foot on the ground, and watched the whole transaction with a grimace of scorn, like somebody watching a bad play. She was there as a bodyguard. Gina opened the handbag, which hung slantwise over her belly and pulled out five crumpled ten-euro banknotes. She then counted them out into the vendor's palm, smoothing each one. A quarrel broke out because the man said the birdcage wasn't part of the price. And as far as he was concerned, he would plonk the bird in her hand if she didn't like it. In the end, Gina asked her sister for another banknote and took the cage from the vendor with the air of a queen who doesn't deign to lower her eyes to gaze upon her subjects.

But she cheered up and smiled when she looked at the bird: it was grey, with a yellow head and an orange splotch on each cheek. The parrot, a male, seemed agitated, and his delicate crest was pressed flat to his head, a sign that he was frightened. The tail consisted of grey and lemon-yellow feathers. Gina wanted to hold the cage herself, so she changed places with her, even though she didn't trust her—she knew she liked to ride recklessly. They tore off on the scooter, the parrot's tuft fluttering in the wind.

'Auguroni!' shouted the vendor after them, stuffing the money in his pocket.

I opened the folder on my desktop labelled *J*. In it were dozens of reproductions of Jonah and the big fish, from various periods, from anonymous illuminations to the Rembrandt drawing in Vienna, from Giotto to contemporary acrylic paintings. I enlarged the one by Jan Brueghel the Elder to fill the entire screen. And because I couldn't do so any other way, moving the mouse, with the arrow pointer I slowly, lovingly caressed the Jonah blinded by the light and his gentle monster, the mother who had released him back into the world without being able to separate him from his fate.

02.02.2020

Acknowledgements

I thank Francisca Băltăceanu and Monica Broșteanu for their careful reading of the manuscript and their philological observations and notes on the translation of the Bible from the Hebrew text, likewise for the chapter 'Jonah' in *Cele mai frumoase povestiri din Biblie* [The Choicest Bible Stories]. I thank Professor Andrew George of the S.O.A.S., London, for his incredibly prompt and clear answers to my complicated and confused questions and for compiling and translating the Penguin edition of *Gilgamesh*. My warm thanks to archaeologist and writer Cătălin Pavel, who provided me with much documentation and whom I asked impossible questions concerning fine details. Moreover, his book, *Arheologia iubirii* [The Archaeology of Love] gave me the confidence that we can consider the ancients quite similar to ourselves. I am extremely grateful to Dr Corneliu Ioan Marinescu for all his expert explanations. I thank once again my old friend Jean Pătrîngenaru of the *Le chemin des philosophes* antiquarian bookshop for the priceless books he gave me about Jonah, about everyday life in the time of the Patriarchs, and about seafaring in Antiquity, which I made use of here, along with other items in an extensive bibliography which, however, has no place in a novel. My best wishes to Vlad Niculescu of Cărturești & Friends, who obtained for me with the greatest celerity the books in English that I was lacking. Many, many thanks to wonderful writer Adriana Bittel, who constantly urged me not to waste my time on trifles and to concentrate on this novel, although I was unable strictly to abide by the first part of this exhortation. And of course first of all, even if I have left it till last as usual, I would like to thank the staff at

Humanitas, who worked on this book during difficult times: Lidia Bodea, who edited the text, Cristian Negoiță, my former student, who proofread it, and Manuela Măxineanu, Florina Vasiliu, Radu Dobreci and Dan Dulgheru of the technical department. With all my heart I thank painter Mihail Coșulețu, to whom I owe all the front covers of my novels and, I have no doubt, a part of their success.

THE AUTHOR

Ioana Pârvulescu is a writer and professor of modern Romanian literature at the Faculty of Letters in Bucharest. She has published more than 20 titles of prose, essays, children books, many of which are bestsellers and perennial favourites in her native Romania. She translated from German and French, Angelus Silesius, Rilke, Maurice Nadeau, Kundera and several volumes of Asterix and Obelix comics, and has coordinated collective volumes, the most important being *I also Lived Through Communism*.

Pârvulescu has dedicated two novels to Bucharest in the Belle Époque, *Life Begins on Friday* (Humanitas 2009, Istros Books, 2016) and *The Future Begins on Monday*, and one to his native Brașov, *The Innocents* (translated into German by Zsolnay and Italian by Voland). The novel *Jonah and His Daughter* (*Prevestirea*, 2020), the story of the biblical Jonah, won the National Prize for Prose in Iasi. Ioana Pârvulescu has won major national awards and, on two occasions, the European Union Prize for Literature, for *Life Begins on Friday* in 2013 and for the short prose *A Voice* (*O voce*) in 2018. Her novels have been translated into 15 languages.

Alistair Ian Blyth is one of the most active translators working from Romanian into English today. A native of Sunderland, England, Blyth has resided for many years in Bucharest. His many translations from Romanian include: *The Bulgarian Truck* (Dalkey Archive Press, 2016), *The Book of Whispers* (Yale University Press, 2017), and *Life Begins on Friday* by Ioana Pârvulescu (Istros Books, 2016). He has translated and annotated three works of Ludovic Bruckstein so far for Istros Books: *The Trap* (2019); *With an Unopened Umbrella in the Pouring Rain* (2021) and *The Fate of Yaakov Maggid* (2023). He is the author of the novel *Card Catalogue* (Dalkey Archive Press, 2020).

www.ingramcontent.com/pod-product-compliance
Lightning Source LLC
Chambersburg PA
CBHW030819090426
42737CB00009B/785